Kirstie Drummond Papworth
Compassionate Leadership

De Gruyter Transformative Thinking and Practice of Leadership and Its Development

Edited by Bernd Vogel

Volume 4

Kirstie Drummond Papworth

Compassionate Leadership

For Individual and Organisational Change

DE GRUYTER

ISBN 978-3-11-076301-0
e-ISBN (PDF) 978-3-11-076312-6
e-ISBN (EPUB) 978-3-11-076318-8
ISSN 2701-4002

Library of Congress Control Number: 2023934193

Bibliographic information published by the Deutsche Nationalbibliothek
The Deutsche Nationalbibliothek lists this publication in the Deutsche Nationalbibliografie;
detailed bibliographic data are available on the internet at http://dnb.dnb.de.

© 2023 Walter de Gruyter GmbH, Berlin/Boston
Cover image: khonkangrua/iStock/Getty Images Plus
Typesetting: Integra Software Services Pvt. Ltd.
Printing and binding: CPI books GmbH, Leck

www.degruyter.com

Advance Praise for *Compassionate Leadership*

Without compassion and kindness, how effective can a leader be? Kirstie has impeccable credentials to illuminate these qualities. She works with leaders, understands the pressures under which they operate and helps address the dysfunction that is an inevitable by-product. This practical guide has all the trademarks of Kirstie's down-to-earth, compassionate approach to leadership.

– Richard Hytner, Former Worldwide Deputy Chairman
of Saatchi & Saatchi, and founder of Blue Hat Man

The author takes a distinctive approach to leadership development and practice by using the concept of compassion to focus on the human and emotional aspects of leadership behaviour . . . the author's definition of compassion and her intent to reinterpret it in a practical and hard-headed way instead of the more conventional soft-centred way has real value. It has the potential to allow leaders to improve the way people feel about their organisation and commit themselves to it, and themselves to become more effective.

– Sir David Pepper, formerly Director GCHQ

The power of this author's approach is to focus not so much on what makes people feel good, or conform to expected standards but to create a clearly actionable fusion of practice with contemporary research and the words of great authorities on what is good and leads to better well-being at the same time: i.e. compassion.

– Dominic Houlder, Adjunct Professor of Strategy and Entrepreneurship,
London Business School

Compassionate Leadership by Kirstie Papworth is a transformative read for managers and leaders seeking personal development with impact. With a pragmatic approach and a new model, Kirstie explores the practical benefits of compassion in organisational life, including improved employee trust, increased productivity, and stronger professional relationships. But what sets this book apart is its emphasis on the mental health and well-being benefits of compassionate leadership, empowering leaders to build a more positive work culture that benefits individuals, organisations, and society. If you're looking to develop your leadership depth sustainably while creating a more compassionate workplace, this book is a highly practical must-read.

– Chris Dalton, Associate Professor, Henley Business School

Compassionate Leadership is an essential read for leaders looking to foster resilient and sustainable workplaces. In this book, Kirstie Papworth draws on robust research to introduce the reader to a practical and user-friendly approach to bringing compassion into their organisation and leadership practice.

– Tatiana S. Rowson, PhD, SFHEA CMBE, Programme Area Director
Business and Management, Henley Business School

https://doi.org/10.1515/9783110763126-202

For TPS, with love

———

Compassionate people are geniuses in the art of living,
more necessary to the dignity, security, and joy of humanity
than the discoverers of knowledge.

(Albert Einstein)

Acknowledgements

This book is the result of many years of work, research, conversation and practice. Sometimes I learned about compassion through its presence and at other times through its absence. I am strangely grateful for both types of opportunity.

With apologies for any omissions or oversights, I particularly want to thank:

My research supervisors, Dr Kellyanne Findlay from Strathclyde University and Dr Trevor Long from Henley Business School, for your combination of challenge and belief.

All the organisations and individuals who participated in my research, so willingly giving your time and energy to these projects.

Those whose compassionate work has informed and inspired me, and who have been generous with their knowledge, especially Dr Jane Dutton, Dr Monica Worline, Dr Tania Singer, Dr Olga Klimecki and Dr Kristin Neff.

The amazing team at De Gruyter, especially Dr Bernd Vogel, Steve Hardman and Jaya Dalal for your guidance, support and compassion around deadlines.

A heady mixture of friends, mentors and colleagues who gave time, insight and nudges. I cannot name you all, but I particularly want to thank Dr Chris Dalton. Also, Sir David Pepper, Dr Kathleen O'Connor, Dominic Houlder and Mrs Mo.

The talented and compassionate Jenny Lee (@daddysangbass) for her creativity and superb design of the images in this book.

Friends whose company, walks, sustenance, laughter and patience were invaluable and deeply appreciated, especially Sabine, Caroline, Leigh, Johanne, Michelle, Neil and the Rotters.

Most of all to my boys: Ed, Calum and Lewis. Thank you from the bottom of my heart for the endless support, compassion and love. You are my world.

https://doi.org/10.1515/9783110763126-205

Foreword

"We need to build compassion into the structure of our organisations and to weave it into the fabric of everyday organisational life. This is not a 'knit your own granola' brand of leadership for people who cannot handle the pressure of modern organisations. Quite the opposite." – Kirstie Papworth, *Compassionate Leadership: For Individual and Organisational Change* (2023, p. 170).

Compassion needs to see the light of day in order to create ripples in organisations

Deep in my inner core you would find that I am a rather cynical, and even more sceptical individual. A book on compassion is exactly what I needed! And if you are similarly inclined, keep reading.

More so, I have noticed that a dichotomy seems to be emerging in organisations where some workplaces are purpose-driven, human-centred and sustainably performing, while other workplaces seem to go down the route of becoming more dehumanised; people feel commoditised, and relations and interactions seem purely transactional.

Compassionate Leadership: For Individual and Organisational Change adds thinking and practices that aim to bridge the seemingly irreconcilable desires to be a profitable, purposeful and sustainably human organisation. We often take these aspects as independent, but in fact, through devastating or exceptionally positive events we learn that they are actually interdependent.

One of the main challenges for topics like compassion and compassionate leading is to not only speak to evangelists and the convinced and help them to strengthen; the real test is impacting those who might be highly critical, less convinced or more sceptical. Engaging the unconvinced and reflecting on our own leadership takes us into the uncharted territory for an idea such as compassionate leadership. This book has the potential to succeed in exactly that terrain.

Compassionate Leadership also addresses an age-old and simultaneously contemporary pressing issue: How can we strengthen our thinking and practicing of leadership for a more desirable world – at all times?

Compassion is hard work – this book is a pathway to organise and motivate your and your organisation's journey

Kirstie's first clever move is to break down and broaden our understanding and practice of compassionate leadership with a new compassion construct that has four main areas of engagement: awareness, feeling an emotional response, appraisal, and taking action in an attempt to alleviate suffering, injustice, pain. In engaging with these, the book helps to access and strengthen compassion in our personal practice and wisdom.

The second clever move is to increasingly expand the footprint of compassionate practice in organisations. I often find that books on personal practice leave the individual alone to embed, reinforce, or strengthen a practice. Kirstie's book goes beyond this insular and disconnected capacity building and introduces a systemic approach

https://doi.org/10.1515/9783110763126-206

to support compassionate leadership. The book develops areas of development and action such as self-compassion for leaders, developing compassionate leadership, and designing a compassionate organisation, which acknowledge that personal agency and the wider context constantly interact. This is where things really start to change. I am convinced that this book can equip organisations to become sustainably compassionate places.

As a non-native speaker it is always a great opportunity to translate key terms to your own language, German in this case, and then literally translate back to English to grasp the meaning. Compassion comes back as *suffering with* or *feeling with*. While Kirstie might agree or disagree with one or the other option, I am interested in the *with*. In some spheres and organisations of the world, it seems to be much more about thinking, acting and succeeding *alone* rather than *with others*. This book convincingly reminds us to relate to people at work and beyond at a deeper level, and by that, make us together more successful in a healthier and sustainable way. This is a proper invitation to leave your own echo chambers in leadership thinking and practice and reach out to an uncharted territory of your own practice in leading. In doing so, you as reader will co-create the sustained impact of this title. Kirstie, many thanks for making this possible by writing this fascinating and indispensable book.

Bernd Vogel
Henley-on-Thames, UK
April 2023

Contents

Acknowledgements —— XI

Foreword —— XIII

Chapter 1
The case for compassionate leadership —— 1
    Human suffering —— 1
    Humanising the workplace —— 2
    Timeliness of compassionate leadership —— 3
    What is compassion? —— 3
    Earlier models of compassion —— 4
    What to expect from this book —— 7

Chapter 2
A new construct of compassion —— 9
    The new compassion construct —— 9
        Awareness —— 10
        Feeling —— 12
        Appraisal —— 14
        Responding —— 27
    When less is not more —— 28

Chapter 3
Mistaken identity: What compassion is and is not, and why this matters —— 30
    The nature of compassion: Vice, virtue, or verb? —— 30
    Mistaken identity —— 33
        Empathy —— 33
        Sympathy and pity —— 38
        Reality and perspective —— 40
        Individualistic versus collective —— 41
        Altruism —— 42
        Interconnectedness —— 45
        Kindness —— 46
        Compassion by comparison —— 48

Chapter 4
Compassion: Dubious reputation and accusation —— 51
    A dubious reputation —— 51
        Compassion in religion —— 52
        Compassion in philosophy and economics —— 54

Compassion in literature —— 56
Compassion in the press —— 56
Common organisational accusations —— 57
Weak leadership —— 57
Compassion fatigue —— 63
Compassion fade or psychic numbing —— 64
Compassion avoidance —— 65

Chapter 5
Research & reality: benefits of compassion —— 67
Leadership benefits —— 68
Reduced cellular inflammation and stress —— 68
Chemical balance and rewiring —— 69
Improved social connectedness —— 70
Organisational benefits —— 70
Affective Commitment (AC) —— 71
Organisational Compassion (OC) —— 72
Enhanced organisational wellbeing —— 75
Improved conflict resolution —— 76
Accountability and psychological safety —— 78
Case study: Compassionate lessons from healthcare organisations —— 79
The dark side of compassion —— 81

Chapter 6
Compassion and cognitive bias —— 84
But I am not biased! —— 84
What are cognitive biases and why do they matter? —— 85
Authority Bias and leadership —— 86
Motivation and intention —— 86
New compassion construct and cognitive biases —— 88
Confirmation Bias —— 89
Self-serving Bias —— 91
Fundamental Attribution Error —— 92
Availability Bias —— 93
Inattentional Blindness —— 94
In-group Favouritism —— 95
Just World Hypothesis —— 98
Naïve Cynicism —— 99
Negativity Bias —— 100
Bystander Effect —— 100
Compassion, bias and compassionate leadership —— 103

Chapter 7
Self-compassion for leaders —— **106**
    Self-compassion: Definitions —— **107**
    Self-compassion reputation and mistaken identities —— **109**
        Self-pity —— **109**
        Self-esteem —— **110**
        Self-criticism —— **111**
    Self-compassion: Research and benefits —— **113**
        Cognitive —— **113**
        Emotional —— **115**
        Behavioural —— **118**
    Actions to build self-compassion —— **119**
        Benchmarking your self-compassion —— **119**
        Self-compassion scale —— **120**
        Leadership research into self-compassion interventions —— **121**
        Adjusting self-talk —— **122**
        Self-compassion mirror —— **123**
        Self-compassion letter —— **124**
        Thank and release the inner critic —— **126**
        Compassion imagery —— **126**
    New compassion construct and self-compassion —— **127**

Chapter 8
Developing compassionate leadership —— **129**
    Compassion as a leadership choice —— **129**
        Why choose compassionate leadership? —— **130**
        Compassionate leadership and organisational outcomes —— **131**
        Organisational elevation —— **132**
    Developing our compassionate leadership —— **133**
        Awareness —— **135**
        Feeling —— **141**
        Appraisal —— **143**
        Responding —— **145**
    Leadership in the firing line —— **148**
    Our compassionate leadership legacy —— **150**

Chapter 9
Designing a compassionate organisation —— **152**
    Greater than the sum of parts —— **152**
        Strategic —— **153**
            The moral psychology of business —— **153**
            Building commitment through compassion —— **154**

Structural —— **156**
    HR policies and the employee lifecycle —— **156**
    Compassionate organisational responses, resources and reward —— **158**
Behavioural —— **160**
    Compassion, behavioural change and nudges —— **160**
    Compassionate leadership opportunities for all —— **163**
Cultural —— **166**
    Psychological safety and trust —— **166**
    Leadership creation and reinforcement of culture —— **168**
What gets measured (sometimes) gets done —— **169**
Key approaches to measuring organisational compassion —— **170**

Chapter 10
The future of compassionate leadership —— 173
The power of compassion —— **173**
Humane leadership —— **174**
Intention, choice and practice —— **175**
The future of compassionate leadership —— **176**

Further resources —— 179

References —— 181

List of figures —— 191

List of tables —— 193

About the author —— 195

About the series editor —— 197

Index —— 199

Chapter 1
The case for compassionate leadership

I have no idea what's awaiting me, or what will happen when this all ends. For the moment I know this: there are sick people and they need curing. (Albert Camus)

The one who plants trees, knowing that he will never sit in their shade, has at least started to understand the meaning of life. (Rabindranath Tagore)

Human suffering

We all suffer. Our suffering occurs in different ways and to varying extents, but none of us are immune. Compassion is a considered and powerful response to suffering. When correctly understood and applied, compassion can be a formidable force for positive change. This book tackles the very human experience of suffering, and shows what compassionate leadership is, the impacts it has and why it is needed now more than ever before.

Suffering may initially sound like a strange word to use with reference to organisational life. That said, have you ever experienced any of the following:

A bad day in the office, which left you feeling despondent?
Experiencing or witnessing bullying in a workplace?
Feeling emotionally or physically exhausted as you juggle competing demands of your work and home life?
Serious illness or death of a loved one?

If your answer to any of these is yes, then you have experienced suffering. Consciously or not, each of us is carrying a load. The size, nature and weight of the load will vary by individual. Indeed, the same event can affect us all in very distinctive ways, and what derails one person might be barely noticed by another.

Consider the last time you experienced suffering at work. Did anyone notice or respond? Perhaps someone took the time to listen and find out what would best support you. Maybe you suffered in silence. If someone acted to support you, did you feel the response was authentic or a tick-the-box exercise? The response you received may have impacted the quality of your work. It likely even had a direct bearing on your feelings about the organisation more widely. Such considerations reveal why our response to suffering at work matters. It concerns us all, impacting how we feel, how we approach our work and how we engage with the people and organisations we interact with. In addition to individual, personal impact, suffering has an immense productivity and financial cost to organisations. Compassion at work matters.

https://doi.org/10.1515/9783110763126-001

Humanising the workplace

To say that there is human pain in organisations is a colossal understatement. Factories of the industrial revolution and modern-day sweat shops are extreme examples of the workplace as a cause of suffering. Indeed, the very word 'sweater' was used in the late 1800s to describe an employer who paid very little for repetitive work done in miserable conditions. Contemporary settings might have changed for the better in some respects, but workplaces are still too often significant sources of employee discontent and distress.

Nor is human misery confined to the working week. Newsfeeds relentlessly update us about the gruesome impacts of political intolerance, war and environmental disaster. The World Bank estimates that approximately 160 million people are in need of humanitarian assistance as a result of natural disasters, conflicts and other crises. In addition, they estimate that around 1 billion people worldwide are thought to have some form of mental disorder and only around 25% of those suffering receive any treatment at all in low-income countries. In middle- and high-income countries, more than half of the population will suffer from at least one mental disorder at some point in their lives. Children are particularly vulnerable; almost half of mental health disorders globally start by the time a child reaches their 14th birthday. World Health Organisation data (WHO 2001) suggests that at least one in four people globally suffer from mental health issues. In short, it certainly seems that to be human is indeed to suffer.

We are struggling to keep pace with this global mental health tsunami. The WHO (2022) report that the pandemic either significantly adversely impacted or completely stopped mental health services in 93% of countries globally. That this happened at precisely the moment where the need for such services was increasing rubs handfuls of salt into an already festering wound. In addition to the individual, decidedly human impact of such mental health trends, the subsequent effects on economies worldwide is also significant. The WHO estimate that over the next decade depression will put more of a humanitarian and economic burden on nations than any other illness. The financial cost of mental health on the world economy pre-pandemic was estimated to be between USD$2.5–$16 trillion; that this figure will be revised upwards now seems inevitable.

In a trend exacerbated by the COVID-19 involuntary global social experiment, increasing numbers of people are reassessing their work priorities, opting to work more flexibly than before, and willing to move jobs in order to have their needs and aspirations met. So, alongside discussions on employee wellbeing at work and stress management, humanising the workplace is now a mainstream management topic. Long overdue, this development is not entirely surprising. Humans are, after all, social beings. No matter how perplexing or frustrating we find other people to be, it is almost impossible for us to live without each other. And, if we need to work together, the contexts in which we do so can be designed for compassion.

The snowballing of evidence about the detrimental impacts of organisational life has been gathering momentum for many years. Voices from across many disciplines encourage a more humane, people-centred voice to be heard in the boardroom. Lead with empathy. The power of altruism. Be kind. Although well intentioned, some confusion has arisen about what these different terms mean and the impacts they have. Such concepts as empathy, sympathy, kindness and compassion remain subtly yet crucially different, and not just semantically. Recent research has demonstrated that there are critical differences between them from a physiological and neuroscientific perspective. As this book will show, these varied responses to suffering are different in both their motivations and consequences. Our leadership intentions may be positive, yet they need to have clear understanding grounded in robust research if they are to have truly beneficial impacts.

Timeliness of compassionate leadership

Our volatile, complex and fragile world will continue to present unexpected challenges and pressing mental health issues for the foreseeable future. These issues, combined with the preference of younger generations to move jobs more frequently, and their desire for more purpose-led employment, make a compelling case for compassion to take on a more significant role in organisations. Compassionate leadership matters because people matter.

Compassion is, in some ways, nothing new. It is a cornerstone of most religions, and has attracted the attention of philosophers, economists and writers for centuries. Sadly, it also labours under an unfortunate reputation problem and is often considered a weakness in an organisational setting. In chapters 4 and 5, as well as exploring where this dubious reputation came from, we will assess more contemporary research which shows why compassion is, in fact, an extraordinarily powerful force for good. The old ways of profit-above-all, great-man leadership have been found wanting. Our world has changed, and we urgently need a new paradigm for leadership.

If the task of compassionate leadership sounds daunting, do not give up. This book will guide you through evidence-based ways to make a real difference. Consider this: every forty seconds, someone somewhere in the world dies by suicide. Forty seconds. Coincidentally, Johns Hopkins University research (Fogarty et al. 1999) found that a simple, verbal compassionate intervention significantly reduced anxiety in cancer patients. Each intervention took just forty seconds.

Sometimes the smallest actions can have the greatest impacts.

What is compassion?

The origin of the word compassion is derived from the Latin *compati*, meaning 'to suffer with'. When we notice someone suffering, we can feel their distress and take action to alleviate their pain. Compassion is, in the simplest terms, an emotional and practical response to suffering.

Earlier models of compassion

Paul Gilbert is a Professor of Clinical Psychology and a leading expert on the psychology of compassion. He writes, "compassion can be defined in many ways, but its essence is a basic kindness, with a deep awareness of the suffering of oneself and of other living things, coupled with the wish and effort to relieve it" (2009: xiii). What Gilbert is describing covers the common tripartite conceptualisation of compassion: noticing someone suffering, having an emotional response to that suffering and then taking action to try to alleviate the suffering, as shown in Figure 1.1.

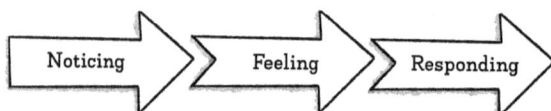

Noticing Feeling Responding

Figure 1.1: Common tripartite conceptualisation of compassion.

This three-part understanding of compassion is appealing in its simplicity. However, although it includes noticing, feeling and responding to suffering, it fails to include some other key elements which are crucial to a more complete understanding of compassion. For example, research scientist Jane Dutton and her colleagues (2014) have produced a substantial body of research on compassion in organisations, and they propose an additional step of 'sense-making', as illustrated in Figure 1.2.

Noticing Feeling Sensemaking Responding

Figure 1.2: Four-part conceptualisation of compassion.

At the simplest level, this 'sense-making' is defined as the observer interpreting what they have perceived in order to understand the situation and to promote a useful response. So, as a simple example, we might see someone struggling to cope with their workload, and yet spend a lot of time away from their work. Through sense-making, we might realise that they are upset about a family issue which is taking up a lot of their time and energy, and so impacting their capacity for work. We might – consciously or otherwise – then make a number of sense-making judgements depending on what we know about that person. Let us explore a few of these sense-making judgements, as they are startlingly prevalent in organisational and everyday life:

Sense-making judgements

1. Deserving of Suffering

Firstly, we can assess to what extent the person suffering has brought this on themselves, and to what extent they deserve their suffering. 'They are always like this, taking on work without thinking about whether they can do it – they only have their self to blame.' A Just World Hypothesis where people are deemed to 'get what they deserve' is explored further in Chapter 6 on cognitive biases; such judgement sounds disagreeable, yet is remarkably common and often made subconsciously.

2. Relevance to Ourselves

The second judgement concerns the relevance of the situation to us as the observer. This is an assessment, again potentially unconscious, where we consider the situation against our own values and gauge whether or not these are congruent with the suffering we observe. So, for example, if I value the stiff-upper-lip of emotional containment, I might negatively judge someone crying in an office environment. Neither is necessarily right or wrong; this is about a misalignment of different values and expressions.

3. Ability to Make a Difference

The third judgement assesses our ability to make a difference in a situation, or even to cope with helping someone else. This judgement might be as simple as 'I can't deal with this right now' or 'they are too upset and I don't have the time it will take to listen'. Equally, our judgement might have its beginnings in our own suffering, and whether we feel able to care for someone else when we ourselves might feel in need of support.

These three sense-making judgements are in many ways a useful supplement to the traditional three-part understanding of compassion. We can recognise that each of us has a unique, subconscious tapestry of experiences and values. Sense-making highlights some of our unconscious judgements, and allows for the ebb and flow of our individual capacity to support one another. Certainly, exploring our biases and blind spots are noble pursuits, worthy of deep reflective practice in our quest for personal growth and development as leaders. Such reflection, though, is typically a more useful pursuit when considered a lifetime's work; more a work-in-progress backdrop to our daily motivations and actions than a momentary response when faced with another's suffering.

The judgement of examining our individual and contextual ability to cope is useful in order that we are compassionate rather than empathetic or altruistic. As we will explore in Chapter 3, truly compassionate responses are resourcing and generative, while empathy and altruism are often detrimental from both a situational and a psychological perspective.

However, these judgements have a worrying undertone of us being in the position of judge and jury as we gaze upon the suffering of another person. They also fail to take into account our inevitable unconscious biases, and there is a distinct possibility that they might result in us reserving our compassion for people who are like us, those who share our values and views. There is a tacit assumption in these judgements that compassion for others is a burden for us to shoulder, rather than something which, if approached from a place of understanding, might be useful and positive for everyone involved. Biases including such in-group favouritism are explored in Chapter 6, and the supposed burden of compassion is investigated in light of recent research in Chapter 5.

A new construct of compassion

The new construct of compassion proposed in Chapter 2 is derived from both recent research and practical organisational application. When clearly understood and deftly practiced, the new compassion construct is a convincing basis for a compelling approach to leadership. This new approach is based on multidisciplinary research and has been applied in numerous organisational settings. It offers leaders something which can be easily brought to mind and applied, whilst also incorporating areas for deeper reflective practice and personal growth.

Even with a strong theoretical understanding, many leaders still struggle to turn new-found knowledge into action. It may be useful to keep in mind the stages of learning competence shown in Figure 1.3 as you develop your compassionate leadership:

Figure 1.3: Conscious competence learning model.

As you use this book, your competence in compassionate leadership might progress like this:

– unconscious incompetence
"I am not entirely sure what compassion is, or if it is useful, and I am worried that I do not know how to be compassionate."

– conscious incompetence
"As I read this book, I am starting to understand what compassion is and where I might already be good at it. I am moving from not being aware of gaps towards seeing which ones I have and want to address. I am trying some of the practical suggestions, and I know that I do not always get it right."

– conscious competence
"I have read the book, and I know how to apply compassion in my organisation. It still takes some effort to get it right, but it's getting easier."

– unconscious competence
"How did I live without this?! It is now second nature to bring compassion into my everyday leadership, and I have started sharing my new-found knowledge and practical skills with others – especially with those who think compassion is a weakness or even a threat."

To further support your compassionate endeavours, this book has an emphasis on everyday application. I distil much of the recent research and debate about compassion into an applied, contemporary approach to leadership. My emphasis throughout this book is on evidence-based practicality, at a time of deep human and organisational need.

What to expect from this book

As with many things in life, there is no absolute, prescriptive 'answer'. Instead, throughout this book, I offer guidance and realistic steps as well as areas for deeper reflection and exploration. You will find questions posed for your consideration alongside proven practices to adopt both as an individual leader and for your organisation more widely.

The new construct of compassion will be used as a frame throughout this book. This new construct includes an additional appraisal step, which is designed to encourage consideration of our motivations, resources, roles and patterns of behaviour. Understanding these enables us to be truly compassionate, in an impactful and restorative way. This new construct clearly distinguishes compassion from other related concepts and provides leaders with a useful guide, which includes psychological, leadership and organisational perspectives. We are no strangers to suffering, yet there is hope: as you learn about the power of compassion and how to adeptly apply it, you will enable compassionate change on a personal and organisational level.

Using the new compassion construct, we will look at the mistaken identities which lead many to confuse compassion with empathy, pity, kindness, sympathy or altruism (Chapter 3). We will also explore the dubious reputation compassion typically labours under and assess this in light of recent research (chapters 4 and 5). Cognitive biases are useful shortcuts to navigate our increasingly complex world, but they have unfortunate side-effects which compassionate leadership must remain alert to (Chapter 6). Compassionate leadership is incomplete if it is reserved only for the suffering of others, and so the beneficial impacts of self-compassion on the wellbeing and performance of leaders is explored in some detail (Chapter 7). Throughout this book, you will find prompts and suggestions in order that you can apply your learning long before you have finished reading this book. Taking this further, chapters 8 and 9 offer a detailed view of how to develop your compassionate leadership and build sustainably compassionate organisations. Chapter 10 will offer some conclusions on the outlook for compassionate leadership.

Above all, this book is an appeal for action; such action begins with each of us as individual leaders, extends to the organisations we influence and continues as our legacy.

Key Chapter Points

- Everyone suffers. It is the timing, nature and impact of our individual suffering that differ.
- Globally, mental health issues are increasing, and we are struggling to keep pace with this in our fast-paced, complex world.
- These issues have serious human, economic and financial impacts and need to be addressed in organisations through compassionate leadership.
- Compassion means to suffer with someone, to share in their pain.
- Traditionally, compassion has been described as a three-part process: noticing suffering, feeling a response to this and taking action to alleviate the pain.
- Sometimes a fourth step of sense-making judgements is included, although there are some limitations of this approach.

Chapter 2
A new construct of compassion

You never change things by fighting the existing reality. To change something, build a new model that makes the existing model obsolete. (R. Buckminster Fuller)

. . . the only genuine moral incentive [is] . . . the everyday phenomenon of compassion . . . all satisfaction and all well-being and happiness consist in this. (Schopenhauer)

The new compassion construct

This chapter offers a new construct of compassion, illustrated in Figure 2.1. The new compassion construct was devised as a result of my research into compassion in organisations, and has been refined through practical application. In essence, this construct has four main sections: awareness, feeling an emotional response, appraisal, and taking action in an attempt to alleviate the suffering. The appraisal step contains a further four considerations, which we will explore in some detail throughout this chapter. These are examinations of safety and intention, our patterns of behaviour, our resources and our roles.

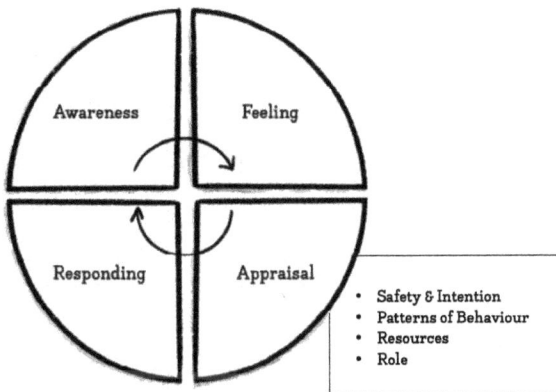

Figure 2.1: New compassion construct.

I will now outline each of the sections in turn, in order to build a robust understanding about compassion and how it applies to leadership. The appraisal step will, perhaps unsurprisingly, receive most attention below as this is a key differentiator from previous definitions of compassion. Each of us has a unique background of upbringing, personality

https://doi.org/10.1515/9783110763126-002

and experience, and so Boxes 2.1 and 2.2 encourage reflection on your individual preferences as you learn about the new compassion construct.

> **Box 2.1**
> Even at this early stage, consider where you are most and least comfortable in these four key areas. How might you step into discomfort to grow and how could you best use your areas of strength?

Awareness

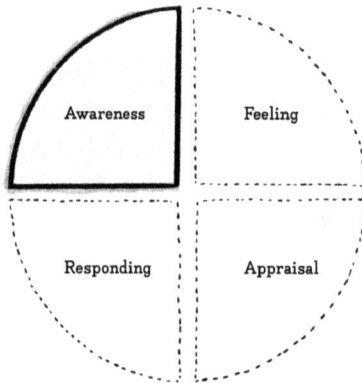

The new compassion construct deliberately chooses 'awareness' over 'noticing'. Noticing is the act of observing something which has attracted our attention, whereas awareness is the almost constant state of being alert to ourselves, to others and to nuance. Awareness includes what occurs, that which is sensed, and the 'white space' of that which is unarticulated, absent or not yet entirely observable.

Are you aware?

Nathaniel Branden was a Canadian psychotherapist whose work and writing focused predominantly on self-esteem. Although self-esteem is better understood and somewhat more palatable to most corporate tastes, self-compassion is increasingly considered a more persuasive device for individual resilience, as we will explore in Chapter 7. Regardless, Branden understood the importance of simple awareness, and encouraged his readers that awareness was the primary movement toward any change. This may seem an obvious statement, but awareness often seems to be in remarkably short supply. Ask yourself whether you are self-aware? Chances are you answered in the affirmative. Most people do. A recent study (Eurich 2018) found that although around 95% of people think they are self-aware, only between 10–15% are considered self-aware by others. The discrepancy, the researchers argue, is down to the difference between how well we understand ourselves and how well we understand how other people view us. From a leadership perspective, the picture looks even worse, as hierarchical power and experience often further hinder self-awareness. Put simply, higher level leaders are more likely to overestimate their abilities than those in more junior roles across a range of important competencies including empathy, self-awareness, trustworthiness and performance (Sala 2003).

Adding to this gloomy picture, author and psychologist Tasha Eurich (2018) also found that those who introspect – examining their thoughts, behaviours and feelings, whilst seeking to understand their underlying causes – are typically even less self-aware and report lower job satisfaction and wellbeing than those who do not. Initially this seems counter-intuitive. Surely introspecting on oneself is the path to increased self-awareness?

Perhaps not. Our minds are less rational that we might want them to be, and are subject to a myriad of shortcuts and biases (Chapter 6). Our unconscious is, by definition, almost impossible to examine, thus denying us access to the understanding we seek through introspection. Self-awareness may be more elusive than it first appears. As George Orwell noted back in 1946, 'to see what is in front of one's nose needs a constant struggle'.

Language of awareness

Tasha Eurich and her colleagues examined the language of those who were considered by others to be self-aware, and noticed that they use the word 'what' more frequently than they used 'why', even though the latter is more commonly associated with introspection. They hypothesise that this subtle shift to 'what' is less likely to result in rumination, and more likely to have a future-focused action orientation. For example, rather than asking ourselves 'why does work cause me to feel so low?', a more useful question could be to consider 'what are the situations at work which I dislike, and what pattern emerges from these?'. Further 'what' questions could then follow, such as 'what can I do to avoid or resolve these issues?' or 'what would my ideal job therefore look like?'.

Awareness of others

If self-awareness is largely elusive, awareness of our own suffering typically is not. We can certainly notice our individual physical pain and mental anguish, sometimes with crippling intensity. Becoming attuned to the suffering in others, though, seems much harder. To some extent, we can tune out of the daily bombardment of news about war, hatred and disaster as a form of self-preservation. In an organisational setting, or even with loved ones, we can simply be too busy or distracted to notice the pain someone is experiencing. This may sound trivial, until we consider that for a person suffering, often being seen and heard is an intensely influential response in itself. In other words, just being noticed can bring some healing.

When awareness is missing

Lack of awareness in an organisational setting is, of course, undesirable for compassionate leaders. Small issues can fester and grow if they are not noticed, and what goes unseen simply cannot be addressed. We do not need to behave with malice in order to harm someone; sometimes not noticing their suffering is enough. Such absence of awareness can result in us missing what truly matters, missing the detail and nuance in the rich fabric of the everyday. If we fail to notice suffering, we deny ourselves the chance to fully be with the people around us and to understand their experience.

Awareness in organisational life requires compassionate leaders to pause in order to allow suffering to emerge, and to hold an openness which allows it to be spoken. This requires us to consider what is not said, or to catch the fleeting glimpse of suffering in the briefest of moments when it bubbles to the surface. It does not require us to become paralysed by the prevalence of suffering, nor to become the organisational agony aunt or uncle. The trick is getting the balance right. An initial step towards compassionate leadership, then, is quite simply to increase our awareness. How we can do this is detailed in Chapter 8.

Feeling

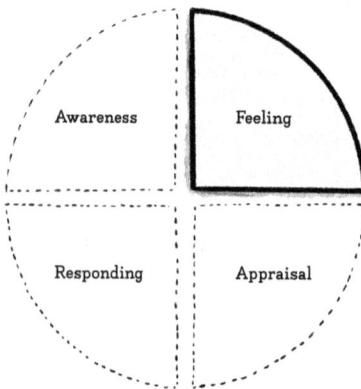

Following directly from awareness is the second step, feeling. This is where we feel an emotional response to the suffering we have witnessed. Feeling our emotional reaction is a cornerstone of empathy, that colloquial ability to be able to put oneself in the shoes of another, to feel their pain. And empathy, as we will see in Chapter 3, is a crucial building block of compassion.

Having such feeling for others impacts us at a psychobiological level, where the interplay between our minds and our bodies meet. At the Netherlands Institute for Neuroscience, researchers have found that observing the pain or actions of another person can result in a triggering of the same neural networks responsible if the pain or action was experienced first-hand (Keysers and Gazzola 2009). This research begs some interesting questions. Does such mirroring allow us to better understand other people? Does the ability to experience our own version of the suffering of another provide us with a vicarious response which is the foundation of compassionate action? Heinz Kohut, the renowned psychoanalyst, certainly believed such empathic feeling to be a fundamental element of human response:

> The empathic understanding of the experience of other human beings is as basic an endowment of man as his vision, hearing, touch, taste and smell.   (Heinz Kohut 2011: 13)

If this feeling response is so fundamental, then it is worth considering those who allegedly lack feeling or care for the pain of others: psychopaths. This may seem extreme in a book for organisational leaders, although the relevance is actually significant. Industrial psychologist Paul Babiak and criminal psychologist Robert Hare, in their fascinating book *Snakes in Suits: When Psychopaths Go to Work* (2007) note that while only approximately 1% of the general population is thought to be psychopathic, between 3–12% of CEOs display psychopathic traits. This is a wide range, as most CEOs are unlikely to respond in the affirmative to a direct question on this, and some may be adept at hiding their psychopathic tendencies under a cloak of charm. Although the term 'psychopath' often conjures up images of Hitchcock's Norman Bates or Leatherface from *The Texas Chainsaw Massacre*, the reality is a little less cinematographically exciting. Psychopathy is a neuropsychiatric disorder marked by deficient emotional responses, a lack of or inability to appropriately access empathy and poor behavioural control. Although not always the case, psychopathy sometimes results in recurrent antisocial deviance and criminal behaviours. Hitchcock's *Psycho* shower scene displays distinctly antisocial behaviour in a vividly memorable manner. Psychopathy in an organisational setting may hopefully be less bloody but can include a lack of empathy, outbursts of anger at subordinates, public humiliations, narcissism, threats or bullying.

Studying the psychopath's apparent lack of empathy can help our understanding of more typical emotional responses to suffering. Further research from the Netherlands Institute for Neuroscience examined activity in the insula and the anterior cingulate cortex; these regions of the brain are typically activated when witnessing the pain of another and during impulse control, respectively. Their research indicates that psychopaths may have the same ability to empathise, but it is their propensity to do this spontaneously which is altered. This research is too embryonic to provide definitive answers yet, but a useful practical step when dealing with lack of empathy from a boardroom 'suited snake' might be to simply remind them to feel the pain of the other person.

On the scale of feeling an emotional response, the extremes of either a psychopathic lack of empathy or, conversely, mirroring the pain of everyone we meet could both be overwhelming. The research of neuroscientist Giorgia Silani and colleagues provides some reassurance in this regard (2013). Their work has shown that the right supramarginal gyrus area of the brain, which correlates with emotional projection and responses, maintains a subtle distinction between our own pain and that of others. In other words, our brains provide a means of keeping our feeling response to the pain of another in a more centred place than either the extremes of psychopathy or empathic overwhelm. As compassionate leaders, feeling a response to the suffering of others enables us to have a human response without becoming overwhelmed.

> **Box 2.2**
> Keep a diagram of the new compassion construct to hand as a reference. Take the time to notice if you tend to or prefer or avoid any particular sections. We will explore in Chapters 8 and 9 what you can do to overcome such inclinations.

Appraisal

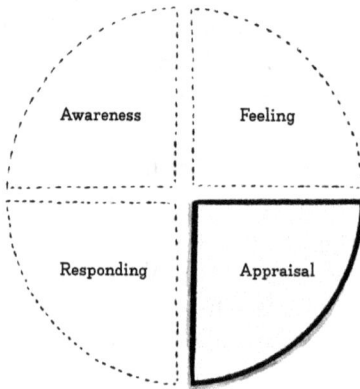

The inclusion of an Appraisal step is the key difference from other models of compassion, outlined earlier in this chapter. Therefore, we will now explore this step in some detail, so that the different aspects of appraisal are well understood and can be skilfully applied to compassionate leadership.

Appraisal and judgement

As we have already seen from Jane Dutton's 'sense-making' step in Chapter 1, the idea of appraising a situation is sometimes used with reference to compassion. However, what I mean here by appraisal differs from such judgements.

Writing about compassion, Aristotle described judgements which are made about the 'deservedness' of suffering. Having reached their verdict, he argued, the observer then acts in accordance with their judgement (in Nussbaum 2001). This approach demonstrates a Just World Hypothesis, of people getting what they deserve in life (Chapter 6) and may easily catch us in the trap of extending our compassion only to those who are similar to ourselves.

Such an approach to appraisal is also in direct conflict with humanistic psychologist Carl R. Rogers's notion of Unconditional Positive Regard (1961). The basic premise of such regard is accepting people just as they are, without judging what they say or do, and without the need to fix or change them. Rogers believed that this allowed people to accept themselves without judgement, which in turn enabled them to take more personal responsibility. Sounds simple enough, but Unconditional Positive Regard is often harder to apply in practice than it is to comprehend. As we will discover, our shortcuts, judgements and biases are deeply ingrained, and it takes awareness and practice to shift our thinking out of such well-trodden trenches.

So, what do we mean by appraisal?

Appraisal in the new compassion construct

Appraisal in this new construct is different to the sense-making notions outlined earlier in this chapter, as well as from Aristotle's judgement of deservedness. Instead, the appraisal step is designed to ensure our resulting response to pain is both considered and in the best interests of all concerned: the person suffering, ourselves, our leadership responsibilities and the organisations we work within. Four areas are appraised within this step:

(i)   safety and intention
(ii) patterns of behaviour
(iii) your resources
(iv) your role

Appraisal step: (i) Appraising for safety and intention

Safety

The first part of the appraisal step considers safety. Appraising for a safe, compassionate response can be illustrated with a simple example: If we see a cyclist who has fallen from their bike, we can dash across the road to help without appraising the wider situation. This not only puts our own safety at risk, as we rush into the path of oncoming traffic, but it may consequently limit our ability to offer support to the injured cyclist. Alternatively, we can choose compassion, where we take action to alleviate suffering once we have considered the wider situation, and have checked that it is safe to cross the road.

In a similar although more nuanced way, we can appraise for safety in an organisational setting. If we rush to respond to all the suffering we see, we may quickly find ourselves entangled and overwhelmed. Thus ensnared, we are unlikely to be able to see wider systemic issues or causes. Our own emotional reserves could quickly become depleted as we take on more and more of other people's pain. When such entanglement and overwhelm combine, our own work and safety will suffer; our desire to support without considering safety will ultimately, inadvertently destabilise us.

Intention

Appraising our intention is subtler than that of safety. Does our compassionate intention derive from a genuine desire to alleviate suffering, or do we want to look like a noble person, and to take the glory for being seen as a Good Samaritan? We know that taking compassionate action to support others releases happy serotonin hormones, pleasurable dopamine neurotransmitters and feel-good oxytocin. We each need to consider whether these are merely pleasant side-effects or a key driving force behind our compassionate actions.

More worryingly, compassion can be used as a smiling mask behind which lies something far more sinister. As the 'American Nietzsche', H.L. Menchen wrote, "The urge to save humanity is almost always a false front for the urge to rule." Clearly, then, intention is an important consideration for compassionate leadership.

Appraisal step: (ii) Appraising our patterns of behaviour

Take a moment to think about your own repeated patterns of behaviour (Box 2.3). These could include almost anything. Maybe you err on the side of conflict avoidance, are invariably the first (or last) to speak in meetings, simply cannot say no, have an over-reliance on formal power or use humour as a defence. We might have similar patterns in our professional relationships: the boss you never openly disagree with, the peer meetings where you typically leave with most of the action points, the colleague who needs you to listen but rarely returns the support, or the team member whose interactions you secretly dread.

> **Box 2.3**
> Reflection: Consider your repeated patterns of behaviour. Which are useful? Which no longer serve you well?

Transactional analysis

Lest we now start to ruminate on explanations for our behavioural patterns – typically a combination of our personality traits, upbringing, childhood relationships with our primary caregivers and unresolved traumatic experiences – it can be useful to consider these within a frame of Transactional Analysis. This is a psychoanalytic theory developed in the 1950s and 1960s by psychologist Eric Berne (1964). It focuses on the communication between people and whether their ego states are in Parent, Adult or Child. Figure 2.2 illustrates a common dynamic between these states:

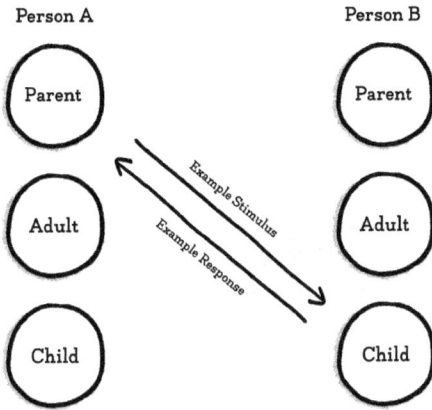

Person A   Person B

Parent   Parent

Adult   Adult

Example Stimulus
Example Response

Child   Child

Figure 2.2: Transactional Analysis: Parent – Adult – Child.

The *Parent* ego state is deeply rooted in the traditions and values of our families of origin. It is concerned with our notions of 'right and wrong' and has many spoken and unspoken rules. These rules can include countless aspects such as how acceptable it is to show emotion or something as simple as whether or not to take your shoes off before going upstairs. When we think that we 'ought' to do something but are not entirely sure why, we are probably hearing parent communication.

The *Child* ego state develops from our early childhood experiences, and is a source of emotional associations or responses. How we experienced criticism as a child, for example, may result in a similar reaction when we find our work critiqued as an adult. Child ego states are often classified as 'compliant' or 'defiant', and most of us recognise our typical pattern in one of these.

The *Adult* ego state is that of mature, rational behaviour. It handles complex scenarios and decisions, and handles its feelings in a calm manner.

As an example of how these ego states might play out, when we are in a Parent ego state we might treat or refer to younger or more junior colleagues as 'children'. Our ego state may be visible in patronising behaviours, or even through excessively protecting people from a known or imagined threat; wrapping them in corporate cotton wool, so to speak. Similarly, we could find ourselves adopting a Child ego state with such a boss and, like actual children, we might either quietly defer to such parental authority or become defiantly disruptive.

When we recognise which ego state we or others are in, we can make an informed choice about whether or not to modify our position accordingly. Particularly in an organisational setting, moving to an Adult-Adult transaction is generally considered optimal. Nobody is permanently in an Adult ego state, though, so we should allow for variation; the key is adopting our state to the context we are in and the outcome we are seeking.

Transactional Analysis is valuable when navigating workplace dynamics, and particularly useful when considering compassion. Compassionate leadership is most beneficial when it comes from an Adult, rather than a Parent, ego state. If someone continually seeks our compassion from a Child state, our ability to recognise this and remain in Adult will be of benefit to both parties, lest we reinforce a parent – child dynamic. Equally, when needing compassion for ourselves, we can reflect upon the ego state we typically adopt in seeking this and consider whether this always serves us well.

Two further concepts are also useful when considering the appraisal of typical behavioural patterns and compassionate leadership: The Games People Play and the Drama Triangle.

The Games People Play

Eric Berne's book, *The Games People Play,* was first published in the mid-1960s. Yet still today, it offers us a sometimes uncomfortably accurate description of psychological game-roles common in human interactions. Although some of the suburban housewife scenarios he describes are rather outdated, many of the games such as 'Now I've Got You, You Son of a Bitch', 'See What You Made Me Do' or 'Why Don't You . . . Yes, But' are still very much in evidence today.

For example, an organisational game of 'Why Don't You . . . Yes, But' might sound something like this:

> Freda: 'I can't get the sales team to take on our new product'
>
> Freda's manager: 'Well why don't you talk to them?'
>
> Freda: 'Yes, but they always tell me they've got too many products to sell already'
>
> Freda's manager: 'Why don't you spend some time with them to understand their needs better?'
>
> Freda: 'Yes, but I don't have time for that – I've got too much else to do'
>
> Freda's manager: 'Why don't you delegate some of your workload in order to free up some time?'
>
> Freda: 'Yes, but people make mistakes so I end up having to do it all anyway'

. . . and so on.

Such game-roles are often subconscious, and can be behavioural patterns which those in the game remain oblivious to. Noticing when we are involved in such a game, and in what role, allows us to make a conscious choice about our subsequent actions and approach. We can choose whether to change the role we typically adopt, to begin a new game or to stop playing entirely. When in the appraisal step of compassion, awareness of the games we typically play or roles we adopt allows us the insight to adopt a more useful stance.

Drama triangle

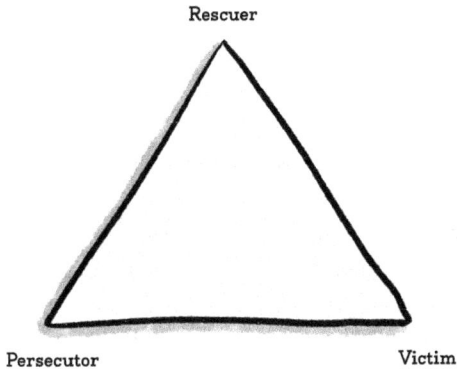

Figure 2.3: Karpman's Drama Triangle.

The three positions in Stephen Karpman's Drama Triangle (1968) are victim, persecutor and rescuer, as illustrated in Figure 2.3. Such roles can be either literal or game-roles, and are a crucial consideration in the appraisal step. In a literal context, the victim may be someone who is being attacked, the perpetrator is the person attacking and the rescuer a passer-by who intervenes. In a game-role situation, the roles are often subtler. Whereas an actual victim may be overpowered and a game-role victim can consider themselves to be equally helpless, the latter are more likely to be underestimating their ability to influence the situation.

Victim
Of the three roles, the victim is often the easiest to notice, often through their use of language: 'it wasn't my fault', 'you're always picking on me', 'I need everyone else to change their behaviour to suit me', or 'there's nothing I can do about it'. In a strange way, the victim role can be an alluring position to adopt, possibly because it receives attention. However, it is an unhealthy place to remain, as it is fatiguing and reduces our own capacity for change.

Persecutor
The persecutor role can be an actual person launching an attack or, in game-role terms, can be someone using and reinforcing a persecutor position through the maltreatment of someone else. Mothers and managers are frequently, albeit unknowingly, cast in the persecutor role. Bearing in mind the discussion on psychopathy in organisations during the feeling step of the new compassion construct, it is important to note that the role of persecutor is typically assigned to someone by the victim, rarely by the persecutor

themselves. When a victim – persecutor dynamic exists, the difficulty comes in understanding what is real versus what is perspective or conditioning of a victim.

Rescuer

Similarly, a rescuer can be literal, where a bystander intervenes to stop an attack, or this can be a game-role rescuer. The latter, sometimes through a desire for recognition or from psychological conditioning, will step in to rescue others. Thomas Harris (1973) would see this as the 'I'm ok, you're not ok' position: I'm ok enough to be in a position to rescue you, whereas you are not ok and therefore require rescuing. Rescuers can inadvertently keep someone trapped in their role as victim whilst they feel good as a rescuer. For example, escorting a little old lady across the road may give the rescuer a momentary dopamine hit, but not all elderly people need such help, and the insistence of the rescuer may have overlooked that the lady did not intend to cross over the road at all. Equally, colluding with a colleague victim about how terrible the persecutor boss is might be temporarily cathartic, but is unlikely to result in a positive change of circumstance and merely reinforces the Drama Triangle roles.

In organisations, whilst a leader is often portrayed as the perpetrator by a victim, a colleague or middle manager will often be recruited into the role of rescuer. If the boss makes us work too hard or does not seem to care about our plight, a victim can waste energy and reinforce their paralysis by simply wishing for a change. Alternatively, they might realise that they have more options available to them than they first thought. Options about how they approach their work, the choices they have within work, and whether or not to remain in the role can all offer a loosening of the bonds of victimhood. By leaping in to save someone from a persecutor, rescuers can inadvertently entrench the role of victims, rather than supporting them to find their own resources and solutions to their perceived or actual situation.

There is, of course, a more effective tactic than the game-role of rescuer, which is of particular interest when considering compassion. To approach someone with the intention of alleviating suffering is a useful, compassionate advance. Yet to do this without strengthening the grip of victimhood requires care and understanding. Unconditional Positive Regard – recognising that we are all capable and perfectly imperfect – supports a more positive, balanced outcome than one which wants to rescue anyone.

All three roles – victim, persecutor and rescuer – are necessary in order for there to be a Drama Triangle. Avoiding entanglement in such a triangle, and in particular the potential allure of the rescuer position, requires us to take a nuanced and neutral stance rather than adopt one of the positions. This can be visualised as standing to the side of the triangle, aware of each role and dynamic between them, yet without being seduced into any of them. Box 2.4 offers more detailed ways to escape the Drama Triangle.

Box 2.4: Escaping the Drama Triangle
If you find yourself in the victim role:
- remind yourself of some things you are grateful for (see this and other prompts in Table 2.1)
- cultivate a growth mindset (see Chapter 7)
- practice self-compassion (see Chapter 7)
- rather than finding others to collude with, consider your options

If you find yourself in the persecutor role:
- consider the purpose of your behaviour and what might serve the situation better
- ask what you are bringing to the issue and how you can change this
- see people more widely, more compassionately, using the new compassion construct

If you find yourself in the rescuer role:
- ask yourself why you are rescuing and what unmet need this might be meeting in yourself
- rather than rescue, consider what might be useful for the other person to support themselves
- coach the other person to find their own solutions, rather than assuming you know best

Karpman's Drama Triangle is a critical aspect of the appraisal step in the new construct of compassion. Through enhancing our understanding of this step (see Box 2.5 for a way to practice this awareness and understanding), and considering our own preferences and behavioural patterns, we increase the likelihood of adopting a more useful, considered approach to the alleviation of suffering. In this way, we can ultimately benefit individual abilities and support options, rather than reinforcing the roles of persecutor, rescuer or victim.

Box 2.5
In conversations, look for game playing or Drama Triangle clues. This will help to develop your awareness of these, in order that you can become more conscious and adept at your own practice and choices.

Appraisal step: (iii) resources
The third element within the appraisal step is a consideration of our own resources or capacity to support others. As we will explore more in Chapter 3, compassion differs from altruism in this regard as altruism looks after the needs of others even if this is to the detriment of ourselves. In order to have a truly compassionate response to suffering, we each have a responsibility for ensuring that we are sufficiently resourced before turning towards others. In this way, compassion can be a sustainable, enduring force for good.

This aspect of appraisal can sometimes make leaders feel uncomfortable. Logically we know that turning to support someone else when we are depleted ourselves often leads to burnout, resentfulness, exhaustion or even illness. We cannot, as the adage goes, pour from an empty cup. Somehow, though, the idea of looking after ourselves first has yet to become the norm.

Resourcing can be thought of as the active, conscious means of nourishing ourselves. There is no one way to do this, and no 'secret recipe' that will work for everyone. For, in the words of Henry Louis Mencken, "there is always a well-known solution to every human problem – neat, plausible, and wrong" (1920/2010: 158). The only 'answer' in this instance is broad guidance, supported by research. We each need to find what resources work for us individually at any given point in time, and then consciously do more of those things.

From working with many leaders over the years, and assessing current research, there are some resourcing suggestions which seem particularly prevalent. Notice which you are drawn to and consider what else may be on your own tailored list, as prompted in Box 2.6.

Box 2.6

Reflection: What makes you feel resourced and how can you make more space for this in your life?

Resourcing ourselves can be thought of in five key areas: physical, social, emotional, mental and spiritual, as shown in Table 2.1. Taking care of ourselves in these areas can increase our energy levels, improve teamwork, enhance relationships and reduce anxiety. In addition, resourcing ourselves in these ways means that we will be better prepared in our quest for compassionate – rather than altruistic – leadership.

Table 2.1: Resourcing Ourselves.

Area	Description	Areas to consider for action
Physical	This area includes how much physical activity you do, how well you are fuelling your body, as well as both the quantity and quality of your sleep. The body and mind need each other, so this is not an area to neglect over purely intellectual pursuits.	– Am I doing enough exercise? – Am I getting enough quality sleep? – Am I eating well?
Social	There is no 'right amount' of time we spend with friends or family. However, investing time in developing close social connections is good for our overall health (see Chapter 5 on social connectedness).	– Am I sufficiently nurturing my relationships with friends or family? – Do I have enough in-person time with people I love?
Emotional	Emotional resourcing gives us the time and space needed to process difficulty and to look after our own emotional needs.	– What support do I have to help me process difficulties in my life (support can be via people or activities)? – What, if anything, do I lack in this regard and how can I begin to source it? – What am I grateful for?

Table 2.1 (continued)

Area	Description	Areas to consider for action
Mental	Mental resourcing includes nourishing our mental wellbeing, as well as keeping our minds sharp and curious.	– Do I read books or watch programmes about areas of interest to me? – Do I have a rich variety of interests? – Am I proactively looking after my mental health, through exercise, connection, rest and practicing self-compassion (see Chapter 7)?
Spiritual	Spirituality has been shown to help us cope with stress and is linked to better physical health (Whitehead and Bergeman 2012). Not necessarily religion, spirituality is considered to include explorations of meaning or purpose.	– Am I nourishing and exploring my emotional or spiritual side, through religion, meditation or other means? – How can I notice and appreciate more moments of awe (natural beauty or art are fertile areas in this regard)?

At this point, overworked leaders may be thinking 'nice ideas, but I just do not have time'. I would counter, quite simply, that you do. That we all do. Arnold Bennett wrote a slim volume cheekily entitled *How to Live on Twenty-Four Hours a Day*, with an emphasis on living rather than simply existing. He notes, "one's programme must not be allowed to run away with one. It must be respected, but it must not be worshipped as a fetish. A programme of daily employ is not a religion" (1908: 58). We are not our jobs. Our jobs are not our lives.

If the ideas noted in Table 2.1 for resourcing versus your lived experience have left you feeling despondent at how few you currently partake in, do not despair. There are many small steps you can take, which will soon add up to a significant improvement in your resources and capacity for compassion.

Firstly, consider that our focus, productivity and creativity are all enhanced by taking regular breaks. Even taking a few moments throughout the working day has been shown to have a host of benefits. Our ability to concentrate and the way we perceive our jobs is improved. The detrimental physical impacts of being desk-bound for the majority of our waking hours can be offset to some extent when we break, stand up, stretch or move around. We are unlikely to allow our technology to run out of charge, and we should apply the same care to ourselves. Nourishing and prioritising ourselves is a smarter approach than putting such resourcing off until after the (endless) to-do list is miraculously done.

Secondly, remember that the victim game-role is not a healthy position to adopt, so before time or work become your persecutors, consider what options you have and what steps you could take in order to change your situation. Examples of solutions for the time-poor include having walking meetings to increase our capacity for exercise and fresh air, spending a few minutes on a Monday morning removing at least three meetings from the week ahead, delegating or declining more often than is comfortable, and asking for additional support in whatever way that benefits you most. If the mere thought of doing these things fills you with dread, then the next stage within the appraisal step – considering the impact of your role on compassion in organisations – should provide further food for thought.

Thirdly, do not assume that resourcing is an onerous task. Micro-experiments can be a rapid, enjoyable way to resource ourselves. Steal like an artist; try what works for someone else, and either adopt, abandon or amend it to suit you. Block a couple of short breaks in your day to do something that does not involve screens or doing things for other people. Making a coffee and drinking it outside without scrolling on a phone can feel like a longer break that the few minutes it actually takes. Taking a couple of minutes to privately write down what you are grateful for each day may feel cringe-worthy initially. However, an increasing body of research suggests that gratitude is strongly correlated to wellbeing, quality of sleep, improved inter-personal relationships and the ability to cope with pressure (Wood et al. 2010). Listening to a short self-compassion meditation once a day has been shown to significantly reduce feelings of stress and anxiety, as will be explore more in Chapter 7.

Above all, remember that the active, conscious resourcing of ourselves is a crucial investment to ensure our effectiveness and longevity as a compassionate leader.

Appraisal step: (iv) Role

The fourth and final area included within the appraisal step is that of role. We have already explored psychological roles within the Games People Play and Karpman's Drama Triangle; the roles which concern us in this section are the more visible roles of our everyday lives, both in an organisational setting and in our lives more broadly. Each of us take on multiple different roles, and these may be extremely important to our lives or to our sense of identity. We are friends, peers, children, leaders, parents, partners, customers and many others, often simultaneously.

Consideration of these roles matters, because we typically access compassion more readily for those we know and love, and for those who we consider to be part of our in-group than those in out-groups (more on this in Chapter 6). Sadly, the reverse can also be true, as domestic abuse and other extreme persecutor behaviours unfortunately demonstrate. More often than not, though, we are simply more likely to give care, time, money and attention to our known acquaintances than to the millions of anonymous others who live in poverty around the world.

So, the challenge we face as leaders is to widen our compassion beyond those who are known, loved or familiar. As we shall see in Chapter 3, Einstein implored us to extend our compassion as widely as possible, especially when this is difficult to do. Dissenting voices, creative non-conformists, those who cut our budgets or challenge our authority – all of these are still deserving of inclusion in our compassionate leadership.

Disproportionate leadership role impact

Compassion is, of course, highly sensitive to both role and context. The role of a parent when their child falls over is likely to be different to that of a passer-by. The role of a firefighter attending a burning building differs from that of someone in the neighbouring building. Similarly, the role of a leader is unlike that of other roles in an organisation.

As my own and other research has shown, whether a leader chooses to be compassionate or otherwise, their actions will be amplified and have disproportionate organisational impact. Box 2.7 offers a case study in this regard, focused on the actions of ex-Starbucks CEO, Howard Schultz.

Box 2.7: Case Study: Starbucks

Starbucks offers a useful example of such leadership impact when compassion is present and also when it appears to be absent. In 1997, three Starbucks employees were shot dead in a Washington branch of the coffee chain during a robbery. Howard Schultz, then CEO, did not do what many CEOs would have done. He did not call his public relations team. He did not call his lawyers. He avoided national television. He did not tweet his thoughts and prayers. Instead, he immediately interrupted his vacation and went to meet the victims' families. As well as simply being with them and listening to them, he was actively finding out what would be useful to each of them over the coming days and months. Consequently, counselling sessions for grieving families and traumatised staff were arranged, a reward for information about the killings was offered and Shultz mourned with the victims' families both privately and publicly. Schultz's compassionate response generated positive PR for Starbucks as a result of his actions and his name became inextricably linked with compassionate leadership.

Compare this outcome with that of the subsequent Starbucks' CEO response to an incident in 2018. Donte Robinson and Rashon Nelson, two black customers, were arrested for allegedly trespassing in a Philadelphia branch of the coffee chain; in fact, they were waiting for a friend and so had not yet placed an order. Social media moved quickly, and protests began outside Starbucks stores. CEO Kevin Johnson called the arrests reprehensible and said "I'd like to have a dialogue with them [Robinson and Nelson] so that I can ensure that we have opportunity to really understand the situation and show some compassion and empathy for the experience they went through" (Gayle 2018). Another press report noted that arranging this meeting might take a little time: "According to a Starbucks spokesperson, the timing of the meeting has yet to be set. The company said it hopes the meeting will come off this week . . ." (Annor 2018). In actual fact, Johnson ultimately met Robinson and Nelson the week after the incident and Starbucks later reached an undisclosed agreement with the men.

As an outside observer, reliant on the accuracy of press reports, we cannot assess the merit or otherwise of the outcomes of these two Starbucks incidents. We can, however, as neutral observers, notice that Shultz displayed timely, action-orientated compassionate leadership. He tailored his response to the individual needs of the victims' families and put their suffering at the centre of his subsequent actions. Johnson's response was different. He appeared on Good Morning America to talk about showing compassion before he found the time to meet the arrested men. We do not know the detailed outcome of their discussions, legal, financial or otherwise. What we do know is that whether the actions of leaders are perceived to be compassionate or otherwise, those with the leadership job title ought to remain aware of their disproportionate visibility and impact.

As a leader, indeed as in many other roles in life, role modelling the desired behaviours you want is far more effective than just espousing them. At home, children are more likely to do what you do than do what you say. Similarly, if you want to understand leadership behaviours, instead of listening to what people say, try watching what they do. When espoused and enacted leadership behaviours are poles apart from each other, people notice. In contrast, where strong value congruence between words and actions exists, employees are more likely to be aligned to the espoused values (Gopinath et al. 2018). So, a further responsibility of the compassionate leader is to consider their role in modelling how a compassionate organisation behaves when resourcing oneself and when responding to suffering. Box 2.8 offers some prompts to support your reflections in this regard.

> **Box 2.8**
> Consider everything we have covered in the appraisal step. Maybe start by thinking about a recent scenario where compassion was warranted: did you consider your safety? Intention? Patterns? Resources? Role? What can you learn about yourself, your preferences & tendencies? Is there anything you might do differently in future as a result of this understanding? What small steps can you take today in order to resource yourself more fully?

Remember, if you are not the CEO, you still make a difference. Such disproportionate leadership impact does not necessarily mean that *only* those with the most senior job titles can have a compassionate effect. Recent research on the emerging notion of followership suggests that influence occurs in many directions within an organisational setting (Brown 2018). In the words often attributed to anthropologist Margaret Mead, "never doubt that a small group of thoughtful, committed citizens can change the world. Indeed, it is the only thing that ever has." Every one of us can make a compassionate difference, in our organisations and in our world.

Responding

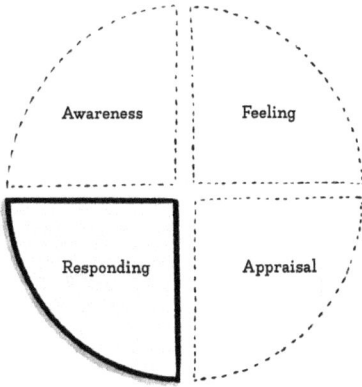

The last step in the new compassion construct is responding. It is specifically this taking of action in order to alleviate suffering which differentiates compassion from empathy. Empathy plus action is compassion.

This final step is necessarily the shortest to describe. Having understood the preceding three steps, the compassionate leader will be in a position to be aware of suffering, feel a measured emotional response, appraised the safety and intention of their response, and will have assessed their own resources, role and patterns of behaviour. They can then respond in a considered and truly compassionate way.

Responding can take many forms, and is most impactful when it is tailored to the specific situation. A leadership response can be as simple as spending time listening to someone. It may involve agreeing for them to have time away from work pressures in order to resolve an issue or emotionally heal. Or it could require a more complex response which involves orchestration of various resources across an organisation. In short, as Howard Shultz adeptly demonstrated, a response which listens to the needs of the sufferer, sits with their pain, asks then delivers what would be most useful to them is that of a truly compassionate leader. Even when you find the content difficult or upsetting, or even when you are told that you are the source of the suffering, this is not the time to argue or dismiss what you hear. Listen. Listen like you are wrong. Listen to understand. Only then, choose your compassionate response.

The choice of the word 'responding' for this step is quite deliberate. Using all four steps of the new compassion construct means that we will be able to respond rather than to react. As Holocaust survivor and psychiatrist Viktor Frankl (1959/2004: 75) noted:

> Between stimulus and response lies a space. In that space lie our freedom and power to choose a response. In our response lies our growth and our happiness.

When less is not more

With understanding and practice, the four steps of the new compassion construct can take place in moments. What matters is that they are all included. When we shortcut any of the steps, our response is not compassion.

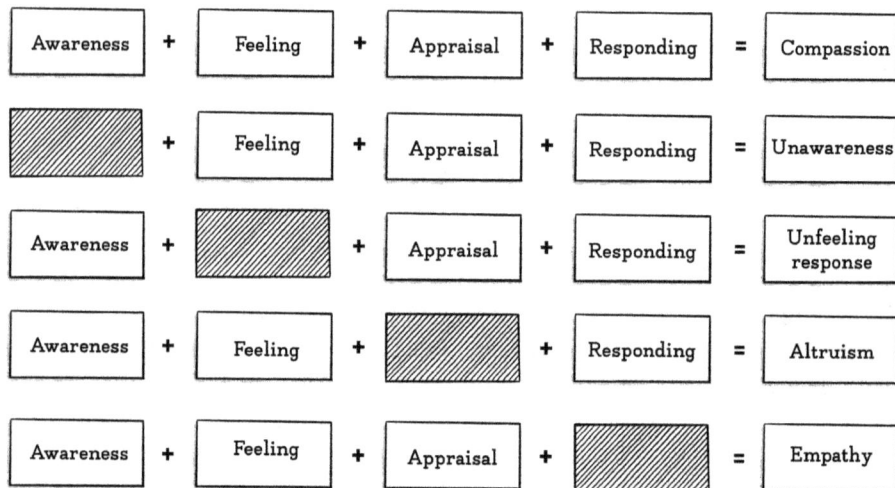

Awareness	+	Feeling	+	Appraisal	+	Responding	=	Compassion
[hatched]	+	Feeling	+	Appraisal	+	Responding	=	Unawareness
Awareness	+	[hatched]	+	Appraisal	+	Responding	=	Unfeeling response
Awareness	+	Feeling	+	[hatched]	+	Responding	=	Altruism
Awareness	+	Feeling	+	Appraisal	+	[hatched]	=	Empathy

Figure 2.4: Compassion maths.

As Figure 2.4 illustrates, all four steps of the compassion construct are required for an effective, compassionate response to suffering. Without awareness, compassion cannot occur as the suffering remains unnoticed. Without a balanced emotional response, any action may be robotic or cold. When the appraisal step is missed, taking action can result in depleted resources, may be inappropriate to our role, might have a Machiavellian intention, could put us in danger or entrench the sufferer in a victim position. Without action, the response is empathy, not compassion. Action without consideration for ourselves is altruism. Why such nuances matter is explored in the following chapter; more than simply semantics, the differences are distinctive both psychologically and in their impact upon others.

Key Chapter Points
- The new construct of compassion has four distinct steps, each of which has been examined in some detail:
  - Awareness
  - Feeling
  - Appraisal
  - Responding

- The additional appraisal step has a further four key areas to consider:
  - Safety and intention
  - Patterns of behaviour
  - Resources
  - Role
- Considerations of the impacts of Transactional Analysis, Drama Triangle and psychological games are all important aspects of appraisal.
- Practical, evidence-based suggestions for improving your resources in physical, social, emotional, mental and spiritual ways are offered.
- The disproportionate impact of leadership is discussed, and a case study of Starbucks is used to highlight an example of compassionate leadership in adversity.
- When any of the steps of the new compassion construct is missing, the result is not compassion. It is either unawareness, an unfeeling response, empathy or altruism.

Chapter 3
Mistaken identity: What compassion is and is not, and why this matters

> Seldom, very seldom does complete truth belong to any human disclosure; seldom can it happen that something is not a little disguised, or a little mistaken. (Jane Austen)

> If we could read the secret history of our enemies, we would find in each person's life sorrow and suffering enough to disarm all hostility. (Henry Wadsworth Longfellow)

Have you ever felt uncomfortable when someone was compassionate towards you? Perhaps you have witnessed a compassionate act which you felt had an unpleasant undertone. Or maybe frequent requests from charitable causes leaves you feeling despondent. If you recognise familiarity in any of these, you are not alone. Compassion has sometimes received attention for its positive benefits and associations, and yet has also been dismissed as immoral, wearisome or self-serving. And sometimes what we think is compassion is actually something else entirely. Because of all this complication and misunderstanding, we will now explore the nature of compassion, and then assess a line-up of the usual suspects when it comes to compassion's mistaken identity.

The nature of compassion: Vice, virtue, or verb?

Vice
Ben Jonson, English playwright and contemporary of Shakespeare, is famed both for his comedic plays and his unusual, upright burial position in Westminster Cathedral. Jonson wrote in his play *The Alchemist*: "I see compassion may become a justice, though it be a weakness, I confess, and nearer a vice than a virtue." Was Jonson really suggesting that compassion was wicked and immoral? Possibly not. *The Alchemist* is, after all, a comedy which satirises the greed and gullibility of humankind, and ultimately punishes the characters who take advantage of their fellow humans. Although Jonson may not have been serious in his reference to compassion as a vice, the reputation remains.

Over 100 years after Jonson's death, in 1785, German philosopher Immanuel Kant wrote that "to act in accordance with the impulse of sympathy, compassion, and philanthropy is not moral at all" (1785/1996: 199). While this is sometimes understood as Kant having an aversion to compassion, he was really arguing that compassion should result from practical reasoning, not from feelings or 'impulses'. Kant was, in effect, advising us to omit the second step of the new compassion construct. Although he accepted that

https://doi.org/10.1515/9783110763126-003

compassion could be a beautiful act, he argued that it was a poor guide for moral action. More tarnish on the reputation of compassion.

Virtue

By contrast, compassion is sometimes considered to be a virtue. The Good Samaritan is the well-known parable of a traveller who was robbed, beaten, stripped and left for dead by the side of a road. A number of others walk past the traveller, and even cross the road to avoid him; perhaps they had succumbed to the Just World Hypothesis and believed that he deserved his fate. The Samaritan, however, does something different: "When he saw him, he was moved with compassion, came to him, and bound up his wounds" (Luke 10: 30–37). Compassion here is clearly regarded as a virtue. Virtue, from the Latin *virtus*, refers to a morally good character trait or behaviour. Although compassion did not make Aristotle's virtue list, it is arguably an example of *phronesis* – an Ancient Greek word typically translated as 'practical virtue'. Compassion has an emotional aspect, as outlined in the feeling step in Chapter 2. This often becomes the focus for its detractors, such as Kant. As the Good Samaritan parable shows, in addition to feeling, compassion requires cognition and volition. Our emotions allow us to connect with how another person might feel, our cognition is needed to understand the situation and what might be useful, and volition is our will to take action.

Professor and best-selling author Brené Brown has written that "compassion is not a virtue – it is a commitment. It's not something we have or don't have – it's something we choose to practice" (2008: xxvi). Brown may not be entirely correct, as researchers are increasingly convinced that compassion IS something we all have. Experiments have observed the preferences of babies for puppets which are compassionate, as opposed to those who are not, and they have noted the different facial expressions of babies and children when they witness compassionate acts. Such an innate biological propensity for compassion may in itself may be insufficient, though, as the twists and turns of our individual life histories can dent or obscure access to our compassionate nature. By developing our practice of compassionate leadership, our capacity for compassion can be developed to great effect. Brown's emphasis on practice is useful, and her indirect introduction of choice is also important. A significant strength of the new construct of compassion is the choices we can make as a result of our considerations within the appraisal step.

Verb

Vietnamese Buddhist monk Thich Nhat Hanh often focused on the action orientation of compassion, asserting that compassion is a verb. Rather than predominantly being an emotion or thought, he considered compassion to be an action of the heart. Such action of the heart, regardless of affection towards the recipient, resonates with the concept of global compassion: "a concern to alleviate the suffering of anyone, regardless of their nationality, language, culture, or religion" (Ekman and Ekman 2017: 41).

Of course, action is what distinguishes compassion from empathy. But such heart-led action does not necessarily mean that compassion requires the presence of love. When a firefighter attends a blaze or any of us come to the aid of a colleague or a stranger in need, we do not need to know, let alone love, the recipient of our compassion. Compassion is therefore more all-encompassing than love:

> Because this is the most important aspect of love, whose other face is compassion: It isn't doled out, drop by drop. It doesn't measure who is worthy and who isn't. It is like the ocean. Unfathomable. Astonishing. Measureless.
> (Divakaruni 2019: 358)

Social process

We return now to Paul Gilbert, whose definition of compassion was described in Chapter 1, and who has written extensively about the nature and function of compassion. Gilbert considers compassion to be a reciprocal co-evolved social process, where the person in need and the compassionate responder perform a sort of 'social dance'. This analogy can be considered as a dance with multiple different dance partners, frequent navigations between lead and follower roles, and with regular changes in tempo. Such a dance is not a simple movement, either in this analogy or in real life, and both require skilful practice. As Gilbert notes, "also core to compassion are courage and dedication [for compassion] is not just automatic but something that can be deliberately chosen and worked at with a deepening of understanding over time" (2019: 112). Like Brené Brown, Gilbert is reminding us about conscious choice and practice; these are fundamental to compassionate leadership and are therefore offered for your use throughout this book.

Behavioural choice

Registered Nurse and Assistant Professor Maria L. Schantz has researched the impact of compassion in clinical contexts, particularly focusing on the behaviours between medical staff during stressful situations. She notes, "Virtues or vices can undergo similar fates. Compassion . . . is just as contagious a behaviour as apathy or indifference" (Schantz 2007: 50). In the situations she describes, as is equally applicable elsewhere in our lives, we have a choice about how we respond to any situation. Choosing to counter conflict with compassion can bridge the void between vice and virtue, bringing us to 13th century Persian poet Rumi's field of curious encounter:

> Out beyond ideas of wrongdoing and rightdoing,
> there is a field. I'll meet you there.

All of the above

Perhaps the true nature of compassion is a blend of these perspectives. In many ways, compassion can simultaneously be a virtue, a verb and a social dance. It includes emotional, cognitive and behavioural components, as found in the new construct steps of feeling, appraisal and responding, respectively. And, if used bluntly, with malicious intent or for individual gain, compassion can also be a vice; maybe this is why, as we considered at the beginning of the chapter, we can sometimes feel uneasy around something masquerading as compassion.

Mistaken identity

Choosing wisely

Compassion is often viewed as being interchangeable with kindness, sympathy, empathy and altruism, amongst others, and all of these seem to be increasingly in the organisational spotlight. We are encouraged to bring more kindness into our workplaces and our leadership (Haskins et al. 2018). Quizzes can inform us about how empathic or what kind of empath we really are (Greater Good Science Center, no date; Riggio 2020). Sympathy is touted as an effective means of approaching customer service issues. For those short on time, lists of quick ways to improve empathy at work are readily available (Forbes 2021). An article in the Academy of Management Perspectives even encourages us to consider altruism as an overarching corporate goal (Kanungo and Conger 1993).

Empathy, sympathy, pity, kindness, altruism and compassion may not be synonymous, but they do have some associations and overlaps. Each has a relational aspect, perhaps unsurprisingly since humans are a social species. These concepts are also predominantly concerned with responses to the pain of another, although kindness may not necessarily include such a concern, as we will explore later in this chapter.

Each of compassion's mistaken identities is appropriate and useful in its own way, in different contexts. We will now examine the differences and similarities between compassion, altruism, sympathy, pity and kindness. Definitions, semantics, psychology and neuroscience all contribute to this understanding, resulting in a view of compassion which is both clear and focused. These differences matter to compassionate leadership in much the same way as selecting a screwdriver will not help when a hammer is needed; applying the right tool for the job allows us to become more adept in our craft of leadership.

Empathy

The need for more empathy (Figure 3.1) has become a common refrain in workplaces and elsewhere, possibly predictably given the wider global context. Divisions and heated debates between opposing factions are rife and political rhetoric is increasingly divisive. Such difficult contextual issues and their impacts have resulted in calls for more empathy at work and beyond. And yet, despite empathy's leading role in the humanisation of the workplace, there is some evidence that there is an unfortunate downside to empathy, as we shall explore later in this chapter.

EMPATHY

Figure 3.1: Empathy.

With its root in the Greek *pathos*, referring to emotion or suffering, the word empathy comes from the German *'Einfühlung'*. This translates as 'feeling into'; more colloquially, to put oneself in another's shoes. Indeed, the UK's Empathy Museum has a touring exhibition entitled 'A Mile in My Shoes', housed in a giant shoe box. Visitors can listen to the stories of strangers whilst going for a walk in their shoes, and the museum produces a podcast for those not able to visit in person. This clever play on the literal meaning of empathy encourages us to consider different perspectives to our own. As outlined in Chapter 6, seeking unfamiliar perspectives can be a useful counterbalance to cognitive shortcuts such as the confirmation or availability biases.

This central aspect of empathy – feeling into the pain of the suffering of another – is a crucial element of compassion. Yet empathy lacks the action orientation of compassion, and has even been accused of being merely ". . . the vicarious experience of another's emotions", without any impetus towards action aimed at alleviating suffering (Strauss et al. 2016: 18). Empathy is still required as part of a sensitive response to suffering and forms the basis for compassionate action. Simply put, empathy and compassion need each other; empathy is an essential component of compassion, yet it is action that turns empathy into compassion.

Different types of empathy

Psychologist Daniel Goleman is renowned for his research on emotional and social intelligence, work he considers crucial in the workplace for:

> If your emotional abilities aren't in hand, if you don't have self-awareness, if you are not able to manage your distressing emotions, if you can't have empathy and have effective relationships, then no matter how smart you are, you are not going to get very far. (Goleman 1996)

Goleman is not alone in his convictions about the importance of human relationships and how they impact both management theory and practice. Peter Druker developed a strategic management system which emphasises the welfare of individuals and wider society, as well as organisations. MIT Professor Peter Senge begins his *Fifth Discipline Fieldbook* with a welcome and underpinning philosophy contained in the Zulu saying *Umuntu ngumuntu nagabantu*, which translates to "a person is a person because of other people" (Senge et al. 1995: 3). Similarly, John Mayer's (2014) personal intelligence research emphasises the capacity for empathy as a crucial trait for adult and leadership development. Another MIT Professor, Edgar Schein, encourages a humble approach to leadership through asking questions and holding positive assumptions about human nature; anything else, he contends, simply results in negative self-fulfilling prophecies (2013).

Understanding empathy in an organisational context has received more attention than the exploration of compassion, maybe because of compassion's reputational problem outlined in Chapter 4. In the course of his research, psychologist Daniel Goleman (2008) suggested that there are three different types of empathy:

– Cognitive empathy:
   Cognitive empathy is the consideration of how other people think and how they perceive the world, as well as what mental models they knowingly or unknowingly use.

   In late 2019, as the word coronavirus was just becoming part of common global vocabulary, the *Financial Times* published an article titled 'What I Want for Xmas – More Empathy' (Foroohar 2019). The author's definition of empathy – 'the ability to understand the point of view of people on the opposite side of the table' – is an example of cognitive empathy.

   Another example can be found in the *Theory of Mind*. This is the ability to imagine how someone else might be thinking or feeling, and to understand that this might be different to our own thoughts and feelings. Thought to develop from around the age of 4 or 5 years old, such understanding is fundamental to the first step of awareness in the new construct of compassion.

– Affective empathy (also known as emotive or emotional empathy):
   Affective empathy reflects how a person resonates with the other, and allows an emotional connection to be established. This form of empathy is most closely associated with the 'feeling' step in the new compassion construct.

   If a colleague experiences the death of a close relative, affective empathy is our ability to connect with a similar pain from a similar experience. We may have this from our own familiarity with such loss or we can relate to similar feelings of grief from another experience.

– Empathic concern:
   Empathic concern occurs when we care about the suffering we see and then communicate this to the other person. Again, this empathy type resonates closely with the feeling step in our new construct of compassion.

Empathic concern is sometimes called 'compassionate empathy' as there is a desire to alleviate the pain we see. However, a desire to act and actual action are close but distinct responses, and so it seems reasonable to maintain the difference between empathic concern and compassion.

Limits of empathy

Although the *Financial Times'* article encouraged understanding the view of those on the other side of the boardroom table, such cognitive empathy alone may not be sufficient in reaching a positive outcome. A study of medical General Practitioners found that such perspective taking alone was a high-risk factor for burnout, whereas combining this with empathic concern resulted in a protective emotional outcome for the GPs (Lamothe et al. 2014).

The outcome of this study has echoes in an increasing body of evidence about the uniqueness of compassion from the field of neuroscience. Neuroscientists Tania Singer and Olga Klimecki's work (2014) in particular has highlighted that different areas of the brain respond to either compassion or empathy conditions. Their research underlines crucial distinctions between compassion and empathy, both psychologically and at a neurological level.

In one series of experiments, Klimecki and colleagues (2014) performed Functional Magnetic Resonance Imaging (f-MRI) scans on the brains of participants before and after they underwent either empathy or compassion training. In simplest terms, f-MRIs measure miniscule changes in blood flow to show which areas of the brain are activated during different activities. These experiments revealed that short-term compassion training over several days was able to increase positive affect and activations in a neural network usually related to positive emotions. Compassion, not empathy, made people feel better. The compassion training used in these studies was based on a simple loving-kindness meditation, similar to that outlined later in this chapter.

Singer and Klimecki then took their research further. Through their use of fMRI scans, they were able to examine the different neural networks activated for either empathy or compassion, as shown in Figure 3.2.

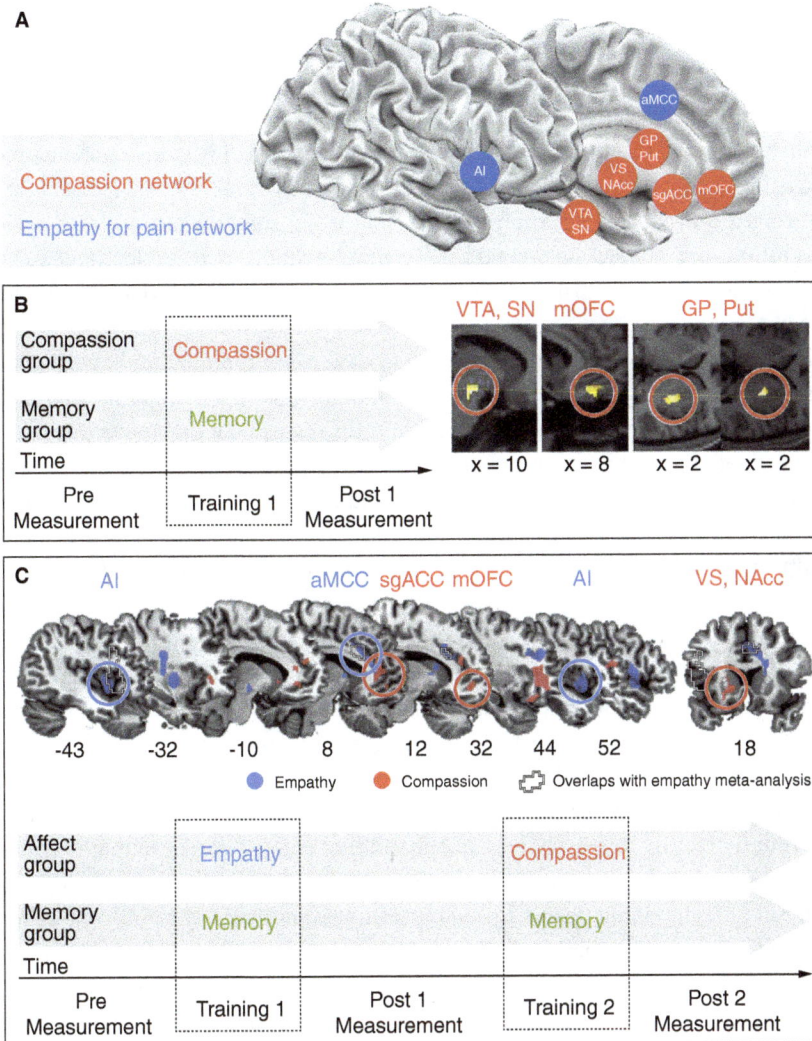

(A) Training compassion or empathy leads to differential plasticity in neural networks. (B) Compassion training compared to memory training augments activations in ventral tegmental area/ substantia nigra (VTA/SN), medial orbitofrontal cortex (mOFC), and striatum, the latter spanning globus pallidus (GP) and putamen (Put). (C) Empathy training (in blue) leads to increased activations in anterior insula (AI) and anterior middle cingulate cortex (aMCC), while subsequent compassion training (in red) augments activations in medial orbitofrontal cortex (mOFC), subgenual anterior cingulate cortex (sgACC) and the ventral striatum/ nucleus accumbens (VS, NAcc). Original brain data in (B) and (C) adapted with permission from Klimecki et al. (2014). (Reproduced with permission from Singer and Klimecki 2014.)

Figure 3.2: Differential neural networks for empathy and compassion.

Even just visually, these images make it clear that empathy and compassion result in subtly different areas of our brains being activated. Upon closer inspection, we can see that empathy recruits the anterior insula and anterior middle cingulate cortex; these are areas whose functions include the detection and modulation of emotions and responses. This resonates with the common definition of empathy, concerned with an emotional response to suffering. By comparison, we can see that compassion recruits the medial orbitofrontal cortex and ventral striatum areas of the brain, commonly associated with social cognition and reward behaviours. As well as helping us to understand each other, the recruitment of reward centres also underlines why being compassionate can feel so good.

Noting these differences, Klimecki and Singer decided to run another experiment. This time, they recruited new participants and initially gave them empathy training, focused on empathic listening skills. After more fMRI scans, they then gave the same volunteers the compassion training mentioned in the first set of experiments, and then ran another set of scans. These results showed that areas of the brain recruited changed between the two different types of training. This matters for compassionate leadership: building on its innateness, we can quickly be trained for, and benefit from, compassion.

Participants during this last experiment were asked to report on how they were feeling during the training. During empathy training, participants reported an increase in negative affect and emotional distress, whilst in compassion training, such distress decreased while positive feelings increased. In other words, compassion makes us feel better than empathy does.

All of this makes a more compelling case for compassion. Through Singer and Klimecki's ground-breaking research, we understand that compassion or empathy training result in very different brain activity, and that there is a significant neurological, psychological and emotional upside to compassion. It is particularly significant as we consider compassionate leadership to note that compassion training led to more positive emotions such as love, positive affect and resilience. These emotions together enable people to cope better with stressful situations. That alone sounds like a useful outcome of compassion for any leader.

Sympathy and pity

Sympathy (Figure 3.3) and pity (Figure 3.4) are considered together here as they are both concerned with feeling sorrow for the misfortune of another and are therefore closely linked. The difference between them is nuanced. Pity can be considered more distant in nature, and can even be considered a condescending perspective on suffering. Sympathy has more caring connotations; having sympathy *with* someone refers to a more common feeling between people.

Figure 3.3: Sympathy.

Figure 3.4: Pity.

Scottish Philosopher David Hume, more commonly known for his empiricist theory of knowledge, contemplated the critical role of sympathy in moral evaluation and rational action. Hume did not believe that humans took action based on rational evaluations alone. Instead, he proposed that moral evaluations were largely influenced by feelings and emotions balancing out our more rational thoughts. "Reason is", Hume wrote, "and ought only to be the slave of the passions, and can never pretend to any other office than to serve and obey them" (1740/1985: 462). Modern research is as yet inconclusive about the extent to which rational thought shapes our emotions, and vice versa, but that there is a complex interplay seems, at very least, a reasonable assertion.

Of Hume's 'passions', he argued that our capacity for moral evaluation particularly required the presence of sympathy. He defined sympathy as the ability to understand the feelings of others. This definition, tuning into the feelings of others, sounds similar to our understanding of empathy. Much like the difference between pity and sympathy, though, the distinction between sympathy and empathy is also nuanced. When we feel sympathy or pity, we feel sorry for the misfortune of another person. This stance is from our own perspective as we observe troubled circumstances. With empathy, we still seek to understand such plight, but we seek to do so from the other perspective rather than our own. Remember, we empathically feel into the emotions of another by metaphorically standing in their shoes.

Neuroscience has also helped to differentiate between empathy and sympathy. Research by neuroscientist Bérangère Thirioux and colleagues (2014) used electrical neuroimaging techniques to examine neural activations in the brain during situations designed to elicit either empathetic or sympathetic responses. They found that neural activations initially occurred in the same areas, regardless of whether the volunteer was under the sympathy or empathy condition. Then, after around 330 milliseconds and again after around 510 milliseconds, differences occurred. Most notably, empathic responses resulted in significantly more recruitment in areas of the dorsolateral pre-frontal cortex (dlPFC). This is one of the most recent areas of brain evolution and is responsible, amongst other things, for executive functions such as working memory and selective attention. As a result of these differences in activity of the dlPFC, Thirioux and colleagues proposed that from a neuroscientific perspective, sympathy is a first person, ego-centric response, whereas empathy is second person, other-centred response. We can see, then, that from both a semantic and a neuroscientific perspective, sympathy is when we feel *for* someone who is suffering as we view it from our perspective, whereas empathy is when we feel *into* someone else's pain.

Reality and perspective

This subtle, yet important, difference of perspective between empathy and sympathy shifts us from our own individual perspective towards attempting to understand that of the other. In order to do this, we must be prepared to challenge ourselves on what we consider to be 'true'. Awareness of the difference between what is reality versus a perspective – or, indeed between fact and opinion – is crucial to such other-centred responses. As Anaïs Nin wrote, "we don't see things as they are, we see them as we are" (1961: 120). Nin beautifully illustrates such differences as she describes characters Jay and Lillian's perceptions of their walk alongside the River Seine:

> Lillian was bewildered by the enormous discrepancy which existed between Jay's models and what he painted. Together they would walk along the same Seine river, she would see it silky grey, sinuous and glittering, he would draw it opaque with fermented mud, and a shoal of wine bottle corks and weeds caught in the stagnant edges. (1961: 120)

Even without the Parisian backdrop, varying perspectives on the same events are commonplace in organisations. Finance and Marketing will have different views on the same operational plans, and perspectives on whether a colleague is assertive or aggressive will depend on a myriad of individual experiences, beliefs and opinions. As outlined in Chapter 6, confirmation bias results in our tendency to seek affirmation of our beliefs, rather than challenge them. Empathy, feeling into the emotion of another, gives us the opportunity, to some extent, to feel into and understand someone else's suffering. It enables us to feel suffering from their perspective, rather than simply observe, and even judge, it from our own.

Individualistic versus collective

This raises questions about the extent to which we care about others. Individualistic cultures tend to regard people as being independent and self-directed, and they typically prioritise individuality and uniqueness as cultural values. Collectivist cultures, by comparison, tend to view people as being interconnected with others within in a wider social context, and emphasise interdependence, social conformity and the importance of family relationships.

Although for some time it has been supposed that Western cultures in particular have become increasingly individualistic, recent research suggests that this may in fact be a world-wide trend. Psychologist Henri Santos and his colleagues (2017) looked at individualistic practices such as number of one-person households, household sizes and divorce rates, as well as individualistic values such as importance of friends over family, prioritisation of self-expression, and importance of instilling independence in children. Overall, they found that individualism has increased by around 12% since 1960 across the world. Only four countries showed a decrease in individualistic practices during this period, and only five countries displayed a decrease in individualistic values. Interestingly, the research found that socioeconomic development, particularly improvements in education and associated wealth, was the greatest predictor of an increase in individualism.

So, what does our predisposition to confirmation bias, our self-centric view of the world, and the global trend towards individualisation mean for our consideration of others? Are we destined to be selfish, to ignore the plight of others? Will we shrug at the sight of pain, and go back to our quiet households, our chosen few friends, continuing to count our own blessings and money?

Possibly not.

The Charities Aid Foundation has, since 2010, compiled an annual World Giving Index. This is compiled by asking three questions about the prior year:

Have you helped a stranger?
Have you donated money to charity?
Have you volunteered some of your time to an organisation?

Comparing Santos's ranked list of individualistic countries with the World Giving Index 2021 provides an interesting perspective. In 2018, many of the most individualistic countries, including the USA, the UK, Australia and New Zealand, were also in the top 10 of the World Giving Index. This is not necessarily simply explainable in terms of these countries being wealthier. The World Giving Index comprises interviews from over 1.5 million individuals across 114 countries each year; it does not look at Government funding. Interestingly, the country which frequently comes first in the World Giving Index is Indonesia, currently ranked 104th in GDP per capita.

These rankings of individualism and giving suggests that increased individualism does not necessarily adversely impact our ability to respond to the suffering of others. Maybe an increase in wealth allows us to open our hearts and our purses to strangers more freely? An optimistic suggestion, perhaps, and there is some grit in this particular oyster. In 2021, the post-pandemic World Giving Index saw the UK and USA drop in the global rankings to 22 and 19, respectively, although Australia and New Zealand managed to retain their top ten positions. Pandemic fear, lockdowns, binary political divisiveness stoking fear of the 'other' may all have impacted our likelihood to give time, money or care to a stranger. Compassionate leadership is needed in today's world, more than ever before.

As you consider your perspective and role in supporting what our world needs, Box 3.1 offers some questions to support your thinking.

Box 3.1
Ask yourself the World Giving Index questions about the last 12 months:
Have you helped a stranger?
Have you donated money to charity?
Have you volunteered some of your time to an organisation?

Also consider another question:
What would you like your answers to be a year from now and what can you do towards making this a reality?

This balancing of the individual versus the collective brings us neatly to another of compassion's frequent mistaken identities – altruism.

Altruism

Auguste Comte, the 19th century French Philosopher and founder of Positivism, first popularised the term altruism. Altruism was proposed as an antithesis of egoism, whose benefit is based on the pursuit of self-interest. The word altruism itself is derived from the Latin *alter*, 'other', as Comte considered positive moral action to be that which resulted in good for others. Superficially this seems a simple enough definition, although as a theory of moral conduct it relies on an elusive, universally agreed definition of 'good'.

Figure 3.5: Altruism.

Altruism has come to describe behaviour which benefits another, even when this oc-curs at some detriment to the self, as illustrated in Figure 3.5. This detriment can be rela-tively small; if I see someone has no lunch, I can give them mine. They will eat whilst I will go hungry for a few hours. Of course, the detriment can be more substantial; if I see someone in a burning building, I can try to rescue them even though I could die whilst doing so. And the detriment can be subtler, less visible; when we see someone suffering at work, we can offer support even when our own reserves are dangerously low.

Altruism certainly has the action-orientation of compassion, although in Comte's later works he deemed the benefit of the whole to be of greatest significance, even if this ultimately proved costly to the altruistic individual. Such sacrifice of the self is not a feature of the new compassion construct, and demonstrates why an appraisal of our own resources is such a crucial additional step.

As a result of this action emphasis, compassion and altruism are often used inter-changeably; this is notably the case in the title of Matthieu Ricard's engaging book *Altruism: The Power of Compassion to Change Yourself and the World* (2013). Ricard notes at the outset that defining altruism is not an easy task. He views altruism as being both a motivation and an action, and encourages us to consider the possibility that altruism is, above all, a way of being. In this respect, his approach is similar to that of compassionate leadership, in that it is not something we do or do not have, it is rather an intention and ongoing practice.

On organisational and economic altruism, Ricard emphasises that it is the ex-tremes of inequality which are unsustainable. He notes that ". . . the pursuit of pros-perity must accommodate an aspiration for the well-being of all citizens and respect for the environment" (2013: 564). In this regard Ricard, a Buddhist monk, and corpo-rate organisations have some common ground. Environmental, social and governance (ESG) criteria are increasingly used to assess corporate investment opportunities. A recent PWC survey of consumers found that over 90% of leaders believe that their company has a responsibility to take action on ESG issues, and younger consumers, between the ages of 17–38 years old, are twice as likely as those over 38 to consider ESG when making purchasing decisions (PwC 2021). Such considerations matter to organisations and everyday consumers, as well as to monks.

There is, of course, an overlap between compassion and altruism. Both are concerned with taking action in order to alleviate suffering. The distinction lies in the extent to which the alleviator will put themselves at risk – hence the crucial appraisal step – and altruism's wider definition of the 'other'. Our own often subconscious designations of in and out groups, as examined in Chapter 6, will influence who we consider to be 'other'. This, in turn, will influence our actions. We are more likely to offer support to someone we know and like, or someone we perceive to be a member of one of our 'in-groups', than we are to someone from an 'out-group'. Box 3.2 offers a short case study of altruism in the workplace.

Box 3.2: Case Study: Altruism at Work

Peter (not his real name) is an exemplary employee, and it was a delight to work with him in a leadership coaching capacity. He has been with the company for years, knows the formal and informal networks well, and has been promoted into a senior role. People like him. He is warm, thoughtful and has a dry sense of humour. Peter cannot but be aware of suffering. As well as his own ability to notice suffering, many others bring their problems to him. They know that he will listen, guide and do whatever he can to support.

Peter is also exhausted. Juggling his own responsibilities whilst trying to soak up the pain of others is sometimes overwhelming. He frequently ends up working late into the evening and at weekends, to catch up on his own work. This leaves him, in his own words, 'constantly tired and grumpy'.

As we worked together, using the new compassion construct, Peter began to make changes. He was more conscious in appraising his situation, working out what was his to resolve and what might belong to other people. He realised that his role was well positioned to solve some of the root causes of pain in the company, and took steps to do this rather than just react to symptoms. His practice of self-compassion took a while; he admitted that he felt 'ridiculous' doing this at first, but soon noticed the benefits. Resourcing himself has become both a practice and a passion. Peter notices his inner state and has even created a spreadsheet of micro-experiments and results, as he develops his own compassionate path of leadership. Life is not perfect, but he now has conscious awareness and practical compassionate tools at his disposal for when things get difficult.

His partner has apparently observed that Peter is much less grumpy.

In organisational life, altruistic self-sacrifice can take many guises: a culture of heroes, swooping in to resolve any crisis, ready to rescue regardless of the impact on their own wellbeing. It can also take the form of burnout when someone is always ready to help and support, without checking their own resource levels or considering their potential inadvertent reinforcement of the Drama Triangle through their actions. Compassionate leadership therefore needs to remain vigilant to the risk of excessive altruism. There is no definitive, neat answer to whether, when or how we should offer our altruistic or compassionate support. Situations, people and our individual levels of resource are in a constant state of flux. Sometimes people will, in the ultimate altruistic act, risk their own lives to save someone in imminent danger. The world will always need those of us who are prepared to speak up, to dissent, to act, to question, to hold up the mirror and to blow the whistle. Each of us can decide in any given moment where our balance is between the self and other, if, indeed there is an 'other'. Let us now look at otherness in contrast to connectedness, and consider what implications these might have for compassionate leadership.

Interconnectedness

As we have seen, Comte's altruism prioritises the interconnectedness of our lives over any one individual. This systemic, interconnected view was not unique to Comte. As John Donne wrote:

> No man is an island entire of itself; every man
> is a piece of the continent, a part of the main.

Similarly, a central concept of Buddhism is the interconnectedness of all beings, where events are informed by multiple causal factors in any given moment of experience. Such interconnectedness, alongside the Buddhist doctrine of no-self (*anātman* or *anātta*) may in part account for Buddhist monk Matthieu Ricard's apparent amalgamation of altruism and compassion mentioned earlier in this chapter.

Over 300 years after Donne wrote his verse, and at least 2,500 years after Buddha's birth, Einstein was similarly aware of the interconnectedness of our fates, and also of the power of compassion:

> A human being is part of the whole . . . He experiences himself, his thoughts and feelings as something separated from the rest – a kind of optical delusion of his consciousness. This delusion is a kind of prison for us, restricting us to our personal desires and to affection for a few persons nearest to us. Our task must be to free ourselves from this prison by widening our circle of compassion to embrace all living creatures . . .
> (Albert Einstein to Norman Salit, 4 March 1950, © Hebrew University Jerusalem)

In these words, Einstein alludes not only to the interconnectedness of our existence, but also the need to extend our compassion beyond those we know and love, or our ingroups. This has similarities in the Buddhist Metta prayer, commonly known as the loving kindness meditation. Many variations of the Metta prayer exist, although all follow a similar wording and pattern, and all can be spoken or silent. Starting with ourselves, the prayer then extends out to those we love, to strangers, and then to our enemies:

> May I be happy.
> May I be well.
> May I be safe.
> May I be peaceful and at ease.
>
> May you be happy.
> May you be well.

May you be safe.
May you be peaceful and at ease.

It may seem strange to include a loving-kindness meditation in a leadership book. However, no one needs to wear saffron robes to benefit. In their research in controlled laboratory conditions, Stanford Psychologists Cendri Hutcherson and colleagues (2008) found that even a few minutes of such silent meditation significantly increased feelings of social connectedness and positivity towards strangers. Research which compared focused-breathing meditations and loving-kindness meditations found the latter resulted in a significant increase of participants' willingness to make amends for their mistakes (Hafenbrack et al. 2022). A version of the loving-kindness meditation shown above was the basis of the training Singer and Klimecki used in their research, mentioned earlier in this chapter.

The distinction between altruism and compassion can become blurred because of their shared action orientation. Each compassionate leader must decide for themselves where their distinction between the two rests, and when each is appropriate. Considerations of human interconnectedness and our own discreet roles do not have formulaic answers; they are individual, existential reflections. As a compassionate leader, holding the distinction between compassion and altruism in conscious awareness (as outlined in Box 3.3) allows us to avoid burnout and exhaustion, whilst still making a compassionate difference.

> **Box 3.3**
> Now that you are clear on the differences between compassion, empathy, pity, sympathy and altruism, start to notice when you are using each one. Take time to consciously select the right 'tool for the job'. In particular, notice if you are languishing in empathy or tipping into altruism.
>
> Do not worry if this feels a little strange to begin with; you will be moving from unconscious incompetence to conscious incompetence (Figure 1.3). With a little practice, you will soon be on your way to conscious then unconscious competence as a compassionate practitioner.

Kindness

Kindness, like many of the areas examined in this chapter, can have many different meanings. To be kind is to be generous, considerate, friendly and motivated by a genuine warmth of feeling for others. Kindness, it seems, is also very popular.

In Aesop's fable of the Lion and the Mouse, the lion, rudely awakened from his nap by the mouse scurrying across his nose, is kind enough to let the mouse go. Some days later, the lion finds himself trapped in a hunter's net. The kindly mouse repays the lion by nibbling the ropes, thus setting him free. The moral of the story, Aesop tells us, is that "no act of kindness, no matter how small, is ever wasted".

From this point onwards, quotes about kindness abound. His Holiness the 14th Dalai Lama encourages us to "be kind whenever possible. It is always possible."

Figure 3.6: Kindness.

Eminently quotable psychiatrist Theodore Isaac Rubin – who, incidentally, wrote *Compassion and Self-Hate: An Alternative to Despair* in the mid-1970s, weaving together psychotherapy and Buddhism – is attributed with saying "kindness is more important than wisdom, and the recognition of this is the beginning of wisdom". And, of course, seemingly endless supplies of t-shirts, mugs and other paraphernalia remind us that in a world where we can be anything, we should be kind.

Beyond fridge magnet philosophy, there is a growing body of research which highlights the power of kindness. Even simply witnessing an act of kindness increases our oxytocin levels and reduces our blood pressure. Kindness stimulates serotonin production, stabilising our moods whilst helping us to feel happy. The kindness we share with others through volunteering has benefits, as it correlates with improved heart health and increased feelings of social connectedness. Some of these benefits of kindness apply to both the person extending the kindness as well as the recipient, regardless of how well they know each other. An intriguing study by Oxford University's Lee Rowland and Oliver Curry (2019) compared acts of kindness between people with both weak and strong social ties, self-kindness, and even the impact on individuals who witnessed, rather than directly received, kindness. Their results were fascinating. Firstly, not surprisingly, they revealed that undertaking acts of kindness for seven consecutive days increased the participants' self-reported levels of happiness. Secondly, they reported a positive correlation between the participants' increases in happiness and the number of acts of kindness; the greater the number of kind acts, the happier people became. Even more interestingly, the correlation between kind acts and happiness was equally positive whether the kindness was between people with weak or strong social ties, whether it was other-orientated or self-kindness, or even when it was simply observed kindness. Kindness, it seems, is incredibly powerful.

If the outcomes of all of this research are motivating you to start a 'kindness drive' in your organisation, a word of warning: Recent findings from psychologists

Netta Weinstein and Richard Ryan (2010) found that people who are kind because they want to be experience far heightened benefits than those who are being kind because they think they ought to or have been told to be so. Similar to compassion, intentionality and authenticity are fundamental to positive outcomes in kindness.

Compassion and kindness are, of course, closely linked. In the UK, the National Health Service constitution even refers to compassion as 'intelligent kindness' (Department of Health 2013). The key difference between compassion and kindness is that kindness may not necessarily be linked to an alleviation of suffering, whereas a compassionate response is exactly that. As shown in Figure 3.6, someone can be kind if they bring you a birthday cake, but that is not necessarily a response to suffering.

Other ways in which compassion and kindness are certainly similar is in their conspicuous absence from organisations and, more optimistically, in their more recent, long-overdue focus of attention. Kindness does not necessarily have the reputational issues of compassion to the same extent, although it does sometimes similarly suffer from being viewed as weak or soft. With individualism on the increase globally, kindness to another person may be perceived as a weakness as it shows a degree of reliance. Yet, as we have seen, research repeatedly shows that kindness is beneficial in a myriad of ways, even when we only witness a kind act.

Compassion by comparison

Figure 3.7: Compassion.

By comparing compassion with other, related concepts, we can now understand the differences and overlaps more clearly. Compassion is different from kindness as the former is a response to suffering, whereas the latter is not necessarily so. Compassion includes an action orientation which is missing from pity, empathy or sympathy.

Compassion has an appraisal of resources that prevents it from tipping into altruism. Although complex, compassion's uniqueness is simply illustrated in Figure 3.7.

Research from psychology and neuroscience have repeatedly shown us, as outlined throughout this chapter and illustrated in the summary Figure 3.8, that these concepts are all quite distinct from each other, and not just semantically.

The knowledge which we have gained in this chapter enables us to select the most appropriate approach for the specific situation we find ourselves in. Through applying this understanding about what compassion actually is and what it is not, we

Figure 3.8: Compassion's mistaken identities summary.

can contemplatively craft our response to suffering most appropriately and in the best interests of all involved. We can consider the wider organisational impacts of this understanding, establishing compassionate systems that best support our individual leadership efforts. As we approach this task, we should remain mindful that compassion still suffers from a reputational issue despite research about its unique benefits. The following chapter therefore explores the genesis of this reputational problem and offers a research-based alternative viewpoint from which to build a compassionate organisation.

Key Chapter Points
- There has been much debate and little agreement on the nature of compassion, and whether it is a virtue, a vice or a verb. These areas are briefly discussed alongside considerations of compassion as a social process or a behavioural choice.
- Compassion frequently suffers from mistaken identities, often being seen as interchangeable with kindness, sympathy, empathy, altruism, and pity.
- However, these are all different – semantically, psychologically and neurologically, as well as in practical application. These important differences and their impacts are discussed in detail.
- This matters from a leadership standpoint because when compassion is well understood and thus properly applied, it is uniquely powerful and generative.
- This chapter also examines the rise of individualism and the interconnected nature of our organisations and lives more broadly.

Chapter 4
Compassion: Dubious reputation and accusation

Lose money for the firm, and I will be understanding. Lose a shred of reputation for the firm, and I will be ruthless.
(Warren Buffett)

Tenderness and kindness are not signs of weakness and despair, but manifestations of strength and resolution.
(Khalil Gibran)

A dubious reputation

Have you heard the term 'compassion fatigue'? Or considered compassionate acts as weak leadership? Seen an eye roll when a compassionate response is suggested? Perhaps you are even a little embarrassed to admit that you are reading a book about compassionate leadership?

Compassion fatigue. Feeble leadership. Sob story. Good guys finish last.

In short, a dubious reputation.

Compassion ought to be the most renowned approach to leadership today. Yet it is not. Instead, it has a centuries old reputation problem, and most leaders do not understand what it is or why it is so effective. When properly understood and applied, compassion can make a positive, lasting difference to us as individuals, as leaders, and for the organisations we serve. Yet compassion is frequently maligned, and finds itself strangely absent from both management theory and organisational life.

Where did compassion's dubious reputation begin? Why does it persist today? What is it about compassion that provokes such an adverse reaction from some people?

In order to address these questions, we will now briefly explore religion, philosophy, economics, literature and the media as contributing factors to this unfortunate reputation. Next, we will look at some common shorthand regularly used to dismiss or decry compassion in organisations: weak leadership, compassion fatigue, career sabotage and psychic numbing. Understanding these areas will help us to comprehend compassion's difficult reputation and, in the next chapter, to assess recent evidence which suggests that compassion can hugely benefit our leadership and our organisations.

There are some glimmers of hope to be found. Compassion is increasingly becoming an area of interest for researchers and leaders alike. As we will see in Chapter 5, the psychological and organisational results of compassionate approaches are both compelling and ideal for our times. And so, in order to understand the current state of compassion's reputation, it is useful to begin by briefly considering its potted history. In this way, the impacts of religion, philosophy and economics will set the stage for compassion's revival in a contemporary leading role.

https://doi.org/10.1515/9783110763126-004

Where compassion's reputation problems began

Compassion in religion

Compassion is nothing new. It is fundamental to most major religions, albeit expressed in different ways. Regardless of whether or not we consider ourselves to be religious, understanding the role of compassion in religion still offers a useful perspective on compassionate leadership.

Every recitation of the Qur'an begins with an invocation to Allah the Compassionate (Al Rahman) and Merciful (Al Rahim); the litmus test for true belief and genuine worship of Allah is that it leads to compassionate living.

Buddhists believe compassion to be a part of everyone's 'Buddha nature', the seed of consciousness or enlightenment. His Holiness the Dalai Lama XIV has written extensively on the importance of compassion in everyday life, and has collaborated with psychologists and neuroscientists in his aim to discover more about compassion. Dr Mathieu Ricard, the Buddhist monk we met in Chapter 3, has participated in numerous studies which examine the power of meditations on the mind and of compassion-focused meditations in particular. Some of the outcomes of his research have shown how meditation increases activity in the left pre-frontal cortex area of the brain, which is associated with positive emotions. Because of this research, and his general demeanour, Ricard is sometimes referred to as 'the happiest man in the world'. In another experiment, Ricard showed how participants who had received meditation training were more likely to help a stranger; as the amount of time they spent practicing compassion meditations increased, so did their pro-social behaviours (Ricard 2013). The research of Ricard and others is useful for our understanding of how to train our brains for compassion; the benefits of such training will be explored in more detail in Chapter 5.

In Judaism, the Torah emphasises the receiving of compassion from God, and also the need to be compassionate towards other people: "Who has compassion with his fellow human beings will be shown mercy in heaven" (Shabbat 151b: 13). A number of Hebrew words can translate as compassion, including rachamim, which is derived from the root 'rechem', meaning womb. This root implies that compassion is felt by a mother for her child, even before the child is born. As we have already discussed, the Latin word for compassion is derived from 'com' (with) and 'pati' (to suffer), thus meaning to suffer with someone. The Hebrew root 'rechem' takes this further, using the closeness of the mother and unborn child as a metaphor; if one suffers, so does the other. These notions of suffering and interconnectedness are central to an understanding of compassionate leadership.

In Christianity, compassion is one of the virtues named in Colossians (3:12), 'clothe yourselves with compassion, kindness, humility, gentleness and patience'. In addition, of course, the parable of the Good Samaritan is one of the most recognisable stories from the New Testament. The Good Samaritan assists someone who was not familiar to him and who others had ignored. This compassion for the stranger or 'other' is discussed in

Chapter 6, specifically when we examine Social Identity Theory and the impacts of sub-conscious group membership.

Many other religions also have compassion at their core. Krishna is the Hindu God of love and compassion. In Sikhism, Daya, or compassion, is one of the five virtues alongside truth, contentment, humility and love. Daya's importance is apparent from this line in the Sri Guru Granth Sahib scriptures, "You have no compassion; the Lord's Light does not shine in you". Daya means to suffer in the suffering of others, again emphasising the notion of interconnection.

Despite compassion's role in most religions, however, human action has sometimes spoken a different dialect from the printed word. Noting this difference, religious scholar Karen Armstrong set up the Charter for Compassion with her winnings of the 2008 TeD Prize. Armstrong's charter is designed to support leaders in promoting world peace and compassion, and to restore compassion to the centre of all faiths. It states:

> The principle of compassion lies at the heart of all religious, ethical and spiritual traditions . . . . Compassion impels us to work tirelessly to alleviate the suffering of our fellow creatures, to dethrone ourselves from the centre of our world and put another there, and to honour the inviolable sanctity of every single human being, treating everybody, without exception, with absolute justice, equity and respect . . . . We acknowledge that we have failed to live compassionately and that some have even increased the sum of human misery in the name of religion. (Charter for Compassion)

To date, the charter has been affirmed and signed by over 2 million people of various denominations globally calling for a restoration of compassion in religion (www.char terforcompassion.org). You may wish to read the charter yourself, as prompted in Box 4.1. Throughout this book, there is a similar call to bring compassion into the centre of organisational life. This is not 'bleeding heart' sentimentality; as we will see, this is both a humanistic and commercially sound approach.

> **Box 4.1**
> Take some time to read and maybe even sign the Charter for Compassion.

In the first century AD, Pope Gregory I – also known as Gregory the Great – noted that he preferred compassion to be shown to the faithful before it was offered to adversaries of the church, in an astonishing example of in-group favouritism. The antagonist in this particular case would likely be considered an 'insider' by many. He was the Archbishop of Grado, who had incurred Gregory's wrath by disregarding his summons to travel to Rome. The Archbishop may have been wise; his refusal was on the basis that he felt Gregory would be a biased judge in a church dispute. In calmer moments, Gregory the Great wrote that being compassionate risked a 'condescension of emotion' which might have calamitous results. His description of compassion, where friends go mad with grief for someone who has suffered, has tones of excessive altruism rather than compassion. Intellectually at least, Gregory the Great seemed to understand this delicate balance, as he includes amongst his list of required qualities for an ideal bishop, "one who through the bowels of compassion is moved to great pardon but is never plucked from the citadel of righteousness by pardoning more than is fitting" (quoted in Richards 1980: 142). Here, Gregory is warning of the dangers of being altruistic, yet he also understood the value of compassionate leadership in his church. Centuries later, one of the accusations levelled at compassion is that it makes for soft or weak leaders; we shall explore this misconception in more detail in Chapter 5, and show how compassion and accountability are actually mutually advantageous in a contemporary organisation.

Compassion in philosophy and economics

At first glance, Adam Smith might seem a little out of place in a discussion about compassion. After all, as the father of modern capitalism, he is renowned for his writing on the division of labour and productivity, and these are not necessarily the most compassionate of concepts. However, before Smith wrote *Wealth of Nations*, he wrote another book, *Theory of Moral Sentiments*. On the very first page of this latter book he talks about compassion:

> How selfish soever man may be supposed, there are evidently some principles in his nature, which interest him in the fortune of others, and render their happiness necessary to him . . . of this kind is . . . compassion. (1759/2009: 13)

Even back in the 1750s, Adam Smith understood the importance of people caring about others and being compassionate when faced with suffering. One wonders what he would think of the stereotypical modern corporation, with its focus on profit and shareholder return above all else.

Over one thousand years after Pope Gregory I, and a few decades after Adam Smith's writings, disagreement about compassion again raised its head, this time amongst philosophers. As we have already noted, in the 1700s Kant saw compassion as an irrational response to human suffering. Early in the next century, Schopenhauer's criticism of Kant was followed by his own treatise on compassion, where he argued that compassion was in fact the very basis of all morality. Schopenhauer wrote that ". . . the only genuine moral incentive [is] . . . the everyday phenomenon of compassion . . . for all satisfaction and all well-being and happiness consist in this" (1839/1995: 140–144). Nietzsche – never one for keeping the peace – aligned his thinking with that of Kant, arguing that compassion is one of the "worst epidemics facing humankind" (1887/2013). Indeed, Nietzsche's comments on compassion are relatively well-known, including the worrying attributed quote that "compassion for the friend should conceal itself under a hard shell".

We can take closer look at Nietzsche, since he is often referenced as being one of the best-known antagonists towards compassion. If we find his comments distasteful, we might console ourselves that Nietzsche struggled with mental illness for much of his life, or remind ourselves that he was often said to have held misogynistic, extreme right-wing views. As ever, things are rarely so simple as they first appear. In her biography of Nietzsche, *I Am Dynamite*, Sue Prideaux argues that Nietzsche was in fact ardently against nationalism and antisemitism, and that his sister Elisabeth was the puppeteer responsible for many of the unfavourable views of her brother still held today. Just before Nietzsche's death, Elisabeth, along with her notoriously anti-Semitic husband, returned from a failed attempt to establish a New Germany colony in Paraguay. It seems unlikely that this homecoming would have cheered the ailing philosopher, as he so disliked Elisabeth's husband, Bernhard Förster, that he had refused to attend their wedding. Elisabeth's posthumous biography of her famous brother was more aligned with her own political views than those of Nietzsche, and she was liberal with her editing of his unpublished works for over three decades after his death. So, we should recognise with some scepticism what Nussbaum terms the "boot-in-the-face" caricature of Nietzsche as an uncaring despot with a particular distaste for compassion (1994: 139).

Much like his characterisation, Nietzsche's comments on compassion should not be taken at face value either. His main concern with compassion – or *mitleid* in German, which also translates as 'pity' – is that one word cannot possibly capture the sheer complexity of potential individual motivations and considerations:

> But we never do anything of this kind out of one motive; as surely as we want to free ourselves of suffering by this act, just as surely do we give way to an impulse to pleasure with the same act, pleasure arises at the sight of a contrast to the condition we ourselves are in; at the notion that we can help if only we want to; at the thought of the praise and recognition we shall receive if we do help; at the activity of helping itself, insofar as the act is successful and as something achieved step by step in itself gives delight to the performer; especially, however, at the feeling that our action sets a limit to an injustice which arouses our indignation (the discharge of one's indignation is itself refreshing). All of this, and other, much more subtle things in addition, constitute 'pity' [*mitleid*]: how coarsely does language assault with its one word so polyphonous a being! (1881/1997: Aphorism number 133)

Much of what we have learned about compassion in recent years corroborates significantly with this view. When we are compassionate, or even view a compassionate act, we experience a dopamine hit which 'gives delight to the performer'. Empathic distress fatigue, as discussed later in this chapter, is somewhat alleviated by compassionate action, as we 'free ourselves of suffering by this act'. Nietzsche also hints at the issue of intention, and whether we are compassionate in order to alleviate suffering or at least in part because of the 'praise and recognition we shall receive'. It seems that Nietzsche understood the complexity, necessity and nuance of compassion; perhaps he was not such a heartless tyrant after all.

The writings, debates and disagreements of Adam Smith, Nietzsche, Schopenhauer and Kant are now hundreds of years old, yet they continue to influence us today.

Such influence can still be seen in the absence of, and sometimes distaste for, compassion in the modern organisation.

Compassion in literature

In the early 1980s Milan Kundera wrote in *The Unbearable Lightness of Being* that ". . . the word compassion generally inspires suspicion; it designates what is considered an inferior, second rate sentiment that has little to do with love" (1984: 19). Kundera's workaholic womanising character Tomas was "sick with compassion . . . tons of steel of the Russian tanks were nothing compared to it. For there is nothing heavier than compassion. Not even one's own pain weighs so heavily as the pain one feels with someone, for someone, a pain intensified by the imagination and prolonged by a hundred echoes" (ibid.: 30). Tomas's experience seems to be, similar to the Pope Gregory example above, excessive altruism rather than compassion. Yet again, though, compassion – Kundera's "curse of emotional telepathy" (ibid.: 29) – is the scapegoat with a dubious reputation.

Compassion in the press

Compassion's reputational issue is not restricted to religion, philosophy or literature. Research conducted by James Walsh (1999) on word frequencies in the *Wall Street Journal* over a fifteen-year period found that words such as win, beat and advantage increased by over 400% during this time, while words such as caring and compassion hardly appeared at all. Hopefully, the situation has improved since Walsh's research, and the 'dog eat dog' approach to business is starting to crumble. Caring about employee mental and physical wellbeing is an increasingly important topic for organisations today, as evidenced through articles about compassion, empathy and kindness in mainstream broadsheet and business publications.

A rather extreme silver lining of the COVID-19 pandemic is that it allowed, or even forced, us to take a fresh look at ourselves, our workplaces, and our priorities. Compassion is finally on the cusp of becoming a more mainstream organisational consideration. The *Financial Times* produced a 'Guide to Compassion' because, with no trace of irony, they add that 'he who cares wins' (*Financial Times,* no date). A recent edition of the *Wall Street Journal* wants to know why bosses are asking about our feelings; the short answer they offer is that this is done in the anticipation that compassion will revive exhausted employees (Smith 2022). Hopefully, organisational focus on compassionate responses to suffering and employee wellbeing are becoming more mainstream.

That said, there is still some way to go, and hundreds of years of discourse and derision have taken their toll on the reputation of compassion in organisations. Box 4.2 offers some suggestions as to how you can become increasingly aware of the reputational issues surrounding compassion. Some of the more contemporary accusations levelled at organisational compassion shall now be examined in light of recent evidence.

> **Box 4.2**
> Notice when compassion's dubious reputation rears its head, either in spoken or written words, or through implication. Decide whether and how you might to challenge this, using the research outlined in this book and with examples from your own growing awareness and practice.

Common organisational accusations

Now that we can see the context compassion sits within, attracting the derision and suspicion of many leaders, writers and philosophers, it is less surprising that it has often been excluded from modern-day organisations. We are now going to look at some common shorthand used to underline compassion's reputational issue: weak leadership, career sabotage, compassion fatigue and psychic numbing.

Weak leadership

Do you consider yourself to be a good leader? How do others view your leadership? Research by Professor Shimul Melwani and colleagues (2012) examined whether the emotions leaders expressed influenced perceptions of leadership. They made some interesting discoveries. Of passing interest, neither love nor anger correlated with associations of leadership. However, people who either expressed compassion or, conversely, expressed contempt were perceived by others to be leaders. Contempt and compassion, though, are obviously very different approaches to leadership. Compassion notices suffering, and takes action to support others, whereas contemptuous leaders consider others to be beneath them, and are less likely to assist someone in need.

That these opposing approaches both correlated with perceptions of leadership is an interesting consideration. Maybe contemptuous emotions are associated with leadership because that has been the predominant model in industrialised countries for so long. The stereotype of leadership as forceful, dominant and even contemptuous is so embedded in the Western narrative that it barely registers.

The research also correlated compassion with leadership. Far from being weak, leaders who are resilient without being brittle, vulnerable without being needy, and compassionate without being altruistic are perceived by others to be successful leaders. Such leaders remind us that we are all human, that we all suffer and that we all sometimes need to be seen. As we will discuss later in this book, such well-regarded leaders demonstrate that they are as willing to be recipients of compassion as they are to provide it for others.

Compassion is not always gentle. A mother who roughly pulls her child away from the path of a car could be described as being fiercely compassionate. Soldiers who weep and hug each other after the death of their comrades may be demonstrating gentle compassion. Leaders who support their teams in times of need may be accused of being 'too compassionate' or 'weak', but their leadership approach will pay handsome dividends of longer-term employee commitment and organisational performance.

Compassion is for women

Compassion is sometimes referred to as being a predominantly female trait. His Holiness the Dalai Lama XIV, in discussing the need for more compassionate leadership, even stated that biologically, females have a heightened potential for compassion. The jury is still out on whether or not this is true, but the question of whether compassion is a female attribute is an interesting one.

This association of compassion with women is not always intended as a compliment. New Zealand ex-Premier Jacinda Ardern, for example, has frequently been criticised for being soft and overly compassionate. Yet the *Financial Times*, amongst many others, favourably commented on her effective leadership approach of "charisma, competence and compassion" (*Financial Times* 2020). Not such an insult after all.

Male and female brains are thought to be far more similar than they are different. To some researchers, the differences that do exist are at least partially due to how the sexes are socialised in our societies; a gendered world, after all, is likely to produce a gendered brain (Rippon 2019). Any differences might be due to nurture over nature. Maybe girls are more likely than boys to be encouraged from an early age to consider how other people feel, to respond to suffering, to be compassionate.

In my own research on organisational compassion and employee commitment levels (Chapter 5), I found that gender had a moderating influence on the compassion to commitment relationship. Simply put, as levels of organisational compassion increased, the rate of commitment increased more quickly for women than it did for men. Interestingly, neurological research by Roberto Mercadillo and colleagues (2011) demonstrated some gender differences in the precise areas of the brain activated during compassionate conditions. Whilst this does not necessarily imply that either males or females are more or less compassionate, it may mean that they experience compassion slightly differently.

Male leaders are just as capable of compassionate leadership as female leaders. Former CEO of LinkedIn, Jeff Weiner, has written about managing compassionately as being his guiding leadership principle. In his address to graduating students of Wharton in 2018, he said, "The advice I would give my 22-year-old self is to be compassionate . . . [because] managing compassionately is not just a better way to build a team, it's a better way to build a company" (Wharton 2018).

So, yes, compassion is for women. But not exclusively. It is an innate, effective leadership approach which is available and useful to everyone.

Career sabotage

This brings us to another question: is developing compassionate leadership a sure-fire way to sabotage our own careers? Will we be seen as too nice, a pushover when it comes to taking tough decisions, in other words: weak?

The perils of power

On battle fields and in the board room, it seems that even if we start being a 'good guy', power can seduce us towards a darker side. Harvard Professors Julie Battilana and Tiziana Casciaro (2021) warn from their research that power can make leaders and their teams less effective over time. Power, they claim, makes leaders susceptible to two particular hazards.

The first vulnerability is hubris: over self-confidence and excessive pride. In one of their experiments, participants were invited to write about a time they either felt powerful or powerless. They were then offered a reward for correctly guessing what number they would roll on a die and, crucially, offered a choice of whether to roll the die themselves or have the experimenter roll for them. While less than 60% of those who wrote about feeling powerless chose to roll the die themselves, 100% of those who wrote about feeling powerful did. Power, the researchers concluded, can lead us to overestimate our abilities, even when it comes to something as random as the roll of a die.

A second hazard noted by Battilana and Casciaro is that power can result in leaders being overly focused on themselves, to the detriment of seeing others around them. A leader who neither notices nor understands the people they work with is likely to miss important information, and so be less effective. We cannot lead people when we are not aware of them, do not care about them, or do not try to understand them. In the new compassion construct, the first step is awareness. Without this, compassionate leadership cannot materialise (see Box 4.3).

> **Box 4.3**
> Be mindful of leadership propensity for hubris and self-focus; staying humble and curious will serve you better.

Do good guys finish last?

Considering these potential pitfalls, an associated question might be to ask if leadership power can corrupt even good people. Is it just 'bad guys' who get to the top, or do the good guys and gals get there too and then, inevitably, turn bad? Power corrupts, no matter how much we want to remain good? If that is the case, is there any point in developing compassion in a leadership context, or are we doomed to succumb to the perils of power once we become leaders? Box 4.4 outlines of the most notorious cases of leadership corruption: the case of Odebrecht.

Box 4.4: Power and Corruption

Transparency International is an organisation whose purpose is to fight the injustices caused by corruption. They co-created the United Nations Convention Against Corruption, which has now been signed by over 140 countries. Over quarter of a million people have accessed Transparency International's legal support and their work with companies has led to commitments from over 8,000 organisations worldwide.

Each of their 'Top 25 Corruption Scandals' makes for jaw-dropping reading, but one which particularly stands out for its abuse of power is the infamous Lava Jato (or Operation Car Wash) investigations. Although these were centred on Brazil, the case eventually uncovered evidence of corruption across a dozen countries, involving over twenty companies and included bribery payments totalling over US$ 1billion.

The company at the centre of the scandal was Odebrecht, a giant engineering and construction conglomerate founded in 1944 by Norberto Odebrecht. Norberto's son, Emilio, and later his grandson, Marcelo, both joined the company straight from high school and eventually became successive CEOs. Under Emilio and Marcelo's leadership, bribery and corruption were rife. During his defence in court, Emilio even commented that bribing politicians was a normal, institutionalised practice.

Odebrecht had to pay nearly US$3billion in fines as a result of Operation Car Wash. The company still exists and is trying to reform and recover from the scandal, although its name has become a byword for corruption. Emilio resigned as Chairman. Marcelo was sentenced to prison and has become estranged from many of his family. Odebrecht family members will no longer be allowed to occupy the role of CEO.

In trying to answer the question of whether power inevitably corrupts, a study by Cameron Anderson and his colleagues looked at the personality profiles of high school students before they entered the world of work, and then assessed their workplace power some years later. In simple terms, the researchers were assessing whether the 'bad guys' would do better than the 'good guys'.

The first issue, of course, is in deciding who is 'bad' or 'good'. As with many polar opposites, such simplistic terms represent a false dichotomy, and there is, of course, no agreement on the precise definition of such terms. Are some people born evil, or do people do bad things because of difficult life experiences? Is anyone all good? Is there such a thing as an entirely selfless act? Whose perspective decides what is good or bad, when one person's freedom fighter is another's terrorist? There are, of course, no simple answers to any of these questions.

What we are starting to understand is that our behaviours are most likely an interplay between nature and nurture, rather than a simple cause and effect. In a bidirectional interaction, our genes influence our behaviour, and our behaviour and environments can influence our genes (Ridley 2000). Some people may be predisposed to antisocial acts, but this alone does not mean they will do bad things. Studies on the personalities of people who enjoyed online trolling found a strong significant correlation between high frequency and enjoyment of such trolling with the 'dark triad' personality traits of narcissism, psychopathy and Machiavellianism (Buckels et al. 2014). Environment, upbringing, education, and other socioeconomic factors all have an impact on individual behavioural outcomes, as these continuously interact with our predispositions of personality. Environment and conditioning, then, can provide a counterbalance to our individual predispositions, or they may exacerbate them.

For his research, Anderson defined 'bad guys' as those who had low psychometric agreeableness scores, and would typically be characterised as selfish, deceitful, aggressive and manipulative. In Costa and McCrae's Revised NEO Personality Inventory (NEO PI-R), they note that ". . . the agreeable person is fundamentally altruistic . . . sympathetic to others and eager to help them . . . by contrast [those with low agreeableness scores are] egocentric, sceptical of the intentions of others, and competitive rather than co-operative" (2006: 16). As with many of the scales in NEO PI-R, this is not to say that one is better than the other. Low agreeableness scores are described here in narcissistic and antisocial terms. Although there are clearly social and psychological benefits to higher levels of agreeableness, people with extremely high propensity towards agreeableness may be susceptible to dependent personality disorders (Costa and McCrae 1990).

If good guys finished last, then the study would show that the bad guys – those with low agreeableness, and more prone to aggressive, manipulative behaviours – would have gained more power. Fourteen years after the original personality assessments, the researchers evaluated the power of the participants in their workplaces. They found no evidence that the bad guys had any more or any less power than the good guys. It seemed that although disagreeable behaviour in some ways increased the perceived power of an individual, possibly through intimidating others into submission, it also alienated people due to lack of cooperative, generous behaviours. In effect, these two particular outcomes of disagreeable behaviour diminished 'bad guy' power overall.

The results of Anderson's study suggest that although good guys do not necessarily always finish last, they do not always come out on top either. The researchers concluded that "nasty individuals reach the top just as often as nice individuals" (Anderson et al. 2020: 22784). Not quite a Hollywood ending, but at least the bad guys do not always win.

Cooperate and evolve

These results challenge the 'tough is best' mentality still prevalent in so many organisations today. Compassionate leaders are weaker, so the narrative goes, and will become prey for those of a stronger, more brutal disposition. There are, of course, plenty of everyday examples of where those of a more contemptuous disposition do seem to triumph, and we have already seen that bad guys do sometimes succeed. A longer-term view on this may be useful to consider.

Game Theory, prevalent in economics, psychology and evolutionary biology, uses mathematical models to examine interactions and behaviours between participants. Although the best overall outcome in Game Theory is generally derived through cooperation, participants frequently opt for a competitive approach as they try to maximise their own, individual outcome.

Evolutionary biologists Christoph Adami and Arend Hintze (2013) have shown that less cooperative, self-motivated strategies in the well-known Game Theory of Prisoner's Dilemma are evolutionary unstable, and that even initially self-interested strategies eventually evolve into approaches which are more collaborative than coercive. As Adami notes, "evolution will punish you if you're selfish and mean" (Michigan State University 2013). In other research which focuses on outcomes of the Prisoner's Dilemma, selfish strategies sometimes fare better in a game with only two players, but typically do much worse in large, evolving populations which are more representative of real human interactions and networks. Strategies which emphasise cooperation and forgiveness perform best in larger, dynamic populations (Stewart and Plotkin 2012). Instead of a short-term approach of dog eat dog, if you want to succeed over the long term, try cooperation instead.

Everything in moderation

So, just as in the best movies, it seems that from an evolutionary biology and Game Theory perspective at least, bad guys will often get their comeuppance in the end. We can succeed without being a terrible person. Power might offer a dangerous dalliance, but it does not cast its spell over everyone. As leaders, we can choose to stay grounded, open, and humble rather than succumb to the perils of power.

A balance needs to be found between extremes of excessive altruism and self-interest, in what author David Bodanis describes as 'monitored generosity' (2021). This approach involves the practice of three simple principles, where listening, giving and defending are most effective when moderated, rather than extreme:
- Listen, without ego
- Give, but audit
- Defend, by not over defending

Bodanis' principles can be illustrated by contrasting Microsoft CEO Steve Ballmer with his successor, Satya Nadella. Ballmer's temper was famed, and Forbes Magazine awarded him the unenviable title of "worst CEO of a large publicly traded American company" in 2012. Nadella, by comparison, is humble, a good listener, and takes responsibility for his mistakes. Under his leadership, Microsoft's culture has come to reflect Nadella's own, more caring, other-centric approach. In his 2017 book, *Hit Refresh*, Nadella discusses the importance of empathy in organisations and in life more generally. Through his actions, he turns such empathy into compassion with impressive results. Under Nadella's leadership, the Microsoft share price has increased almost ten-fold over the seven years from when he took the helm in February 2014. His compassionate, balanced, humble approach has reaped considerable organisational, financial and shareholder benefits.

Far from being weak, compassion is a successful, commercially astute, long-term approach to leadership.

Compassion fatigue

Compassion fatigue is probably the main protagonist in compassion's reputational struggles. It has been described as the emotional and physical price people pay for looking after the needs of others. Characteristics of compassion fatigue are wide-ranging and include burnout, physical and mental exhaustion, anger, increased alcohol consumption and excessive rumination.

Yet . . . is there any such thing as compassion fatigue?
Not necessarily, according to the neuroscientists.

Klimecki and Singer (2011) in particular have been pivotal in challenging the existence of compassion fatigue. In Chapter 3, we explored their research which examined the neural differences between compassion and empathy by focusing on the brain activity of people in compassion and empathy conditions. Remember, the empathy group reported feeling significantly more negative affect and they also perceived neutral situations more negatively than the compassion group. The areas of the brain activated by the two groups also differed. Compassion training was associated with areas responsible for positive affect, social connection and care for others, while the empathy condition recruited areas of the brain which detect and modulate our emotions and responses.

Their research lead Klimecki and Singer to assert that, from a social and developmental psychology as well as from a neuroscientific perspective, cultivating compassion in fact has a positive, restorative effect on the caregiver. It does not fatigue. By comparison, it is the less action-orientated 'empathic distress fatigue' which causes the negative symptoms commonly associated with compassion fatigue, as mentioned above. The differences between empathy and compassion are of critical importance in this area, and are summarised in Table 4.1.

Table 4.1: Comparison between Compassion and Empathic Distress Fatigue (adapted from Singer and Klimecki 2014: 875).

Compassion	Empathic Distress Fatigue
Other-related emotion	Self-related emotion
Positive feelings, e.g., love	Negative feelings, e.g., stress
Good health	Poor health, burnout
Approach and pro-social motivation	Withdrawal and non-social behaviour

So, perhaps there is no such thing as compassion fatigue. 'Empathic distress fatigue' may be more of a mouthful, and requires an understanding of the difference between compassion and empathy, but it is a more accurate description than 'compassion fatigue'. The restorative benefits of compassion are becoming increasingly clear. It is time for empathy to accept its limitations, and for compassion to take a more leading, restorative role in our lives.

Compassion fade or psychic numbing

Another reason for compassion's poor reputation is 'psychic numbing' or 'compassion fade'. Simply put, this tendency impacts how compassionate we tend to be when faced with the suffering of more than one person. Numerous studies have shown that as the number of potential or actual victims of suffering we perceive increases, our likelihood of being motivated to act decreases.

Charities who are aware of psychic numbing will try to overcome this phenomenon by, for example, featuring a photograph of one particular child in need rather than emphasising how many children are suffering. One study found that increasing the number of children referred to from one to many had a corresponding decrease in donations of around 12% (Västfjäll et al. 2014). The same study noted that compassion fade was also in evidence when assessing large scale disasters, resulting in apathy and inaction.

Consider the Syrian refugee crisis as an example of compassion fade. With over 7 million registered refugees who have fled Syria at the time of writing, there are no signs of this flow of human suffering abating. Yet this large-scale humanitarian crisis gets far less press coverage or public reaction than did photographs of one particular Syrian refugee: three-year-old Aylan Kurdi, whose small, lifeless body washed up on a Turkish beach in 2015. In a way in which the number 7,000,000 could not, Aylan's untimely death forced us to stop, to notice, to feel, to think and to take action.

To combat compassion fade, we need to make large numbers more meaningful and emphasise more individualised suffering (see Box 4.5). The UN Refugee Agency tries to do this by noting, for example, that if the current global estimate – and almost incomprehensively large number – of 60 million refugees was a population, it would be 24th largest country in the world. Infographics can help to mitigate compassion fatigue, as they make large numbers more comprehensible and digestible. Another approach is to focus on individuals, bring them to life through storytelling and detail, as this can help to maintain our compassion in the face of major disasters and suffering. In an extreme way, generating more compassion was Aylan Kurdi's untimely legacy.

Box 4.5
Use your understanding of psychic numbing to create compelling compassionate narratives for action.

Focusing on an individual in order to retain compassion was taken to the extreme by Harvard Law Professor Roger Fischer. Fischer had an unusual, and rather memorable, suggestion of how to overcome compassion fade. In his highly readable and unexpectedly entertaining paper entitled 'Preventing Nuclear War', he wrote a proposal for how to ensure the President of the United States of America would consider the impact of their actions before pressing the 'nuclear button':

My suggestion was quite simple: Put that needed code number in a little capsule, and then implant that capsule right next to the heart of a volunteer. The volunteer would carry with him a big, heavy butcher knife as he accompanied the President. If ever the President wanted to fire nuclear weapons, the only way he could do so would be for him first, with his own hands, to kill one human being. The President says, "George, I'm sorry but tens of millions must die". He has to look at someone and realize what death is – what an innocent death is. Blood on the White House carpet. It's reality brought home.

When I suggested this to friends in the Pentagon they said, 'My God, that's terrible. Having to kill someone would distort the President's judgment. He might never push the button.' (Fisher 1981: 16)

Compassion avoidance

With compassion's dubious reputation and disrepute in organisations, it is unsurprising that some people will avoid compassion. They might avoid receiving compassion or giving it, and many choose to take a leadership path which excludes compassion entirely. You might recognise these tendencies either in yourself or in others.

However, compassion avoidance may not be in your best interests. A study by Marcela Matos and colleagues (2021) assessed the impact of compassion avoidance on the mental health of over 4,000 participants during the COVID-19 pandemic. In short, compassion avoidance was found to significantly amplify the pandemic's impact on the participants' mental health. The researchers found that fear or avoidance of compassion significantly increased the participants' vulnerability to psychosocial distress across measures of stress, anxiety, depression and social safeness. Moreover, these results were cross-culturally valid, occurring across all of the twenty-one countries in the study. These adverse impacts on mental health which resulted from the avoidance of compassion remain of importance to organisational leadership, despite the decline of COVID-19. COVID-19 was not the first pandemic and we do not know what the future holds for our fragile world. We need to learn lessons which can benefit future generations.

Compassion avoidance may be so extreme that someone would actively avoid picking up a book with the title *Compassionate Leadership*. Yet, as we will discuss in Chapter 7, those who avoid compassion are, in fact, likely to experience its benefits in an even more heightened way. We can support compassion avoiders by sharing evidence-based, practical guidance and role modelling compassionate leadership and the benefits it brings.

Psychological studies, neuroscientific research and organisational performance show that succumbing to hubris and self-focus, as well as avoiding compassion, are all unfortunate leadership choices. They are detrimental to our individual mental health, are a poor choice of long-term strategy, and are a far from promising approach to successful, sustainable leadership. Instead, as the next chapter will show, there are numerous individual, leadership and organisational benefits we can quickly reap when we sow the seeds of compassion.

Key Chapter Points

- Compassion has a reputation problem. It has described over many years as immoral, fatiguing and weak, and is particularly absent from much of organisational life.
- To understand where this reputation problem came from, we examined the role of compassion in religion, philosophy, economics, literature and the media.
- Common organisational accusations levelled at compassion include it being a by-word for weak leadership and career sabotage. Detractors sometimes comment on the well-known, but perhaps fictional, notion of compassion fatigue.
- Evidence increasingly shows that these accusations are unfounded. Power can undermine leadership effectiveness, and there are many hazards such as hubris or over-confidence which must be navigated. Yet compassionate leadership is shown to be a successful long-term approach for individuals and organisations.
- Remember moderation: Listen without ego, give but audit, defend, by not over defending.
- Compassion avoidance is also discussed, as this has serious implications for the wellbeing and everyday functioning of leaders.

Chapter 5
Research & reality: benefits of compassion

I would rather make mistakes in kindness and compassion than work miracles in unkindness and hardness. (Mother Theresa)

When it comes to love, compassion, and other feelings of the heart, I am rich. (Muhammad Ali)

Perhaps compassion is acceptable to a point, but when the going gets tough, leadership needs to get tougher? Few would argue that looking after the wellbeing of employees is an important management task; after all, staff costs are typically among the biggest in any organisation, and most organisations crave a productive, engaged workforce. Yet whilst wellbeing of employees clearly matters, does it only matter to a limited extent? Or, maybe worse, is compassion used as a superficial veneer ('compassion washing') whose mask quickly slips when profits are under pressure, or take-overs loom?

As we have seen, compassion is often thought to have no place in organisational life, and is still notably lacking from most organisational and leadership theory. Adam Smith's economic theories about productivity were embraced, but his caveat of compassion has been largely disregarded. The ramifications of this error are finally understood, and that mistake now needs to be rectified.

The pace, quantity and complexity of global change continues unabated, and it can be difficult for leaders to keep up. This sometimes results in people being forgotten, their pain going unnoticed, and their subsequent disengagement from work. Yet engagement matters. According to a recent survey (Gallup 2021), employee engagement levels worldwide average around 20% and Gallup estimate this low engagement level costs the global economy c.$8 trillion each year. Engagement impacts both people and profits.

We have an opportunity to permanently adopt a more compassionate approach to leadership. This will not only benefit sustainable organisational performance, but will also befit a world whose fragility we are finally starting to comprehend. Addressing the emerging leadership challenges of sustainability, climate change impacts and inequality requires compassion, honesty and humility. Self-interested, profit-hungry leaders are entirely at odds with what the world's future actually needs.

Let us now explore some of the main benefits of compassion, firstly to leaders and then to organisations more widely. The areas we will examine in this chapter are the tip of an increasingly large body of evidence about just how uniquely impactful compassion is, despite its dubious reputation. After this, I offer a word of warning about the dark side of compassion; ignore this at your peril.

We will start by focusing on three main leadership benefits: a reduction cellular inflammation and associated stress, chemical balance and rewiring, then social connectedness and associated benefits.

https://doi.org/10.1515/9783110763126-005

Leadership benefits

Reduced cellular inflammation and stress

Let us start by putting the benefits of compassionate leadership under the microscope. Indeed, we are going to begin our examination at a cellular level. The body's immune system has a natural defence mechanism in response to harmful stimuli: inflammation. When this is an urgent, short-term response, it usefully allows us to minimise injury or infection. However, when this continues over a longer term, or when there is no actual stimulus to fight, this inflammation response can result in chronic inflammatory disease. In this case, instead of dealing with an issue then returning to normal, cellular inflammation levels remain high for some time. Such chronic inflammation plays a central role in heart disease, depression and even some cancers (Harvard Health 2020). Of particular note to leaders, high cellular inflammation levels are frequently found in people with ongoing significant levels of stress, and it is a rare individual who does not find some aspects of leadership stressful.

So, what can leaders do about this? One insight comes from research by Barbara Fredrickson (2013), who examined the cellular inflammation levels of adult participants and also asked them about their happiness levels. She particularly focused her research on those participants who described themselves as 'very happy'. Through asking them about their happiness, Fredrickson found that there were essentially two distinct groups: those whose happiness was hedonic, and those whose was eudaimonic. Hedonic happiness is achieved through enjoying pleasurable experiences and avoiding painful ones. Going on holiday or treating ourselves on a shopping trip are examples of this. Eudaimonic happiness, by contrast, results from experiences which align to a personal purpose or meaning, and which often impact others rather than being focused on self-gratification. Volunteering – compassionate action to alleviate the suffering of others – is an example of eudaimonic happiness.

What Barbara Fredrickson found was that although the participants rated themselves at the same high levels of happiness, those who derived this from predominantly hedonic means had higher levels of cellular inflammation than those whose happiness was eudaimonically derived. In other words, although at a conscious awareness level participants considered themselves to be equally very happy, their immune systems differentiated between hedonic and eudaimonic sources of this happiness.

The implications for compassionate leadership are significant. Taking action to alleviate the suffering of others and practicing other-focused compassion can reduce the stress levels of leaders and even reduces their cellular inflammation levels. Compassion, then, is a pathway to longevity.

Chemical balance and rewiring

Leadership is, in some ways, a constant recalibration of the chemical reactions involved in our everyday emotions and behaviours. A chemical approach to self-management, if you like. Cortisol is our alarm system. Serotonin helps to regulate our mood. Dopamine influences our motivations and happiness. Oxytocin helps us to build trust.

Compassion increases activity in the areas of our brains involved in dopamine and oxytocin, and can make us more understanding of others (Lutz et al. 2008). Compassion also helps to manage and augment our chemical balances, improving our happiness levels and helping us to build trust. Leaders can benefit from this understanding and become their own mixologist through compassionate practice.

This may sound fanciful, but we are not entirely at the mercy of our genes or our emotions, and we can take an active role in influencing our brain function. Neuroplasticity is the brain's ability to adapt and change, and we can alter our neural pathways through conscious intention and practice.

One of the simplest practices is writing a gratitude journal or letter. Although this suggestion sometimes provokes an eye roll, the evidence is compelling. Studies often focus on the benefits for adults without mental health concerns, yet even studies where the participants were seeking psychotherapy for depression or anxiety found that the impact of gratitude writing on self-reported wellbeing was significant (Kini et al. 2016). This was the case after only a few weeks, and the benefits continued to accumulate over time. The same study found that increased gratitude was associated with increased activity in the medial prefrontal cortex; again, this matters from a leadership perspective as this is an area associated with decision-making and complex planning.

Another practice, described in more detail in Chapter 7, is a compassion meditation. Again, this may initially feel like an awkward practice in a leadership book. And again, the science is persuasive. Compassion meditations have been shown to have a plethora of benefits. They result in reduced levels of anger and depression in patients suffering from Post-Traumatic Stress Disorder (Kearney et al. 2013). They can reduce the frequency and severity of migraines (Tonelli and Wachholtz 2014). Chronic back pain patients report improved psychological wellbeing and reduced physical pain after such meditation practices (Carson et al. 2005). Compassion meditations have been shown to improve concentration whilst simultaneously lowering stress and anxiety. They have even resulted in an increase in the grey matter of the brain, notably in the areas responsible for emotional control of anxiety and overall mood (Leung et al. 2013). Such benefits are available to everyone, not just those in positions of leadership, yet the benefits of lower stress, improved wellbeing and emotional regulation should make compelling reading for any aspiring compassionate leader.

Self-compassion is a further useful consideration for compassionate leadership, as it results in a reduction of stress, anxiety and depression, as well as delivering a plethora of other physical and psychological benefits. This, and research into the effects of self-compassion specifically in leaders, will be addressed more fully in Chapter 7.

Improved social connectedness

Social connectedness is a largely subjective appreciation of having close, positive rela-tionships with other people. There is no ideal number of social connections, and the form these take varies considerably by individual.

It probably does not come as much of a revelation to find that compassion is good for social connection. Common sense could fairly quickly lead us to the conclusion that taking action to alleviate someone's suffering is likely to result in people feeling close and connected to each other.

What is extraordinary is just how important social connection is for us as individ-uals and as leaders. Strong social connections reduce anxiety and depression, improve our physical and mental health, and enhance our own perceptions of our wellbeing (Seppala et al. 2013). People who report having strong social connections also report higher than average levels of happiness and higher resilience to stress (Lee et al. 2001). From an organisational perspective, social connectedness has the beneficial side effect of reducing in-group bias. Rather wonderfully, when research participants were primed for social connectedness, they sat closer to strangers, displayed more willingness to help, and were happy to celebrate in the joy of others (Seppala et al. 2013). Another study (Brown et al. 2003) even found that people who regularly pro-vided compassionate support to those close to them were less likely to die than those who did not provide such support. Compassion, it seems, can even save your life.

No great surprise, then, that the converse is true: poor social connections are ex-tremely bad for us. The seriousness of this detriment, though, is worse than might initially be assumed. Poor social connection is highly correlated with aggression and antisocial acts, impulsive behaviours and a lack of warmth for others. If that was not bad enough, low social connectedness is a greater risk to our individual health than obesity, smoking or high blood pressure (Holt-Lunstad et al. 2010).

Compassion, then, has many leadership benefits. It enhances our social connect-edness and is demonstrably beneficial to our physical health, our mental wellbeing and even our longevity. We shall now examine the benefits of compassion to or-ganisations, whilst keeping in mind that the individual leadership benefits we have just explored will, of course, also bring benefits to those we work with in our organisations.

Organisational benefits

Studies of organisational compassion are still in their relative infancy, partially because of compassion's reputational issue. Reassuringly, such research is becoming more main-stream, and the results are fascinating. We can now explore these, primarily using the lenses of Affective Commitment (AC) and Organisational Compassion (OC).

Affective Commitment (AC)

In the early 1990s, psychologists John Meyer and Natalie Allen wanted to understand why people stayed with or left organisations; in other words, employee commitment. They developed a model which proposed three distinct types of commitment: Affective Commitment (AC), Continuance Commitment (CC) and Normative Commitment (NC). These three types can be most simply explained as the level to which an individual wants to stay (AC), needs to stay (CC), and feels that they ought to stay (NC) in an organisation, as summarised in Table 5.1.

Table 5.1: Meyer and Allen Commitment Types.

Affective Commitment (AC)	Continuance Commitment (CC)	Normative Commitment (NC)
'I want to stay'	'I need to stay'	'I ought to stay'

Since Meyer and Allen's original model, many others (e.g., Cohen 1996; Culpepper 2000; Meyer et al. 2002) have conducted analyses and meta-analyses of these commitment types, and have repeatedly found a strong, positive association between AC and a host of organisational benefits. These benefits include higher employee retention, increased occupational commitment, better attendance and improved job performance. AC also correlates with organisational citizenship behaviours; that is, those which benefit the organisation as a whole, but which are entirely discretionary to individuals and are beyond any contractual role requirements.

Of the three parts of Meyer and Allen's model, it is AC which has the strongest positive correlation with all of these desirable employee behaviours, much more so than CC or NC. The importance of AC to any organisation is remarkably clear, given these strong correlations to lower staff turnover and improvements in attendance, job performance, job commitment, as well as other, wider pro-social behaviours.

Benefits of affective commitment
– Lower staff turnover
– Reduced absenteeism
– Increased pro-social behaviours
– Increased job satisfaction
– Improved performance in role

Other research (Barsade and O'Neill 2014) has similarly found that such a caring, relational, prosocial culture results in improved teamwork and employee satisfaction, alongside less absenteeism and emotional exhaustion.

Organisational Compassion (OC)

What is organisational compassion? There is no consensus on this, although emerging research can be broadly divided into three main categories:

a) Individual Compassionate Acts and Meaning-Making

In simplest terms, OC can be thought of as a collection of individual compassionate acts and the meaning we each make when we witness these. Although the compassionate acts we see are often small in magnitude, such as emotional support, flexibility in times of need, or material goods if needed, their significance is frequently magnified through inference and creation of meaning for individuals (Lilius et al. unpublished). Each of us as individuals will make meaning about ourselves, others and organisations when we notice either compassionate acts or their conspicuous absence.

Meyer and Allen (1990) also mentioned this creation of meaning in their research. They noted that behaviours which result in individuals feeling more cared about will in turn encourage self-identification with the supporting organisation. In other words, individuals reflect the meaning they make from small compassionate acts into their wider organisational system, which then reinforces the meaning back to the individual. In this way, a mutually reinforcing interaction between the individual and the organisational system is established.

b) Part of Organisational Character

Alternatively, OC can be viewed as more than just the sum of individual compassionate acts and meaning-making. Jason Kanov and colleagues (2004) described how compassion becomes embedded into organisational character through practices and routines. These then effectively legitimise, co-ordinate, and ultimately create further compassion. We will examine some of these structural practices and routines for developing a compassionate organisation further in Chapter 9.

Importantly, this research concluded that building organisational compassion does not need to wait for the supporting structures to be in place. Compassion can, at least initially, be a very individual act. Our role as leaders, then, is to simultaneously be a source of individual compassionate acts, whilst also creating an environment in which compassion can both flourish and become woven into the fabric of our organisations.

c) A Systemic, Social Process

A growing number of researchers have argued that because compassion is so strongly correlated to pro-social behaviours, organisational compassion is effectively a 'social process' which occurs within networked systems (Grant et al. 2008; Lilius et al. 2008, 2011; Rynes et al. 2012). Laura Madden and colleagues (2012) emphasise that organisational compassion can self-organise and self-regulate through such social processes. This view of self-regulating systems is increasingly popular in many fields, including coaching, applied sciences and management theory. It also resonates with the notion of compassion as an evolutionary benefit; survival of the most compassionate, rather than the fittest, perhaps. In both biological and organisational terms, some researchers have argued that compassion is the most effective long-term approach to individual and group survival (Gilbert 2009; Goetz et al. 2010).

Understanding such a systemic approach to compassion helps us to consider what the ideal organisational conditions might be that could enable compassion to flourish. We will explore this more in Chapter 9.

OC can most usefully be considered to be a combination of these three perspectives, where each organisation has its own unique blend of individual meaning-making, organisational character traits and social, systemic interactions. In the absence of consensus, it can be practical to use what Jane Dutton and her colleagues (2014) propose as the six factors which affect the process and outcome of organisational compassion, and which include aspects of all three of these perspectives. The six factors are: shared values, shared beliefs, norms of expected behaviour, formal organisational practices, structure and quality of relationships, and leadership behaviours. A brief description of each of these is shown in Table 5.2.

Table 5.2: Organisational Compassion Factors (adapted from Dutton et al. 2014).

Factor	Description
Shared values	What people in an organisation consider to be important including, but not limited to, the approach to caring for others.
Shared beliefs	What people in an organisation believe to be true, such as whether or not it is acceptable to show emotion at work.
Norms of expected behaviour	Also known as 'feeling rules', these are behavioural norms which are shaped and expressed over time.
Formal organisational practices	These formalise what is important to the organisation, and impact the likelihood and nature of responses in an organisation.
Structure and quality of relationships	The number and quality of relationships in an organisation will impact the speed and nature of responses to suffering.
Leadership behaviours	The formal power, role modelling and even symbolic gestures of leadership in response to suffering all impact the organisation.

Together, these six factors impact the nature, process and outcomes of compassionate responses to suffering in organisations. These factors were the basis for the Organisational Compassion questionnaire created by the Greater Good Science Center at the University of Berkeley. This questionnaire is a useful gauge for considering individual organisational levels of compassion, and was the Organisational Compassion measure used in my own research in this area, which we will now explore.

Organisational Compassion and Affective Commitment

We will now examine how Organisational Compassion (OC) and Affective Commitment (AC) relate to each other, and why this is so important for leaders and their organisations:

Research by Jacoba Lilius and colleagues (unpublished) concluded that the experience of receiving compassion in an organisational setting significantly reduced individual job stress and likelihood of leaving, as well as increasing both Affective Commitment levels and pro-social behaviours. Their research also concluded that such experiences resulted in employees making positive inferences about themselves, about their peers and about the organisation as a result.

Their findings intrigued me and this, combined with my own interest in compassion, led me to research whether or not there was a relationship between how compassionate people perceived their organisations to be and their levels of commitment to that organisation.

To begin with, all did not go according to plan. During my initial approaches to organisations for research participation purposes, one financial institution responded that the organisation would not participate as the HR Director was "concerned about the nature of the questions, [which they didn't think] . . . would fit the profile of a very egotistical ventures business . . ." and suggested that "a more American or a John Lewis type business might work better where they actually care about their staff" (personal communication, 2016). Whilst this was a disappointing response to receive, it was not entirely unexpected in light of research highlighting that people with elevated Social Dominance Orientation (SDO) – a competitive, hierarchical trait common in many assertive business contexts – ". . . might be actively resisting participating in compassionate behaviours" (Martin et al. 2015: 8). Ironically, as will be discussed below, those focused on strong business results would do well to consider organisational compassion, both for their own health and that of the organisations they work for.

Luckily, many other organisations from across a variety of sectors did choose to participate, and I am grateful to all of those who engaged in the research. My investigation included a combination of survey data analysis and individual interviews, and the resulting evidence was compelling: OC and AC are strongly positively correlated with each other. Of course, correlation does not necessarily imply causation, but does it really matter whether people wanting to stay results in high levels of compassion or if high levels of compassion mean people want to stay? The correlation is what matters most here. The fact is, where we find high levels of compassion in organisations, we also find high levels of affective commitment – and that, as we know, results in a host of organisational benefits.

In a compassionate organisation, people are more satisfied and perform better in their roles, resulting in a myriad of tangible and intangible benefits. The extracurricular pro-social behaviours we see with AC benefit both the organisation as a whole and the individuals within it. Lower staff turnover means that organisations retain institutional knowledge for longer and this, along with reduced absenteeism and lower hiring costs, has direct beneficial impacts on profitability.

In the interviews conducted as part of my research, one of the respondents directly – and without prompting – directly linked compassion to resilience:

> If you give people the time and space to deal with their life, they will deal with it more quickly, then their capacity and performance will bounce back quickly.

This comment associating compassion with organisational resilience is worthy of closer inspection. Some research has found that compassion may indeed contribute to the health and even survival of an organisation. In one fascinating study, Professor Jody Gittell and colleagues (2006) examined the differences in airline outcomes following the 9/11 terrorist attacks in the US. They found that while financial robustness was an important consideration, this alone was an insufficient buffer in time of crisis. Companies which survived the economic aftermath also had 'relational reserves' that had a significant part to play in determining whether or not the company survived. Even without such a traumatic event, it seems reasonable that relational reserves of organisational compassion may indeed bolster the viability of organisations in our complex, uncertain world.

Organisations can clearly reap the benefits of AC through organisational compassion. This, as discussed above, can be a combination of individual, relational and systemic approaches which together build the compassionate capacity of an organisation.

Outside of the OC and AC relationship, there are other benefits associated with compassion in organisations. We will now briefly explore three of these: enhanced organisational wellbeing, improving outcomes of difficult conversations and improving both accountability and psychological safety.

Enhanced organisational wellbeing

One common example of organisational compassionate infrastructure is employee assistance programmes (EAPs). These are an increasingly familiar benefit, often tailored to an organisation's particular needs, and are typically focused on practical and emotional support. They usually include some mental health provision, critical incident care and confidential advice lines. In some respects, these could be viewed as an organisation providing a compassionate response to employee suffering. Yet beyond the obvious benefits of such formal compassionate infrastructure, there is a greater organisational value to these EAPs. Well-known psychologist and author Adam Grant and his colleagues (2008) found that such programmes additionally enable employees to *give* support, as well as to receive it. They do this, Grant argues, through a subtle 'sensemaking' process which results in employees experiencing compassion and then becoming more compassionate themselves. This delicate exchange increases the likelihood of a prosocial identity, both individually and organisationally, which weaves compassion into the very fabric of the organisational culture. Even such formalised compassion as an employee assistance programme, it seems, joins in the delicately balanced dance of compassionate give and take, and improves both organisational and individual wellbeing. Compassion is not a one-way street.

Improved conflict resolution

Difficult conversations are a fact of organisational life. Whether we enjoy the challenge they present or try our best to avoid them, whether we instigate them or unwittingly find ourselves in them, they are inevitable. In the world more generally, disputes over differences of opinion seem increasingly common. Binary notions of right and wrong or good and bad leave little room for discussion, consideration and difference.

Can compassion help?

Yes, it can. As we have seen, acts of compassion foster goodwill and result in positive chemical reactions for the compassion provider, the recipient and even for observers. A compassionate response, with its inclusion of feeling in our response to another's suffering, emotionally attunes us to others. Even if only momentarily, compassion can take us from seeing the world merely from our own viewpoint, as we metaphorically, empathetically stand in the shoes of the other person.

Peter T Coleman is a Psychology Professor at Columbia University, where his research focuses on conflict resolution. Since the early 2000s, he and his colleagues have studied hundreds of conversations between people with widely opposing views. In their laboratory, participants have discussed healthcare, gun control, police reform, global warming and many other contentious subjects. Drawing on the results of his research, Coleman offers a number of lessons to support healthy conflict resolution. Most fundamental of these is to embrace complication. "Certainty" he notes, "is the collapse of complexity" (2021). If we are convinced that we are entirely right and the other is therefore completely wrong, then the resulting conflict will be unhealthy and is unlikely to be resolved.

Another of Coleman's proposals is that we should accept that conflict is emotional, and therefore use emotional connection to build trust and rapport with our adversary. Compassion, as a relational process, allows us to make such an emotional connection. Coleman encourages us to switch off our autopilot responses so as to listen with the intention of understanding. In order to do this, we can choose to simply become aware – that first stage of compassion – rather than to react or to assume understanding.

Coleman's conflict research aligns well with our approach to compassionate leadership. In fact, we can see in the new construct of compassion that each step can help support effective conflict resolution. This is illustrated in Figure 5.1.

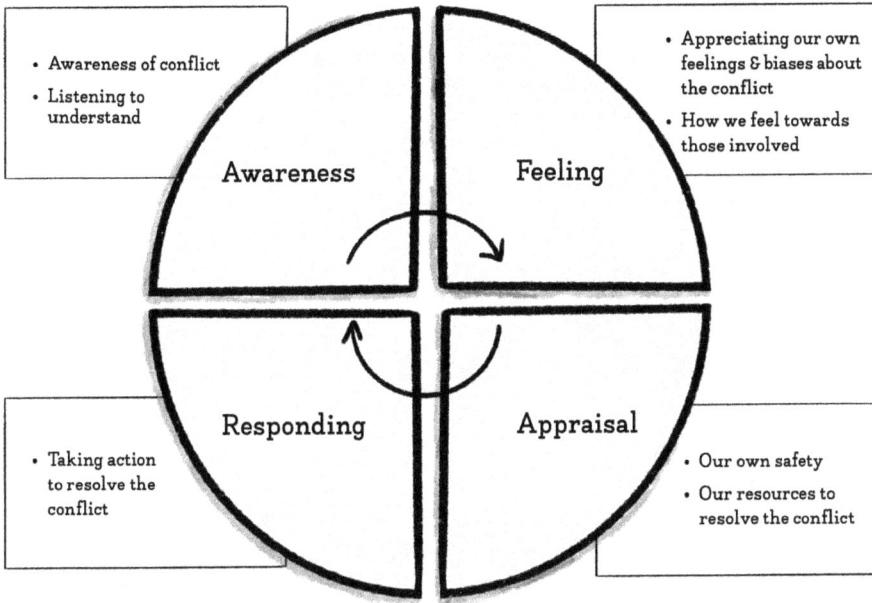

Figure 5.1: New Compassion Construct and conflict resolution.

Compassion's initial awareness step, its emotional attunement with others, listening to understand and feeling into another person's perspective are all fundamental to effective conflict resolution. The new compassion model encourages us to be aware of how resourced we are to safely take action, to notice our potential biases and behavioural patterns at work, and to stay mindful of the impact of our role might have. Far from being soft or weak, compassionate leadership can, in fact, facilitate healthy debate and conflict resolution. A short case study about approaching conflict with compassion is outlined in Box 5.1.

Box 5.1: Approaching Conflict with Compassion

John, a senior manager in a large organisation, dreaded his meetings with Helen. Helen was a Director in another division and she had a fearsome reputation. Whatever work John produced, she would find issue with it, often criticising him loudly in the open plan office. When he tried to talk to Helen about her effect on him, she rolled her eyes and told him to stop taking things so personally.

At first, the idea of treating Helen with compassion seemed a ridiculous one to John. Why on earth would he? She was the one behaving badly and he was in the more junior role. Reaching an impasse, I somewhat desperately asked John if he would feel differently if he discovered that Helen had a sick parent to look after at home. His eyes softened. "Yes," he said. Then he looked at me, quizzically. "Does she?" I had never met Helen and explained that I had no idea about her actual situation. However, since we all suffer, we could perhaps imagine that Helen was experiencing suffering in some form.

Having crossed this initial hurdle, John decided to apply what he had learned about compassion. He scheduled meetings with Helen for times in the week when he was likely to feel more resourced. Before each meeting, he would take some time to imagine (entirely fictitious) scenarios about what

Helen might be experiencing; he felt that this allowed him to see her as more than a Director. When she became agitated, he listened to understand and quietly noticed his own feelings. Importantly, John also applied his understanding about his own preferences in Transactional Analysis ego states, and carefully chose to remain in Adult. John reports that their relationship has improved, and he no longer dreads their interactions. There was no Hollywood ending or lightbulb moment in this tricky professional relationship dynamic, but there was a subtle rebalancing due to John's knowledgeable, compassionate work.

With conflict often comes anger. Behind anger there is typically pain. Handled correctly, a compassionate approach to conflict can produce more fruitful results for everyone involved.

Accountability and psychological safety

During the COVID-19 pandemic, compassion became an increasingly mainstream leadership topic. As the pandemic eased, however, compassion's reputational problem again raised its head. Compassion seemed fitting in the 'Blitz spirit' of a pandemic, but was that just a moment in time? Do we now take off our masks, lace up our gloves and get back in the boxing ring? A recent *Harvard Business Review* article tackled this issue, noting that managers were questioning how to balance compassion with the need to get work done (Gallo 2021). The notion of 'bleeding heart' sentimentality where compassion sits in direct opposition to commercial acumen again raises its head.

Compassion and accountability for results are not, however, diametrically opposed. A leader who uses 'toughness' might see short term results, but is undermining the psychological safety of their team. Psychologically unsafe teams hide mistakes, are low on creativity and innovation, and are more likely to leave than thrive. Instead, compassion and accountability can be integrated to great effect. Compassionate leaders make it ok for people to not be ok, and to talk about their issues. People who are seen, heard and supported are more able to regroup and refocus.

Numerous studies have shown that compassion from leaders results in higher employee engagement, increased pro-citizenship behaviours and less individual burnout. One particular study noted that supervisor compassion towards customer-service orientated employees even resulted in improved satisfaction ratings from customers as well as from employees (Eldor 2017). Building a culture where mistakes can be made, discussed and learned from, without fear of reprimand, humiliation or punishment, builds psychological safety. This results in improved innovation, higher employee engagement, lower staff turnover, and less costly re-work.

Compassionate leadership, whilst seeking to understand perspectives, is not a barrier to dealing with poor performance or unethical behaviour. We must acknowledge that there may occasionally be unfortunate behaviours in any organisation. Allowing such behaviours to continue unchecked will be to the detriment of others in the team more widely. Therefore, in order to successfully integrate compassion and accountability, compassionate leadership needs to constantly calibrate the needs of the individual with those of the wider team. There is no one solution to what this calibration should look like, as the stage and actors will constantly vary.

Let us consider an example, where a team member has been dishonest about the amount of annual leave that they have taken. A compassionate approach seeks to understand the reason for a behaviour, so that a response can be calmly considered from more than one perspective. If the reason behind the behaviour is that the individual has recently received a terminal health diagnosis, or they are feeling bullied at work, then the response to this is likely to differ from the remedial action needed if they just wanted extra time off for reasons of hedonistic pleasure. Seeking to understand before considering a course of action demonstrates that a compassionate response is measured and considered, not weak and reactive.

Compassionate leadership is neither weak nor lenient. It is flexible, considered and supports people and organisations to perform at their very best. The majority of us want to perform well at work, although there will occasionally be exceptions to this; it is better to sort a few 'bad apples' than have a 'bad barrel'.

Case study: Compassionate lessons from healthcare organisations

Stephen G Post, a Medical Professor of Preventative Medicine has written a particularly compelling article on the benefits of compassion in medical settings. This is included as a case study, for the lessons are applicable far more widely than only in healthcare organisations.

Post begins by noting that compassion is an emotional and social intelligence which is beneficial to the patient and practitioner, and which is essential to positive clinical outcomes. He then goes on to argue that there are four main beneficiaries of a compassionate approach to healthcare, as outlined in Table 5.3.

Table 5.3: Beneficiaries of Compassion in Healthcare (adapted from Post 2011).

Beneficiary	Benefit
Healthcare professionals	Can focus on patient care rather than administration or targets
Medical students	Wellbeing and learning improve by working with positive compassionate role models
Patients	Receive better care and medical outcomes
Healthcare organisations	Improved staff and patient outcomes result in a side-effect of reputational gain

Other research overwhelmingly supports these assertions (e.g. Sinclair et al. 2016), and the results are quite astonishing. Compassionate doctors reach more accurate diagnoses more quickly than those who lack compassion or are neutral. Why? The answer is not yet clear, although perhaps patients are more at ease and therefore willing to volunteer information to someone who is compassionate. The information more easily offered might then help the doctor to more accurately diagnose the ailment. Patients with a compassionate doctor are significantly more likely to adhere to their treatment plans, and therefore have better clinical outcomes, in a wonderful example of compassion being more of a shared dance than a one-way flow (Vermeire et al. 2001). Diabetic patients who consider their doctor to be compassionate are more likely to skilfully self-manage their ongoing care than those who report feeling that they have a less compassionate caregiver. Compassionate healthcare is also associated with improved wound healing outcomes, potentially because the safety of a compassionate response results in lower cortisol levels and thus allows the body a chance to heal its wounds most effectively.

Far from the gloomy scenarios of so-called compassion fatigue, the reality is that compassionate care benefits healthcare staff. It results in lowered depression and burnout rates, elevated meaning and purpose, and more diligent technical care. This conscientious technical attention in particular may, of course, be strongly linked to the improved patient outcomes, and seeing patient recovery can further benefit the caregiver.

Compassionate care benefits healthcare organisations through reputational gains which do not require additional time or resources; these are most likely a result of the improved patient and staff outcomes noted above. Furthermore, a study conducted by Medical Professor Gerald Hickson and colleagues (1994) directly challenged the perception that being compassionate is uncommercial. They found that medical staff who were perceived as being rushed, uncommunicative and lacking in concern for the patient were significantly more likely to have medical malpractice claims brought against them; the opposite was true for those who were considered by patients to be compassionate, communicative and concerned about their patients' wellbeing. Defending malpractice claims is a costly endeavour in both time and money for any healthcare organisation; that compassionate healthcare can reduce such claims is an important example of how commercially sound a compassionate approach is. Interestingly, throughout these studies it is people's *perception* of how compassionate they believed their doctor to be that was measured. How people feel and perceive may not be an exact science, but they certainly matter in terms of outcomes.

Post described what he considered to be a balanced compassionate approach for physicians, summarising how they can care for patients without becoming overwhelmed. His list, shown in Table 5.4, is equally applicable and useful outside of healthcare, and fits well with our new construct of compassion:

Table 5.4: Post's Healthcare Approach and the New Compassion Construct.

Post's Compassionate Healthcare Approach	Correspondence with New Compassion Construct
Realise that you cannot fix everything	Appraise when this is your role and if you have the resources
Entrust your colleagues	Appraise your intention and build a compassionate organisation
Step back from your initial emotional reactions	Notice your emotional response then move to the appraisal step, so that you respond rather than react
Have some sort of 'spiritual' practice	Appraise and develop your resources including, but not limited to, spiritual practices such as meditation
Keep in mind the meaning and privilege of being a healer	Appraise your role as leader and remember that leadership amplifies actions, as well as their absence
Have a balanced life and claim the time for it	Appraise your resources, and do not tip into altruism
Be empathic, but the patient's suffering is not your suffering	Stay in compassion, not altruism, and do not become stuck in empathy when overwhelm means that you take no action

Ultimately, organisations are, at their core, groups of people interrelating around a common purpose. Compassion's place in organisations is therefore central. It is a fundamental, innate part of human functioning where we recognise the suffering in others and ourselves then take action to alleviate that pain. Questioning the relevance of compassion in organisations is like questioning the need for oxygen. As we saw in Chapter 3, Einstein encouraged us to have ever widening circles of compassion. In order to do this, a key function of leadership is to nurture compassion: in ourselves as individuals and as leaders, in the people we work with regularly, in those we do not know and even in our competitors.

The dark side of compassion

Just in case all of the research about the benefits of compassion sounds too good to be true, a word of caution. Compassion has a dark side.

Jung observed: "Everyone carries a shadow, and the less it is embodied in the individual's conscious life, the blacker and denser it is" (1938: 131). Awareness of our Jungian shadow, and how its murky, primitive impulses may influence our actions, is critical to understanding the potential dark side of compassion (see Box 5.2). As compassionate leaders, we need to be vigilant to the ever-present dangers of our shadow. Organisational Behaviour Professor Peter Frost and his colleagues briefly hinted at this possibility from an organisational compassion perspective, noting that compassion ". . . can be motivated less by a desire to alleviate suffering than by instrumental goals" (2013: 861). The risk of being compassionate because we want to look good as a leader, rather than because of a more positive, other-focused intention, requires us to pay attention to our shadow.

Box 5.2
Gently, bravely, look into your own shadow. Recruit support to do this, if needed.

Paul Gilbert takes this further, noting that the human need to belong is so strong that it may overwhelm the brain's ability for compassion: "If there's one thing we need from compassion, it's to open our minds to the ease by which we're led to perform immoral acts and then truly believe them to be justified" (2009: 471). Research on the impact of leaders' moral excellence shows that consistently demonstrated ethical behaviours are a reliable predictor of key outcomes such as Affective Commitment, compliance and compassion across the organisation more widely (Vianello et al. 2010). Ethically and morally sound leadership, and constant vigilance of our own shadow, then, are critical in order to avoid the dark side of compassion. History has repeatedly demonstrated the power of morally corrupt leaders who lacked compassion for those excluded from their in-group; Box 5.3 offers a prompt to find compassion for others and lessen in-group bias.

Box 5.3
Look for opportunities to collaborate, and to break down in-group walls.

This warning notwithstanding, the evidence for compassion in organisations is compelling. Compassion is restorative, it allows us to recover quickly from setbacks, it lowers our stress and inflammation levels and can even prolong our lives. It is good for us as individuals, as leaders, as organisations and in our wider societies. Compassion enables us to reap the benefits of Affective Commitment, with a more engaged, positive workforce who are less likely to leave and whose resilience helps the organisation to survive in times of crisis. Even in easier times, when compassion is embedded into our cultural fabric, organisations benefit from better psychological safety and improved reputation. The profitability of compassionate organisations is enhanced through a resilient workforce, less costly conflict and happier customers. Compassion's reputation problem, it seems, is undeserved.

Particularly because of this reputation problem, being a compassionate leader takes courage. Unlikely a source as this may seem, the creator of Sesame Street and The Muppets provides an insight into compassionate leadership as a courageous choice:

> I know that it's easier to portray a world that's filled with cynicism and anger, where problems are solved with violence. That's titillating. It's an easy out. What's a whole lot tougher is to offer alternatives, to present other ways conflict can be resolved, and to show that you can always have a positive impact on your world. To do that, you have to put yourself out on a limb, take chances, and run the risk of being called a do-gooder.   (Jim Henson 2005: 161)

If being called a do-gooder is the worst of our fears, it is tantalisingly feasible that compassionate leadership needs a mere step, rather than a gigantic leap, of courage.

Key Chapter Points
- We have examined in some detail three of main leadership benefits which derive from compassion, and noted the associated advantages of these:
    - Reduction of cellular inflammation
    - Chemical balance and rewiring
    - Social connectedness
- Organisational benefits of compassion have been discussed in light of recent research from many fields. These benefits include:
    - Affective Commitment, when people want to stay with an organisation
    - Organisational Compassion and its relationship with Affective Commitment
    - Enhanced organisational wellbeing and how this is developed
    - Improved conflict resolution and how the new compassion construct can support this
    - Improving accountability and psychological safety
- Compassionate lessons from healthcare contexts are covered in some detail, as these are applicable to organisations more widely.
- The dark side of compassion is briefly explored, as a warning to all aspiring compassionate leaders.

Chapter 6
Compassion and cognitive bias

Our comforting conviction that the world makes sense rests on a secure foundation: our almost unlimited ability to ignore our ignorance.
(Daniel Kahneman)

I can promise to be upright, but not to be without bias.
(Johann Wolfgang von Goethe)

But I am not biased!

Thinking of skipping this chapter? Maybe it does not apply to you? Perhaps you are not biased. You might already know everything there is to know about this subject, since cognitive biases have entered mainstream parlance to a greater extent than much psychology research? Before succumbing to these temptations, it may be worth at least reading this introduction. Consider the two cognitive biases it introduces, and then you can make an informed decision about whether or not you still want to leave this chapter out.

Let us start with the bias about bias. A series of studies by Pronin and colleagues (2002) found that an overwhelming majority of individuals see themselves as being less biased than others. They discovered that although we are typically quick to recognise biases held by other people, we repeatedly fail to recognise our own biases or their impacts. Even when study participants were then told about this so-called Blind Spot Bias and how it may impact their behaviour, most still insisted that their self-assessments were objective, accurate and lacking in bias. Blind Spot Bias is the bedfellow of the Superiority Illusion, where most people think that they are above average in many areas of life, such as driving ability or passing exams, even though this logically cannot be the case. Most of us cannot be better than average. The Superiority Illusion is a cognitive bias which results in individuals overestimating their own positive qualities whilst simultaneously underestimating their less favourable ones. This combination of noticing biases held by others, yet not seeing them in our allegedly above-average selves, means that we are more likely to overestimate our performance and consider ourselves to be more objective than other people, even when we know about these biases.

Still think you should skip the chapter?

Such blind spots and illusions of superiority have serious consequences for our interactions with others, and for successful leadership. Naïve Realism, the belief that we see the world objectively, together with Blind Spot Bias makes for a devastating combination. If we are 'right' and others are 'wrong', curiosity (that holy grail of entrepreneurship) is improbable at best, and conflicts are unlikely to be resolved. Our inability to see our

https://doi.org/10.1515/9783110763126-006

own biases and to consider ourselves likely to be right means we are susceptible to becoming more competitive with the person with whom we disagree. The ability of a leader to accurately assess complex situations, to resolve disputes and to adeptly handle conflict can be enhanced if their own biases are understood and brought into conscious awareness. Taking the time to consider alternatives, even – indeed, especially – when we are convinced that we are right is a useful step towards addressing these potential pitfalls. Reminding ourselves of the Superiority Illusion, and right-sizing our egos accordingly is a leadership practice worth cultivating. If we can incorporate these practices into our leadership habits, we may be capable of more useful conflict resolution and be more inclusive of diversity of thought.

What are cognitive biases and why do they matter?

In the early 1970s, Psychologists Amos Tversky and Daniel Kahneman wanted to understand more about how people made decisions in a complicated crowded world of information and choice. It is generally accepted that our personal and organisational lives are increasingly complex, and in some respects this may have already exceeded a sustainable level. The American Institute for Economic Research note in an article titled 'Life is Complicated, and That is Good' that although societal complexity offers increased opportunities for humans to develop and flourish, it ". . . will also make many feel at least uneasy and uncomfortable" (Davies 2018). It was this human response to complexity and decision-making which interested Kahneman and Tversky.

Their previous research had focused on two main areas. Firstly, they had researched the emotional impact of losses versus gains, finding that the pain of loss had about twice the impact of the pleasure of winning. Secondly, they explored the seemingly irrational behaviour of humans when making economic choices, hypothesising that many traditional economic theories did not play out in real life because emotions were not taken into account. Kahneman and Tversky's research then evolved into what we now refer to as cognitive biases, and fundamentally changed how we think about how we think. They introduced their ideas to a wide readership in their book *Thinking, Fast and Slow*. The popularity of this book brought the terms *heuristics* – shortcuts or rules of thumb to aid decision-making – and *biases* – the resulting impacts caused by such heuristics – into mainstream parlance.

Cognitive biases affect our daily interactions, our decisions, our judgements and our views of the world. Such biases are not necessarily always negative or detrimental, however. Firstly, we use them simply in order to make sense of the overwhelming volume and complexity of the world we live in. Sometimes a shortcut is useful. Secondly, a conscious use of a cognitive bias can be valuable. It can enable us to be more effective in managing conflict or being more inclusive to differing perspectives. Also, as will be outlined in this chapter, we can work with some of our biases, rather than trying to overcome them, in order to use our leadership position to best effect.

Cognitive biases are an important consideration for compassionate leaders. We have already seen how compassion suffers from a reputational issue and is often confused with other concepts such as sympathy, empathy or pity. In addition, we need to consider the impacts of cognitive shortcuts and biases which can inadvertently undermine our attempts at compassionate leadership. Knowledgeable application of compassion allows us to transcend our biases.

Authority Bias and leadership

As mentioned earlier, leaders have a disproportionate impact on their organisations, and so it is useful to consider this more fully in the light of cognitive biases.

Authority Bias means that we trust and are disproportionately influenced by figures of authority. Sadly, human history and organisations are littered with examples of where this has resulted in downfall, death and destruction. Obvious examples from history include Hitler or Stalin, but there are many more recent examples of leaders using authority in pursuit of self-interest. Conversely, there are leaders whose motivations are more pro-social and whose legacy is arguably more positive: Nelson Mandela, Ruth Bader Ginsburg, Mahatma Ghandi, Martin Luther King Jr, to name but a few. (As an aside, it is interesting to note that three of these are people with strong moral reputations who emerged from situations of oppression. Perhaps the pressure of their suffering heightened their compassion.) Specific individuals on our own such lists may differ (see Box 6.1), but the point about leadership influence remains. Leaders have a disproportionate impact on others, courtesy of the Authority Bias, and so their words and actions count.

> **Box 6.1**
> It can be a useful reflection to consider leaders whose compassion has impacted us, and others who ruled through fear. What did we learn from these styles of leadership? And, importantly, what will we do with that understanding?

Motivation and intention

This necessarily bring us back to considerations of motivation and intention. If we can understand cognitive biases and so use them to our advantage, how do we use this influence? As a leader, are we compassionate because we genuinely want to make a positive difference to suffering or because we want to look good? Do we practice compassionate leadership because we know a happier workforce will work harder and therefore do more for the same money? Do 'enlightened' organisations offer health perks such as meditation apps or fitness classes because they genuinely care about people's wellbeing, or because they want their employees to be as efficient and effective as possible? Sweating their assets, just via a yoga class instead of a sweat shop? Motivation matters. As Roman Philosopher Seneca cautioned, in writing about generosity of acts, the spirit or intention from which an action is derived matters more than the act itself. This is a liberating thought. There is no one, correct compassionate response to pain, and the criticality of intention is within our gift to assess.

Joshua Coombes provides an interesting case study when considering motivation and intention. Coombes, a London-based hairdresser, has given free haircuts to homeless people throughout the city regularly since 2015. More than just a haircut, for Coombes this is about challenging preconceptions about homelessness, connecting with people as fellow humans, and being a listening ear to those in need. Of his latest fundraising book *Do Something for Nothing*, he says, "I've got to be honest with you . . . that idea, do something for nothing, it's not true at all. Because it's not for nothing for me. I get a huge amount out of this too" (Adams 2021). In addition to his haircuts beautifully demonstrating compassion in action, Coombes' observation is accurate from a neurological perspective.

As we saw in Chapter 2, when we give support to others, our brains are positively impacted in many ways. Oxytocin, the so-called 'love hormone', which regulates our emotions and can increase our feelings of trust, empathy and other prosocial responses, is released. Serotonin, responsible for stabilising our moods, enabling communication between our nervous system and brain, and helping to regulate our sleep and digestion is activated. Dopamine, that neurotransmitter of pleasure, joins this joyous cocktail with its release of 'feel-good' chemicals in our brain. The result of all this is that we relax, our mood improves, and we enjoy a counterbalance to cortisol, the main stress hormone which curbs anything not essential in a fight-or-flight situation and increases sugars in our bloodstream. A recent study (Inagaki and Ross 2018) has shown that providing targeted social support, that is, support to an identifiable individual such as in the example of Joshua Coombes' haircuts for homeless individuals, reduces the amount of activity in the amygdala. The amygdala, as well as having a key role in our memories, is the main fight-or-flight centre of our brain and is therefore linked to stress responses, so the suppression of this may provide a further reason why doing good for someone else feels so wonderful. So, in some respects Coombes is accurate when he states that he is not strictly doing 'something for nothing'.

Two main areas of our brains are particularly activated when we support others. These are the ventral striatum, which is associated with reward, and the septal area, which plays a central role in feelings of bonding and social connection. This is significant because social connection is fundamental for humans as social beings. As well as improving our quality of life, strong social connectedness boosts our mental wellbeing, decreases risks of depression and suicide, and can even help us to live longer. A recent meta-review indicates that individuals with strong social relationships increase their likelihood of survival by over 50%, even when allowing for factors such as general health, age, sex and cause of death (Holt-Lunstad et al. 2010).

The implications of these findings are important. If our brains and hormones work to reward us for doing good, perhaps there is no such thing as entirely selfless act. As leaders, we need to therefore reflect upon whether our compassionate intentions are predominantly about ourselves, our organisations, or our people. Any benefits of compassionate action should perhaps be best considered a pleasant, rewarding side-effect, rather than a driving motivation.

New compassion construct and cognitive biases

The ten biases which follow are not an exhaustive list. Many others have been identified, even in addition to those originally outlined by Kahneman and Tversky. The biases outlined below have particular resonance with compassion, as we will explore throughout the chapter. Awareness of these biases is useful both generally and with specific reference to compassionate leadership. The very first step of the new compassion construct is awareness; becoming aware of these biases will allow us conscious choice over adapting our behaviours. As we will see below, and in Figure 6.1, such biases correlate to specific steps of our model. They remain, then, a critical consideration for compassionate leadership:

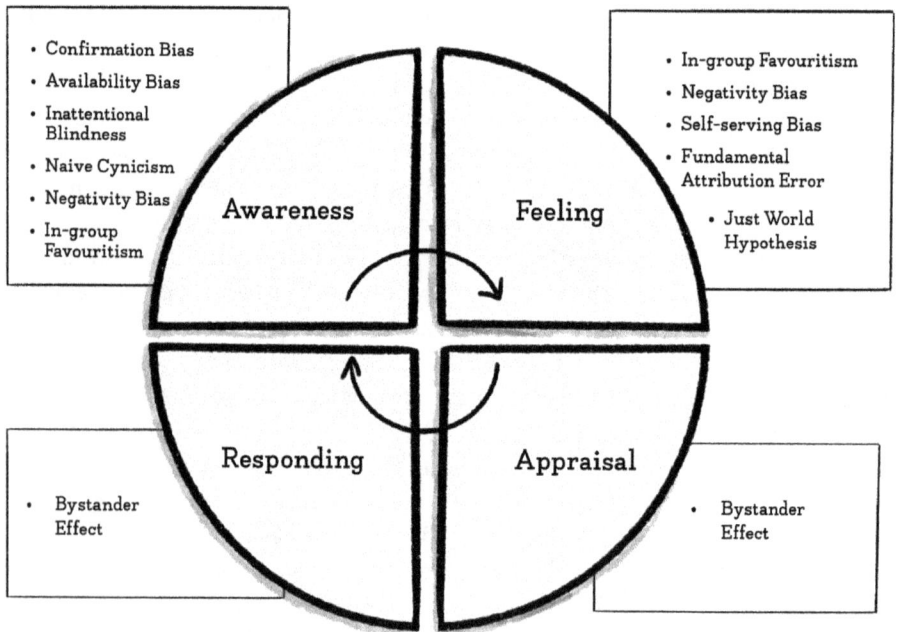

Figure 6.1: Cognitive Biases and the New Compassion Construct.

Confirmation Bias

Ahmed is moving to a new role in Belinda's department. Ahmed's current Director, Charlie, mentions in a corridor conversation to Belinda that Ahmed can be loud and has a tendency to dominate conversations. A few months later, Belinda remarks to Charlie that his earlier observations were accurate. Ahmed's voice can be heard throughout the open plan office, and some quieter members of the team seem to be dominated by Ahmed's vivacity in meetings.

This scenario, so familiar in organisational life is, in a nutshell, Confirmation Bias. The tendency to look for, find and remember information which confirms our preconceptions.

Was Charlie right? Did he have an ability to distil the essence of another complex, non-linear, multi-dimensional person into just a few words? Or did he summarise his perceptions, and then Belinda found what she was therefore expecting? If Charlie had described Ahmed as joyful, caring and energetic, maybe Belinda would similarly have found those observations to be accurate.

Wherever you are now, look around. Look for anything yellow – a sticker, a mug, a book spine, a flower. Now pick another colour, and notice how that now takes over the centre stage in your observations. This is a simple example of Confirmation Bias in what we see, but the bias is also prevalent in how we interpret what we notice. Was Ahmed being loud and dominant, or fun and energetic? The same situation can be interpreted very differently, depending upon the lens through which it is viewed. What about the times when Ahmed was quietly diligent, or listening intently to a colleague? Confirmation Bias makes it likely that Belinda would either ignore, give less importance to, or even fail to notice these behaviours from Ahmed.

The simple example above is a fairly commonplace scenario based on fictitious individuals. However, the impact of Confirmation Bias has more wide-ranging and serious implications. In the 1960s, Robert Rosenthal and Lenore Jacobsen – a Harvard psychologist and head teacher, respectively – published the results of an unusual experiment. They had given teachers information which indicated that some of their students were intellectually gifted, although they were not. In what has been dubbed the 'Pygmalion Effect', many of these students subsequently improved their IQ test scores as well as their academic results overall, possibly due to the positive beliefs that their teachers held about them. Although the results of this research have sometimes been questioned, recent empirical studies, meta-analyses and reviews have demonstrated evidence for the effect (White and Locke 2000). Recent research has also found evidence for the Pygmalion Effect in organisational settings, particularly when an employee's initial performance was poor (Kierein and Gold 2000).

Although studies are less prevalent, it seems that the opposite, Golem Effect is also true; when a person in a position of authority believes that an individual is not capable of success, then the individual will perform less impressively as a result. One study assessed the impact on business school student performance when an instructor verbalised their expectations. For cognitive tasks, the Golem Effect adversely impacted student performance. To mis-quote Henry Ford (attrib.), "whether your boss thinks you can or thinks you can't, they're right". Or, more candidly, as a manager of people, you will find and influence what you are looking for.

Compassionate leaders need to be vigilant to these Golem and Pygmalion effects. Whether intelligence, class, gender or race is being used as a shortcut judgement, higher or lower the expectations from those in positions of authority will likely create results to match beliefs. This takes the 'awareness' step of our new compassion model to another level. We need to remind ourselves to become aware of what is less obvious, rather than just noticing what re-confirms our beliefs and assumptions about people.

We are all susceptible to Confirmation Bias, although our cultural context and individual levels of media trust may moderate this; recent studies have shown higher levels of confirmation bias in the USA than in Germany or Japan, for example (Knobloch-Westerwick et al. 2019). Not only do we tend to seek out information sources which align with our own opinions and politics, we incline towards such harmony in our friendships and social groups. Google's algorithms give us more of what we already like, thus further reinforcing the walls of our echo chambers. We often avoid those whose opinion differs from our own, or information sources which challenge our existing views. To some extent this is understandable human behaviour. It helps to know who is in your 'tribe', and grouping is a normal cognitive process. Indeed, Henri Tajfel, a Polish social psychologist and author of Social Identity Theory, proposed that such groupings are an important source of pride and self-esteem for most individuals. These groups can be sports teams, social class, university attended, amongst many other examples. According to Tajfel, these groups give us a sense of social identity, helping us to understand and convey who we are, and giving us a sense of belonging within a social world. Members of an in-group (us) will seek to strengthen their group and enhance their self-esteem by comparing themselves favourably with the out-group (them). Social Identity Theory results in us reinforcing our perceived 'in' and 'out' groups, while Confirmation Bias makes us susceptible to avoiding interactions with 'them'. Box 6.2 offers simple suggestions to start reducing your own in-group biases.

Box 6.2
Read books or watch films created by people who are not like you. Look for differences which are more obvious and perhaps less so. At work, even informally meeting with people of different backgrounds will lessen the grip of confirmation bias.

Much as we might like to be, we are not always right. Those who hold a different opinion are not necessarily wrong. Our tendency to seek confirmation of our beliefs only entrenches us further in our viewpoints, and it is difficult to truly understand a situation from deep inside the trenches. Compassionate leadership requires us to seek out opposing views and to challenge our assumption that we are right. Rather than engaging solely with those who agree with us, seeking out opposing views forces us to think. Simultaneously, in engaging with an 'other' from an out-group, we may start to understand their perspective, see their challenges, and thus allow a more compassionate stance to develop.

Self-serving Bias

Imagine you have just attended an important client meeting. It went well. The client was impressed with your presentation, everyone in the meeting was supportive of the ideas presented, and you left with the contract signed. Back in the office, you are happy to take the credit. After all, you worked hard on this deal, had thought about the questions in advance, and went to the meeting calmly prepared.

Later that week, you attend another important meeting. This time, however, things do not go so well. The presentation fails to engage the audience, the attendees are restless, and the client sends you away with a list of questions rather than a contract. On your way back to the office, you fume silently. The technology let you down, so the presentation was not as impactful as you had intended. The others in the room were downright rude. Your colleagues did not offer enough support in your preparation. The client is being unreasonably demanding in their requests.

This is a simple illustration of the Self-serving Bias. In short, we prefer to take personal credit for our successes, and blame external, situational factors when things go wrong. Most likely, we do this in order to protect our self-esteem. Our brains do not really want us to take responsibility when things go wrong, lest we dent our fragile confidence.

On a positive note, this bias is one of the easier ones to overcome.

The first step is recognising when we are in the grip of the Self-serving Bias. When we are taking either sole credit or exclusive blame, we are probably succumbing to this bias.

Step two is to accept some responsibility, regardless of the outcome. This should be fairly easy to do:

> Won the deal? Got the promotion? Scored the goal? Congratulations. Remember, no one is an island, so it was not all down to your individual brilliance. Consider who else contributed to the outcome and thank them accordingly. Long-winded Oscar acceptance speeches are not required; specific thanks for relevant individuals will have more impact.

> Lost the customer? Messed up the interview? Missed the penalty? Condolences. Continue to remember that no one is an island, and so you were part of the issue too. Tempting as it might be, do not resort to blame or retribution. Work out how you can fix issues and consider the ways in which you contributed to the problem.

> Step three is to practice self-compassion. This is not about wallowing in self-pity, nor is it futile navel gazing. Self-compassion is a simple, yet incredibly effective way to bounce back more quickly from setbacks, and to suffer less from anxiety and stress in difficult situations. The organisational and psychobiological research on self-compassion is covered in more detail in Chapter 7, where we will also discuss why self-compassion is a better response to pain than our attempts to protect our

self-esteem. For the purposes of overcoming the Self-serving Bias, practice acknowledging that everyone makes mistakes, remember that we should be gentle on ourselves, and take a balanced view of the situation. Things may not have been perfect, but none of us are either entirely incompetent nor completely heroic.

We can link this bias to the feeling step of the new compassion construct. If we are feeling proud or annoyed when we notice a particular outcome, then we would do well to keep this bias in mind. Using the new compassion construct as a guide, we can notice what our feeling, emotional response is to a situation, and calibrate this before choosing a response.

Fundamental Attribution Error

Hot on the heels of self-serving bias is Fundamental Attribution Error. We tend to judge others on their character, but ourselves on the situation. For example, when someone else is late for our meeting, we might describe them as lazy or unreliable. When we are late, we are more likely to blame external factors such as traffic or train delays. We do not want to either see or show the less-than-perfect parts of our own character, and yet we fail to take into account situational factors which can impact other people's behaviour.

Compassionate leaders need to be vigilant to this bias, both from an awareness and a feeling perspective in the new compassion construct. In the awareness step, we can ask ourselves what we are looking to have re-confirmed and what we might have missed. In the feeling step, we can consider how we are feeling when things go wrong, either for ourselves or others. If we respond to ideas or constructive challenge with derision or dismissal, we undermine the psychological fabric of an organisation, as others will know that they are being judged for failing to meet someone else's idea of perfection. Harvard Professor Amy Edmondson is a leading expert on psychological safety, and has written about it extensively (2018). She reminds us that by reducing the fears associated with proposing something new, different or challenging, we are simultaneously nurturing the conditions in which organisations and their people can thrive.

In addition to considerations of psychological safety, if we consider Fundamental Attribution Error in conjunction with Confirmation Bias, it seems that we will most likely continue to find what we look for. The employee who was late for the meeting and therefore considered lazy, begins their journey on a negative spiral as a result of these biases combining and conflating.

A more compassionate approach to this late employee scenario would be to see them more fully, as a whole person. Doing this can happen in three main ways. Firstly, was there a reason for their lateness which would make compassion a more appropriate response? Finding out more about the people we work with supports this approach, getting to know about their life outside of work, their situation and their challenges. Secondly, we can practice a compassionate stance which assumes that, due to the inevitability of suffering, this person would benefit from compassion, regardless of whether we know the exact reason why. Thirdly, when we find ourselves falling prey to the Fundamental Attribution Error, we can choose to consciously consider some positive characteristics about the other person. They may have been late for the meeting, but they are good listeners, they bring fresh ideas and insight, and they never leave someone else out of a conversation. This more balanced perspective allows us to see others more accurately – for we are all, ultimately, complex, multi-faceted, perfectly imperfect humans.

Availability Bias

Availability Bias is the name given to our tendency to evaluate an event, situation or topic by the ease with which it comes to mind. In other words, its ease of availability to us. In short, what is readily brought to mind is considered to be more common than it actually is. Technically, this is a heuristic rather than a bias, but it has been included in this chapter because of its relevance for compassionate leadership.

One of the most common examples of Availability Bias is evaluations of the likelihood of aeroplane crashes. The actual chance of dying in an aeroplane crash is miniscule, around one death for every 7.9 million passenger boardings. This already tiny possibility has decreased by a factor of two each decade since the 1960s (Barnett 2020). To look at this another way, an individual would need to take a flight every single day for 21,643 years before they would statistically die in a plane crash. Indeed, the risk is so low, MIT Professor Arnold Barnett argues, that "being afraid to fly is a little like being afraid to go into the supermarket because the ceiling might collapse" (Dizikes 2020).

Despite the infinitesimal likelihood of dying in such a crash, it is estimated that somewhere between 2–40% of people have a fear of flying, and for around 5% the fear is severe enough to be classified as a clinical phobia (statistics for people afraid of supermarket ceilings falling in are less readily available). So why is the fear so prevalent when the likelihood is so low? Much of the answer may be due to Availability Bias. When aeroplane crashes occur, media sources allocate this news a high profile, show images of aeroplane wreckage, and even provide pen portraits of the victims. All of this combines to make the event readily accessible, and thus easily brought to mind. This is the Availability Bias at work. We can readily access vivid, detailed information about crash events, and so we think that they are more likely to occur than they actually are. It is worth remembering that much of the reason why aeroplane crashes are newsworthy is because they are so rare.

While aeroplane crashes are a useful illustration, this bias is also prevalent in everyday organisational life. With an overload of information and competing demands, many decisions are based on the most immediately accessible information, regardless of whether this accessibility is due to recency, personal experiences, emotional impact or external influences such as media coverage. This mostly occurs outside of conscious awareness, and our reliance on the Availability Bias increases when we experience high cognitive load or when we are under time pressure. Being asked to make complex, quick decisions is when we start to rely even more heavily on Availability Bias.

Knowing that the Availability Bias is at work can serve as a reminder to consciously seek out alternative information, data, sources and perspectives. This approach can lead to a more inclusive environment where diversity of thought is encouraged, and where an absence of 'right or wrong' or fear of reprisal for speaking up supports organisational psychological safety.

Understanding the impacts of Availability Bias is crucial for compassionate leadership, particularly in the awareness step of the new compassion construct. If we work with this bias rather than against it, Availability Bias can be a useful means of accelerating compassion in organisations. Keeping the new construct of compassion in mind, and thus readily available, means that we can more easily access and apply it. Hacking the Availability Bias in this way allows us to hijack the heuristic to a positive, compassionate effect. Akin to practicing a cognitive martial art, we can choose to work with the heuristic energy rather than against it.

Inattentional Blindness

Inattentional Blindness is the name given to our astonishing failure to notice completely visible, yet unexpected, objects because our attention is focused elsewhere. Ulric Neisser and colleagues published much of the original research in this area in the 1970s, although the term 'inattentional blindness' itself was coined by Arien Mack and Irvin Rock in their 1998 book of the same name. Probably the most well-known example of this phenomenon is in Dan Simons and Christopher Chabris' basketball video. No spoilers here, but the short video on Simons' website is worth viewing for an impactful experience in this regard (http://www.dansimons.com/videos.html). Another common example is road traffic accidents where the car driver states that they looked, but simply did not see the unfortunate cyclist. Bumper stickers urging drivers to 'think bike!' are an attempt to overcome this Inattentional Blindness.

Within an organisational setting, Inattentional Blindness is an important consideration particularly for the 'awareness' step in the new compassion construct. When our attention is directed to operational issues, finances or competitor threats, there is a very real danger that we miss what it completely visible and staring us in the face. I should confess that I initially considered the 'noticing' or 'awareness' step of any compassion construct to be somewhat pointless. Surely no one could fail to see suffering around them? Then, as I shared the new construct of compassion with more and more executives, many told me that they would like to do more to support people, but that they just did not notice when someone was in need, often until issues had significantly deteriorated. Perhaps their attention was elsewhere.

By contrast, other leaders seem to 'read' people well, and have a finely tuned sense for when 'I'm fine' means exactly that and when it means the opposite. Such variance in individual ability to 'read' others is central to the Theory of Mind. As already mentioned, this is the ability to consider and attribute mental states to ourselves and others. It is thought to start developing in humans at around 12–15 months, although children are usually around four or five years old before true Theory of Mind starts to emerge. Development of the Theory of Mind generally follows a number of steps, outlined in Figure 6.2 below. The sequencing of these varies by culture, possibly for reasons associated with varying cultural emphases on knowledge acquisition, collectivism and filial respect. Theory of Mind is, of course, an essential foundation for humans as social beings. It allows us to consider and understand the behaviour of others, and thus to display appropriate social interactions such as compassion.

The 5 steps, outlined in Figure 6.2, increase in complexity:

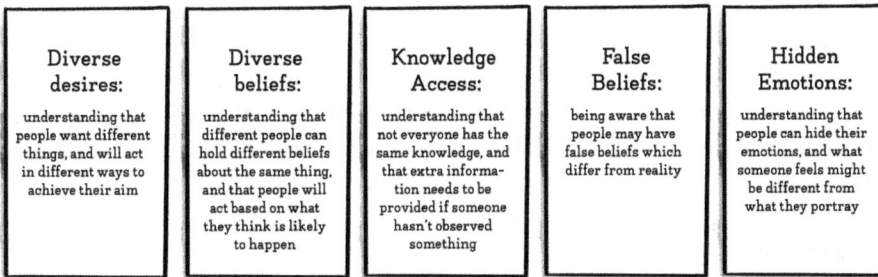

Diverse desires:	Diverse beliefs:	Knowledge Access:	False Beliefs:	Hidden Emotions:
understanding that people want different things, and will act in different ways to achieve their aim	understanding that different people can hold different beliefs about the same thing, and that people will act based on what they think is likely to happen	understanding that not everyone has the same knowledge, and that extra information needs to be provided if someone hasn't observed something	being aware that people may have false beliefs which differ from reality	understanding that people can hide their emotions, and what someone feels might be different from what they portray

Figure 6.2: Theory of Mind development steps.

All of these steps are crucial to social development, but the hidden emotions step of Theory of Mind is particularly important for compassionate leadership. Understanding hidden emotions, combined with a conscious awareness of Inattentional Blindness, can lead us to start becoming more aware of what was previously hidden in plain sight.

Taking some small steps to improve our awareness often has disproportionate results. Implementing regular 'check-ins' at the beginning of meetings is a useful example of how to do this, explained in more detail in Chapter 8. Varying our inner and outer pace can allow us to notice quieter voices and unspoken suffering. Asking others what they have noticed gives us additional perspectives on situations, thus bolstering our own awareness.

In-group Favouritism

Also based on Henri Tajfel's Social Identity Theory, In-group Favouritism is the tendency to give preferential, more positive or helpful treatment towards people who belong to the same 'group' as us. Sadly, this bias tends to go hand-in-hand with out-group bias where people hold negative judgements about a group to which they do not belong. Examples can be found across a wide range of varied sources, from football clubs, religions, sports teams and even nations.

Muzafer Sherif's studies at the Robber's Cave boys camp in the 1950s are a colourful, if somewhat dated and occasionally disputed, illustration of how such in-group favouritism can result in conflict over resources. In this experiment, 22 children were divided into two groups of 11. They were encouraged to establish their own group norms and rituals, and then competed against each other in various events. Relations between the two groups became increasingly antagonistic. Even after the competitive events had finished, the children still described their in-group in favourable terms and the other, out-group, more negatively. It seems that group isolation heightened the in-group salience and exacerbated the perceived differences between the groups. As in-group identity developed, individuals became increasingly likely to hold favourable biases about their own group and less favourable biases about the other group. The Robber's Cave experiment crucially noted that simply exposing the groups to each other after the competitions did not reduce the conflict. Having the two groups work together towards common goals, which they could not achieve without each other, was far more effective in reducing conflict and prejudices.

There are some concerns about Sherif's research. All of the children were male, white and middle class, so the findings cannot necessarily be applied more widely. The research itself was predominantly a field study, lacking the scientific – and, indeed ethical – rigour which would be required of it nowadays. Still, we owe much of our understanding about In-group Favouritism to Robber's Cave, and Sherif's observations about conflicting groups requiring a common purpose in order to reconcile still resonates in organisations today.

More recent research also illustrates that In-group Favouritism still occurs when the groups are entirely arbitrary. Even when individuals are randomly allocated to meaningless groups, such as the red or blue team, In-group Favouritism develops. Pascal Molenberghss' (2013) investigations into the neural mechanisms of in-group bias has produced some interesting results. Our responses to those we perceive to be in our in- or out-groups are more than superficial. Not only do we perceive the behaviours and facial expressions of the two groups differently, but we also have different neural responses in our brains according to our in- or out- categorisation. Molenbergh has noted that we empathise more with those in our own in-group.

There may be good evolutionary reasons for our brains to have developed in this way. Belonging to a group might provide improved security and better access to food, for example. Yet we need to consider whether this function still serves us well in a contemporary organisational context. Molenbergh notes that it seems likely that our cultural and familial contexts influence our neural correlates. As we have mentioned earlier, our brains are capable of neuroplasticity, the ability to adapt and change in response to experience. It seems reasonable that we can therefore positively influence our neural responses to in- and out- groups. To do this, we can reflect on some important questions (see Box 6.3).

Most of us have experienced In-group Favouritism, either as a member of an in-group or of a less fortunate out-group. Regardless of which group we find ourselves in, we need to remain vigilant to the cognitive and social forces of this bias. These forces impact how we behave and how we relate to each other, both positively and otherwise. The assumptions or ideas we hold about people are frequently based on their group identity, and are often inaccurate. Noticing when we have biases about someone based on their group identity or membership is a first, important step towards limiting our reliance on such a bias.

In the new compassion construct, developing awareness of the suffering of those who are not necessarily in our in-groups is an important way for compassionate leaders to overcome this bias. In the feeling step, our emotional response to those who belong to our in-group may differ in nature or strength to those from an out-group. Compassionate leaders can use their awareness of this bias to bring a more inclusive compassionate approach to all.

Closely linked to the In-group Favouritism is the Halo Effect: the overspill of perceived general positive traits into other attractive characteristics. So, if we consider someone to be friendly, we are more likely to attribute to them other positive characteristics such as intelligence or kindness. In the workplace, this can impact hiring or promotion decisions. If an interviewer considers the interviewee to have attractive characteristics such as sociability, they are more likely to consider them capable or intelligent. And, of course, if we consider someone to be part of our in-group, we are more likely to attribute positive characteristics to them in the first place. Conversely, if we interview someone who is not easily identifiable as a member of our in-group, we are far less likely to attribute positive characteristics to them. Compassionate leaders need to be vigilant to the potential impacts of the Halo Effect throughout the employee lifecycle, not just in hiring biases. The Halo Effect within an in-group makes for an uneasy choir of angels, where diversity of thought or dissent may struggle to find a voice.

Compassionate leadership which is reserved for our own in-groups is incomplete. Ethical and moral considerations aside, all in-group membership is ultimately meaningless anyway, as Figure 6.3 illustrates. Sports fans from neighbouring cities put their rivalries to one side when supporting a national squad. Sales and marketing quickly resolve their differences when a competitor out-manoeuvres them. If in-groups are social constructs, although not without their uses, a compassionate leader must learn to see the danger in inadvertently creating out-groups.

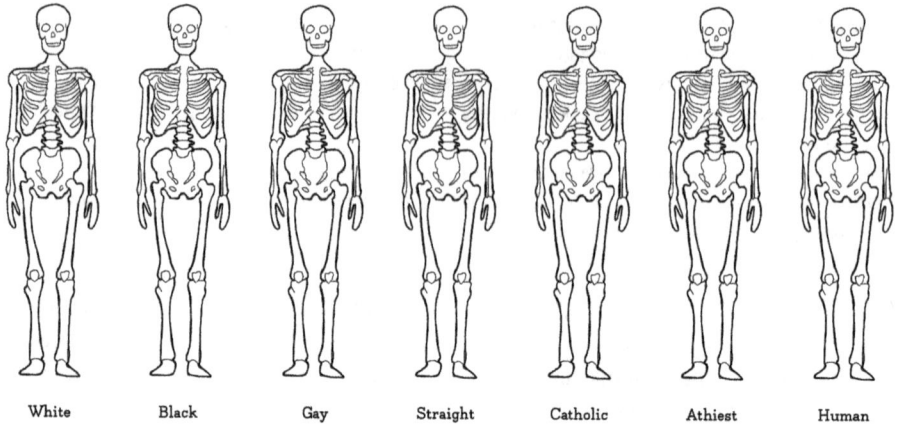

White   Black   Gay   Straight   Catholic   Athiest   Human

Figure 6.3: All the same underneath.

Just World Hypothesis

The Just World Hypothesis states that individuals need to believe that their environment is a fair and logical place in which people typically get what they deserve. Put simply, this is not dissimilar to a Hollywood ending: Batman's noble actions will be rewarded, and The Joker will be punished. Although outside of cinemas this is patently not the case – sadly, bad things happen to good people, and sometimes evil triumphs – decades of research have shown that belief in a just world is cross-culturally generalisable, with no sign of abating either across populations or through a typical human lifespan (Furnham 2003).

This belief is likely to be prevalent simply because without it the non-linear, chaotic and sometimes downright unfair world we live in would be incredibly difficult to cope with. As Lerner and Miller (1978) beautifully summarised, the Just World Hypothesis:

> . . . enables the individual to confront his physical and social environment as though they were stable and orderly. Without such a belief, it would be difficult for the individual to commit himself to the pursuit of long range goals or even to the socially regulated behaviour of day to day life. Since the belief that the world is just serves such an important adaptive function for the individual, people are very reluctant to give up this belief, and they can be greatly troubled if they encounter evidence that suggests that the world is not really just or orderly after all. (pp. 1030–1031)

Just World Hypothesis is a double-edged sword. On the one hand, it is an adaptive coping mechanism which enables us co-exist within our social contexts, and to work towards our long-standing ambitions and dreams. Studies have shown that people with high belief in a just world tend to see potentially stressful tasks more as opportunities than threats, and self-report lower levels of stress than those who hold low levels of belief in the Just World Hypothesis (Tomaka and Blascovich 1994). On the other hand, belief in a just world can result in an unfeeling response to human suffering, with victim blaming and derogation, and negative treatment of victims considered to be from an out-group.

Just World Hypothesis in itself, then, is not necessarily exclusively positive or negative. Perhaps it is a binary, unexamined belief in a just world which is most dangerous. While belief in a just world might provide a useful coping mechanism for us as individuals, and form part of society's cohesion, an unrelenting hold on such a world view is likely to present an immense barrier to compassionate leadership. Victims do not necessarily 'deserve' their suffering, and those on whom fortune is currently smiling are neither 'better' nor even deserving of their comfortable situation.

We can appreciate that the Just World Hypothesis has a protective intention, and also notice when this becomes a barrier between us and those who would benefit from our compassion. Compassionate leadership requires us to remain aware of this bias, especially in the feeling step of the new construct. If we only feel an emotional response to people in our own groups, or have a muted emotional response when someone is 'deserving' of their suffering, then we need to remind ourselves about the inherent danger in the Just World Hypothesis.

Naïve Cynicism

If you ask everyone in an office to estimate what percentage of the time that they each clear up the coffee mugs, the total will most likely add up to more than 100% of the time actually spent on the task. Similar results can be found when estimating division of housework between partners (Kruger and Gilovich 1999). These are simple examples of Naïve Cynicism at work. This is the expectation that other people's judgements and actions will have a self-serving interest, whilst simultaneously believing that our own opinions and beliefs are objective and less self-focused. This is why we overestimate how much we contribute to the coffee cup clearing or household tasks.

Naïve Cynicism is the bedfellow to Naïve Realism, which is the belief that we see the world as it really is, while the views of others will be biased. Availability Bias is also at play here; we are much more likely to be able to access evidence of our own housework or coffee mug clear-ups because, simply, we are always there when we do them, but are not always present when others do.

To lessen the impacts of Naïve Cynicism, the compassionate leader can reduce in- and out-groups. By encouraging more cross-group working, they can enhance people's exposure to different outlooks and opinions. They can work to build psychological safety, in order that the organisation is a happier, securer place of belonging, where debate and innovation can thrive. In Kruger and Gilovich's research, above, the happier a married couple reported themselves to be, the less cynical their beliefs about each other were. Using the new compassion construct, leaders can improve their awareness, not only of suffering, but also of noticing and acknowledging when quiet work is done, whether this is clearing away coffee mugs or quietly supporting others in times of need.

Negativity Bias

Also known as positive-negative asymmetry, Negativity Bias is our tendency to both notice and then ruminate on negatives rather than positives. We feel the pain of the argument more than we feel the joy of the party that preceded it.

In an organisational setting, this bias can be seen in a myriad of ways. In performance reviews, we are more likely to focus on, recollect and worry about the negative feedback we receive rather than the positive. We will recall insults more readily than praise. A hurtful, off-hand remark from a colleague can ruin our perception of our whole day. This bias starts long before our first employment. One study conducted at Yale University indicated that even infants as young as 3 months old will prioritise negative information over that which is neutral or positive (Hamlin et al. 2010).

Psychologists Paul Rozin and Edward Royzman (2001) noted the adage that a spoonful of tar can spoil a barrel of honey, but a spoonful of honey does nothing for a barrel of tar, thus illustrating the dominance of Negativity Bias and its contagion. Kahneman serves this view to us in a slightly more vivid, if somewhat stomach-turning, way: "a single cockroach will completely wreck the appeal of a bowl of cherries, but a cherry will do nothing at all for a bowl of cockroaches" (2011: 302).

Compassionate leadership requires us to notice the cherries as well as the cockroaches, and to keep the latter from contaminating the former. We can do this in a myriad of ways. We can, quite simply, notice the positives. Catch people doing something right, so to speak. When we give feedback, we can ensure a balance, and check that the positive feedback has been heard. And when things go wrong, we can seek to understand, catching and dealing with a cockroach without necessarily throwing away the whole bowl of cherries.

Bystander Effect

Strictly speaking, the last in our whistle stop tour of biases is not strictly a bias. Rather, it is a theory developed by social psychologists John Darley and Bibb Latané in the 1960s, but its implications are important for compassionate leadership, hence its inclusion in this chapter. The findings of this theory have been both replicated and questioned, and seem to vary according to context, so it is a useful consideration for leaders of diverse organisations.

Darley and Latané's interest was sparked by a newspaper report about the murder of a woman, Kitty Genovese, in New York. The report was later shown to be hyperbolic in its reporting, particularly with regards to the number of bystanders who were said to have witnessed the murder but who did not act to save the woman. Still, the resulting Bystander Effect proposed a hypothesis that individuals would be less likely to intervene to rescue a victim when other bystanders were present. Darley and Latané (1968) conducted experiments which involved volunteers overhearing an epileptic seizure, whilst not being aware that this was staged. They found that participants were more likely to intervene when there were no other bystanders, and that they acted more quickly when they were alone with the seizure patient. Darley and Latané hypothesised that this was because the consequences of intervening lay solely with the decision of the lone participant about whether or not to intervene. A bystander's response, they proposed, had more to do with our response to other bystanders than to the victim. Their argument that sole bystanders were more likely to intervene gave rise to the 'Bystander Effect', a mainstay of undergraduate psychology textbooks.

As the discipline of psychology has developed, more focus has been given to the ethical considerations of research, such as the fictitious seizures in Darley and Latané's work. Therefore, more recent research used surveillance footage of actual public conflicts across a number of countries in order to examine evidence for the Bystander Effect. This research, by Richard Philpot and colleagues (2020), offers a more optimistic outcome. Over 200 video clips of aggressive episodes captured by CCTV footage were used, and the researchers discovered that in over 90% of cases someone intervened to help the victim. Moreover, they also reported that the likelihood of intervention actually increased when there were more bystanders.

These conflicting results between the laboratory and CCTV footage may in part be explained by the different situations taking place, and the multitude of variables in real-life contexts. These could include considerations such as whether the attack is physical or verbal, or whether the gender of the perpetrator or victim impacts the likelihood of intervention. A meta-study of bystander effect experiments found that dangerous situations are understood more quickly and more clearly as being genuine emergencies. This prompts higher levels of psychobiological arousal and is thus more likely to result in bystander action.

We should also consider that every potential individual bystander will have a multitude of variables at play: what else are they thinking about that day? Have they been a victim of a similar situation in the past? What sort of mood are they in? Are they in a hurry? This last variable may sound trivial, but John Darley and Daniel Batson's famous Good Samaritan Study in the 1970s demonstrated that higher levels of induced hurriedness significantly reduced the likelihood of a bystander stopping to help someone in need. Slowing down can help us to focus on what truly matters, both in life and in leadership.

Conflicting results are found, then, in the laboratory and on the streets. But what about in the workplace? Unsurprisingly, such studies are rare. After all, it would be difficult and likely unethical to set up problematic situations at work in order to test for the Bystander Effect. In addition to individual variables, organisational culture, roles, hierarchies and other factors need to be taken into account. Indeed, in a recent study by Catherine Hellemans and colleagues (2017), participants reported that both internal and external factors contributed to their decisions about whether to publicly intervene in situations where a colleague was being bullied. The researchers asked what participants felt they would be most likely to do in a workplace bullying situation. The results indicated that non-intervention in a situation was associated with low self-efficacy; in other words, people who did not feel that they could take actions which would have a desired result were less likely to intervene than people who believed that their actions would have a useful outcome. Respondents also reported that within the workplace, perceived severity of the event was the mainly determinant of the likelihood of helping behaviour occurring. The more serious the incident, the higher likelihood of intervention. Whilst understandable, and to a certain extent driven by our psychobiological responses to threat, this finding has serious implications for the workplace. If the likelihood of individuals standing up to micro-aggressions in the workplace is low, then these may continue to proliferate unchecked, and develop into serious cultural or individual incidents.

Compassionate leadership can manifest as quiet assertion, peaceful support or reasoned responses to the smallest difficulty. Sometimes micro-compassion can be disproportionately effective: examples include calmly stating 'I'm not sure that's appropriate', speaking up to someone who can offer formal support, or simply standing next to someone in order to show that you are literally and metaphorically on their side. In the words of Howard Zinn, "We don't have to engage in grand, heroic actions to participate in the process of change. Small acts, when multiplied by millions of people, can quietly become a power no government can suppress, a power that can transform the world" (2007: 270). Zinn was a political scientist, but his assertion rings true for most organisations, not just for governments.

As we have learned, the Achilles' heel of altruism occurs when we do good for others even when this is to the detriment of ourselves. Could it be that the reason why people appear more likely to intervene when there are more bystanders is because there is some 'safety in numbers'? Do we trust in fellow humans to keep each other safe, so that if I intervene and subsequently become a victim myself, someone else will intervene with compassionate action on my behalf too? We all suffer and would benefit from assistance at various times in our lives, so the subconscious dance of giving and receiving compassion keeps our human social system in a delicate balance of exchange. As Buddhist nun Pema Chödrön notes:

> Compassion is not a relationship between the healer and the wounded. It's a relationship between equals. Only when we know our own darkness well can we be present with the darkness of others. Compassion becomes real when we recognize our shared humanity. (2004: 74)

Taking action is the crucial step which distinguishes compassion from empathy, and the Bystander Effect offers us perspectives on possible reasons as to why people take action or not. It is heartening that the overwhelming majority of people appear willing to intervene in real-life scenarios, although our hurriedness and perception of incident severity may attenuate this response. To the awareness step of the new construct of compassion, we may observe someone being verbally abused on the street more readily than we notice the quiet distress of a familiar colleague. The role of the compassionate leader is to notice unspoken pain as well as that which is highly visible, and to listen for the unsaid as well as that which is voiced. A range of compassionate responses attuned to each situation is likely to be a more impactful form of compassionate leadership than an occasional, highly visible responses to extreme situations.

Box 6.4 offers a practical approach aimed at starting to overcoming our own biases. Small adjustments and practice are crucial to overall progress.

> **Box 6.4**
> Each of the biases described above has specific reference to compassionate leadership. This chapter is a resource to re-visit time and time again. Pick one or two areas of focus to begin with, then come back to widen your practice.

Compassion, bias and compassionate leadership

Understanding these, and other, cognitive biases does not make us immune to them. To revisit the blind spot bias from the opening paragraphs of this chapter, individuals still see themselves as less biased once when they know about biases. Even when we are aware of biases and their effects, they still cause us to act in predictable ways: focusing more on negatives, seeking confirmation of our beliefs, creating in and out groups, over-estimating our personal brilliance and the ineptitude of others, taking personal credit for chance, not noticing what is in front of our noses, idle thinking patterns, being in too much of a rush to help, and even believing that people justly get what they deserve.

The allocation of biases, as shown in Figure 6.1, appears unbalanced across the steps of the new compassion construct. However, biases significantly impact what we are aware of and our emotional responses, so this imbalance makes some sense. For each of the areas of the new compassion construct, prompts are offered in Figure 6.4 to offset some impacts of the biases.

New Compassion Construct Area	Bias	Prompts to Offset Bias
Awareness	Confirmation Bias	What were you expecting to hear? What did you actually hear or see?
	Availability Bias	What happened recently that might be impacting your thinking?
	Inattentional Blindness	What might you be missing? Who else could you ask for a view?
	Naïve Cynicism	Are others really being so self-serving? Are you not?
	Negativity Bias	What positives can you notice?
Awareness and Feeling	In-group Favouritism	What common goals could groups work on together?
Feeling	Negativity Bias	Do you notice when events or your feelings are positive, not just negative?
	Self-serving Bias	Who else deserves credit? What errors did you contribute?
	Fundamental Attribution Error	Notice when you judge or label. Can you seek to understand instead?
	Just World Hypothesis	Does anyone 'deserve' their suffering? In what circumstances?
Appraisal	Bystander Effect	Have you appraised for safety, intention, patterns, role and resources?
Responding	Bystander Effect	When and how will you take action?

Figure 6.4: Prompts to offset bias and the New Compassion Construct.

Being aware of the biases discussed in this chapter, and understanding their impacts on our thinking and our leadership can keep us vigilant. We can choose to consider the influence of biases on our thinking and practice attenuating for these. We can remain open to others' perspectives, notice our judgements and choose when to set these to one side. We can create psychologically safe contexts where our words and actions repeatedly show that errors and dissent are permissible. We can offer experiences which challenge and impact our neural responses to those in perceived out-groups. We can share credit for our luck and success in the service of others and, ultimately, we can develop a more compassionate approach to leadership.

Key Chapter Points
- Heuristics are unconscious cognitive shortcuts, which can result in cognitive biases. These often become more entrenched over time, especially when they remain unconscious.
- We use heuristics to quickly make sense of our complex, ever changing, and sometimes overwhelming world.

- Cognitive biases impact how we view our world and interact with others. They colour our assessments and judgements, and influence our decision-making.
- Although these shortcuts are unconscious, we can become aware of the ones we predominantly use and the impacts they have. Such awareness allows us more choice in how we think and behave. We can, to some extent, adopt new patterns of behaviour and moderate the impacts of our biases.
- This chapter is slightly different in structure to the others, as it outlines ten common cognitive biases, and discusses their application with specific reference to compassionate leadership.

Chapter 7
Self-compassion for leaders

> If your compassion does not include yourself, it is incomplete. (Jack Kornfield)

> Don't remain a dependent, malleable patient:
> Become your own soul's doctor. (Epictetus)

So far, most of our discussion about compassion has been centred on relieving the suffering of others. We often find it easier to have compassion for other people than we do for ourselves. Somehow, it can seem more straightforward to bestow compassion upon those currently less fortunate than us than it does to apply it to ourselves, even when we too are suffering. Yet compassion for ourselves is a crucial, if often overlooked, aspect of compassionate leadership. Rather than falling into the trap of being our own toughest critic, choosing instead to be self-compassionate boosts our psychological wellbeing and makes us more resilient as leaders. In fact, self-compassion is an incredibly effective means of resourcing ourselves, within the appraisal step of our new compassion construct. Self-compassion may initially seem self-indulgent, but it is quite the opposite. As we will see, a compassionate connection with others requires us to be deeply grounded in ourselves and therefore self-compassionate.

Self-compassion for leaders merits an entire chapter to itself for three main reasons:

Firstly, leaders who are authentically and appropriately vulnerable in times of need are more likely to be viewed positively by others and less likely to be cast into the perpetual role of 'rescuer' in Karpman's Drama Triangle. At the same time, they are role modelling an emotionally healthy approach and reinforcing organisational psychological safety. It is ok to not always be ok.

Secondly, self-compassion is an important cornerstone of our own self-care and enhanced self-awareness. These are critical from a leadership perspective because, as Dr Mee-Yan Cheung-Judge noted, "use of self as an instrument is at the heart of our uniqueness and effectiveness" as a leader (2001: 11). This Organisational Design concept of 'self as an instrument' is the conscious and intentional use of our entire selves in our leadership roles. It enables us to remain aware of our own biases, judgements and other psychological impacts. Such awareness enables us to maintain our ability to operate effectively, cutting through interference with clarity of our intention and choices.

Thirdly, some of my own psychology research into the effects of self-compassion on leaders has shown this to be a crucial resource which significantly reduces stress, anxiety and depression, whilst building individual resilience. We will explore this research in more detail later in this chapter.

The new compassion construct can easily be applied to ourselves as well as to others. We can become aware of our own suffering, starting to notice our quiet inner voice as it gently chides us for not listening to it. In the feeling step, we allow ourselves to feel an emotional response, without becoming overwhelmed. We can appraise our

https://doi.org/10.1515/9783110763126-007

own safety, typical behaviour patterns, role and particularly our resources. And, as we respond to our own suffering, we can treat ourselves with the same thoughtful compassion with which we would treat another.

Sounds so simple. Yet, much like compassion more broadly, many people have an aversion to self-compassion. Self-pitying navel gazing, which has no place in life generally, let alone in organisations. Right? Wrong. To challenge this misconception, this chapter will begin by outlining the three distinct yet intertwined elements of self-compassion. Findings of research into self-compassion will highlight some of the benefits of this approach, and recent investigations on the impact of self-compassion on leadership mental health will be highlighted. As well as noting the important differences between self-compassion and some other, closely related, concepts such as self-esteem and self-pity, this chapter will provide practical guidance on building your resources and developing your own capacity for self-compassion.

Directing compassion towards ourselves, while perhaps initially uncomfortable, is critical for our leadership. Only directing our compassion to others implies a 'healer – wounded' relationship which is both unhealthy and erroneous. As noted earlier, compassion is a social dance; we all benefit from compassion during difficult moments. Self-compassion reinforces our own self-leadership and develops our instrumental selves. Our ability to offer compassion inwardly improves our own mental wellbeing and resilience, and provides us with a resourced stance from which to offer compassion to others.

Self-compassion: Definitions

Clinical Psychologist Paul Gilbert is the founder of Compassion Focused Therapy (CFT), which integrates Cognitive Behavioural Therapy with elements of evolutionary and social psychology, alongside Buddhism and neuroscience. CFT is particularly used with people who are highly self-critical or who have extreme levels of shame. Gilbert notes that many people with severe mental health problems are frequently self-critical, rather than self-compassionate. This is an important point because, as Gilbert writes, "if you want one recipe to make you unhappy, it would be to focus on the things you criticize or don't like about yourself" (2009: 70). Gilbert's view is echoed by meta-review research focused on self-compassion (Barnard and Curry 2011) which found that wellbeing and self-compassion are consistently correlated.

Kristin Neff's widely accepted definition of self-compassion (2003) is comprised of three aspects: self-kindness, common humanity and mindfulness. These are illustrated in Figure 7.1, and a practical application is offered in Box 7.1. Let us now examine each of these three aspects in more detail.

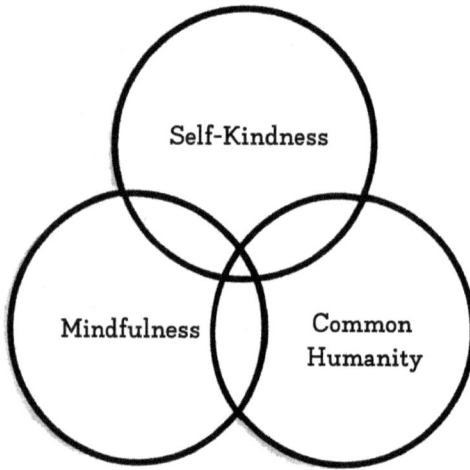

Figure 7.1: Self-compassion (adapted from Neff 2003).

Mindfulness: Although the recent veneration of mindfulness can put some people off, Harvard's Ellen Langer cuts to its essence with a scalpel of simplicity: mindfulness is the simple act of actively noticing things (1990). In the context of self-compassion, mindfulness is taken to mean such awareness of our thoughts and feelings when we are suffering, but neither over-identifying with them nor being overwhelmed by them.

Common humanity: By recognising that suffering is a universal experience for humankind, albeit in different ways and at different times, we can feel less isolated in our pain. Given the universality of suffering, this helps us to put our own distress into perspective. Instead of asking ourselves 'why me?', we can consider 'why not me?' or accept that it is our turn to suffer.

Self-kindness: This is the ability to be gentle, kind and understanding towards ourselves when we make mistakes or are otherwise suffering, instead of being self-critical. To many, such self-kindness sounds simple enough in theory, even though it can prove tricky in practice. For some, though, fear of compassion can be crippling. Gilbert and his colleagues (2011) have studied these fears in a clinical context, and developed scales to measure fear of self-compassion, fear of compassion for others and fear of compassion from others. In their research, the fears of self-compassion and receiving compassion from others were strongly correlated with self-criticism, stress, anxiety, depression and insecure attachment. The latter of these, the result of childhood psychosocial stress, occurs if a child is not confident of their caregiver's support (Bowlby 1969). In adulthood, such an insecure attachment legacy can result in difficulties with establishing and maintaining emotional connections with others. As we will explore further below, moderate self-criticism is fairly common, and those who are highly self-critical may benefit disproportionately from self-compassion interventions.

Box 7.1
Next time you make a mistake or do not live up to your own expectations, practice the three steps of self-compassion. Mindfully become aware of your feelings without overwhelm, remind yourself that everyone suffers sometimes, and be as gentle on yourself as a good friend would be to you. Remember, by doing this you will be making yourself more resilient and quicker to recover from adversity.

Self-compassion reputation and mistaken identities

Similar to its compassionate sibling, self-compassion suffers from a reputational problem. This seems especially true in the West and particularly in corporate life. Self-compassion is, for many, just another form of navel gazing. Not in the Ancient Greek sense of *omphaloskepsis*, where one literally contemplated one's navel as an aid to meditation, but rather in the modern sense of pointless self-absorption. Indeed, many individuals take pride in being their own harshest judge. Proclamations about being 'my own toughest critic' are worn like a badge of humble-bragging honour. But is this approach healthy? Not necessarily, as we shall now explore.

A little self-critique can indeed be useful. It assists us in monitoring our responses and behaviours; important skills as social beings. Not being too lenient on ourselves can be a useful foil to laziness, and can drive us to achieve success. Self-criticism, then, when applied in moderation and in pursuit of our own development, can be a positive thing. Too much self-criticism, though, and an inner narrative focused on negatives, mistakes or issues can begin to dominate our thoughts.

As well as these reputational concerns, self-compassion has interesting associations with self-pity, self-esteem and self-criticism. We will now briefly examine the main semantic and psychological differences between these and self-compassion:

Self-pity

Sometimes, things just do not go our way, we have a streak of rotten luck, or life can just feel like one long, hard slog. When we become preoccupied with such troubles, and feel sorry for ourselves, this is self-pity. Sometimes, self-pity is warranted, and without it we might miss gratitude and joy when life has more ease. As expressed in Rumi's poem, Birdwings, we would be paralysed:

Your grief for what you've lost lifts a mirror
up to where you are bravely working.

Expecting the worst, you look, and instead,
here's the joyful face you've been wanting to see.

Your hand opens and closes, and opens and closes.
If it were always a fist or always stretched open,
you would be paralyzed.

Your deepest presence is in every small contracting and expanding,
the two as beautifully balanced and coordinated
as birdwings.

– Rumi

Self-pity largely presupposes that things happen to us and that we have limited control over our own lives. The work of Psychologist Julian Rotter (1954) on locus on control is a useful consideration here. An internal locus of control orientation expresses a belief that our actions impact our outcomes; an external locus of control believes that events which impact us are outside of our control. People with a high internal locus of control will take responsibility for events or outcomes, while someone with a high external locus of control will attribute outcomes to external events like luck or fate. These are, of course, opposite ends of a spectrum of perceived control, and most of us will sit somewhere in the middle. Self-pity typically arises when we slide towards the external end of the scale, and attribute our perceived failures to uncontrollable external causes or events. In other words, when we consider ourselves a victim of circumstance.

This view on self-pity has echoes in Karpman's Drama Triangle, as outlined in Chapter 2. Here, self-pity puts us firmly in the role of victim. Lingering in the victim role encourages excessive rumination, which has adverse impacts on our mental health. Staying in this victim position depletes our power and our personal responsibility for change.

Self-compassion is a strong antidote to self-pity. Mindfulness allows us to notice the thoughts of self-pity, but not to dwell on them or allow them to engulf us. Common humanity reminds us that everyone struggles sometimes, so it is not only us who suffers; now is just our turn. Self-kindness encourages us to treat ourselves the way we would a friend, with gentleness and warmth.

Self-esteem

Self-esteem is our own view of our personal worth or value, or how much we like and appreciate ourselves. Although it is typically described as our own subjective perspective, it is one which has almost certainly been informed and moulded by the views and actions of many others during our lives.

A relatively stable personality trait, self-esteem is important because it impacts almost every aspect of our lives: our relationships, our decision-making abilities and our overall sense of wellbeing. As with many measures, it is best thought of as a spectrum, where most of us occupy a middle ground. When people have low self-esteem, they may lack confidence, struggle to express themselves in relationships and feel unworthy.

At the other end of the spectrum, high self-esteem can result in an over-estimation of our abilities, combined with an unwillingness to partake in self-development activities: after all, we cannot improve upon perfection . . . right?

This is not to say that self-esteem is entirely bad for us. In moderation, it is correlated with positive wellbeing. Even narcissists, with their extremely high levels of self-esteem, benefit from elevated happiness levels much of the time.

The relentless pursuit of high self-esteem, though, can becoming an exhausting, endless competition with ourselves. Self-enhancement bias describes our preference to show ourselves in a positive light and highlights our aversion to average. Social media and the cult of celebrity feed this insatiable addiction. Narcissism levels are increasing in many populations, and studies have repeatedly shown that high self-esteem is linked to higher levels of aggression and prejudice. Of course, another issue with the precarious pedestal of high self-esteem is that even once we have achieved it, we have to endlessly feed its voracious appetite lest we slip towards something more middling.

So, why does self-esteem matter in relation to self-compassion? Often, when things are tough or we are feeling low, we try to rely on our self-esteem to feel better about ourselves. This rarely works. When we are feeling low, this is the most difficult time to remember the more positive aspects of ourselves which we might typically value. Instead of self-esteem, applying self-compassion is a more viable approach as it can be accessed even when we are at a low ebb. Self-compassion is quite simply more readily accessible than self-esteem in the moments when we need it most.

Research by Kristin Neff (2011) has shown that self-compassion results in greater emotional resilience than self-esteem does. Our self-esteem wants us to be better than average. To achieve this, we must evaluate ourselves to be superior to others. We must talk ourselves up whilst putting others down. By contrast, self-compassion does not require evaluation versus others, and so allows our focus to be on ourselves and having a response of gentle, considered self-kindness to our inevitable failures, mistakes and imperfections.

Self-criticism

Some self-criticism can be useful. It helps us to change behaviours or habits we dislike in ourselves and, when used in balance, can assist us in assessing our achievements. Disproportionate self-criticism, however, can be crippling. Those who suffer from this generally experience strong feelings of unworthiness, inferiority and shame. They will often blame themselves for things outside of their control. They may allow a mistake to become a negative for their whole being: not 'I made a mistake', more 'I am a failure'. Developmental feedback will likely be perceived as a threat or taken personally, and even compliments will likely be deflected. Unsurprisingly, self-criticism is common to many anxiety disorders and is a predictor of depression. It also adversely impacts friendships and relationships throughout life stages. The research of Paul Gilbert noted above examined compassion in relation to self-criticism, self-coldness and insecure attachment. Of these, only self-criticism was a significant predictor of depression. Self-criticism turns failure into despair.

Our brains, for all their brilliance, are easily fooled. In particular, they find it difficult to distinguish between what is real and what is imagined. Our mirror neurons activate whether we are thinking about doing something or actively doing it, or indeed whether we are watching someone do something or doing the action ourselves. In many ways, these neurons are the basis of empathy, as they provide direct, subconscious access to another person's experience.

However, this mirroring has a downside. If someone else were to constantly criticise and belittle us for perceived and actual mistakes, telling us that we are useless, worthless, and noting that we do not belong, the chances are that we would find this behaviour shockingly inappropriate. We can easily imagine the impact this sort of personal denigration would have on our wellbeing. Yet we rarely stop to consider how our own internal criticisms impact us. If our brains cannot entirely distinguish between real and imagined, self and other, then our internal critic is effectively bullying us.

If we constantly criticise ourselves, we can trigger our sympathetic nervous system and increase our cortisol levels, making us fearful, stressed and anxious. Significant traumatic stress causes cortisol to flood the amygdala and hippocampus, the areas responsible for emotional processing and memory respectively. Recounting traumatic experiences causes activity in the same areas of the brain, and chronic trauma can result in a lack of emotional self-regulation. Neurological studies have repeatedly demonstrated that traumatic events can permanently change our brain structure.

Self-compassion is an effective counterbalance to the effects of self-criticism. Increasingly, research is demonstrating just how powerful self-compassion can be. In numerous studies, self-compassion provides protection against anxiety and depression, across many different cultures (Warren et al. 2016; Yamaguchi et al. 2014). Even firefighters who have been exposed to severe levels of trauma in the course of their duties have demonstrated that self-compassion provides a protective factor against depression (Kaurin et al. 2018).

One study, which leveraged the brain's inability to entirely distinguish between real and imagined, involved participants simply imagining being the recipient of compassion. The result was lower levels of the primary stress hormone, cortisol (Rockliff et al. 2008). We do not even need to receive compassion to benefit from its power; we can simply imagine its presence for ourselves.

Interestingly, some recent clinical studies have further shown that those who have a strong preference for self-criticism show the greatest benefit from self-compassion interventions. Ironically, those self-proclaimed 'own toughest critics' have the most to reap from practicing self-compassion.

Self-compassion: Research and benefits

In contrast with self-pity, self-esteem and self-criticism, research into the impacts of self-compassion offers promising results. Far from being vain, self-absorbed navel gazing, self-compassion has many psychological and physiological benefits generally and for leadership in particular. We can now examine these through cognitive, emotional and behavioural lenses, and then take actions to boost our self-compassion in all of these areas:

Cognitive

(i) Developing a growth mindset

The idea of a growth, as opposed to fixed, mindset comes from psychologist Carol Dweck's work in this area (2017). People who believe that their abilities and talents can be enhanced through their actions, smart strategies and feedback are said to have a growth mindset. Conversely, those who believe talent is fixed, even bestowed upon them, are considered to have a fixed mindset. The benefits of a growth mindset for individuals include better performance in tests versus of those with more fixed mindsets, increased intellectual abilities and more energy being allocated to learning. In organisations where a growth mindset is prevalent, collaboration and innovation are more common, and employees report feeling more dedicated and empowered. Interestingly, companies with a predominantly fixed mindset only out-perform growth mindset organisations in one area: dishonesty and deception amongst employees. As with many areas of psychology, these two mindsets can be seen as opposite ends of a continuum, and it is almost impossible to have a purely growth or fixed mindset. Awareness of our preferences gives us a useful perspective from which to develop new habits.

Juliana Breines and Serena Chen (2012) have shown in their research that self-compassion can result in adoption of a growth mindset. In one study, they asked participants about their greatest weakness, then asked them to write about this either from a self-compassionate ('consider this from a compassionate understanding perspective') or a self-esteem ('validate your positive qualities') perspective. All the participants then responded to carefully worded fixed and growth mindset questions about how they felt towards and whether they had tried to overcome their weakness. The participants in the self-compassion group showed significantly more growth mindset thoughts than those in the self-esteem or the control group.

However, what we think we will do and what we actually do are not always the same thing. So, the same researchers ran another study, this time looking at actual behaviours. They gave all participants an extremely difficult vocabulary test. The participants, all university students, were told that they had performed badly in the test, and were then randomly assigned to one of two groups. The first group heard an observation from a researcher which deliberately emphasised self-compassionate aspects such as feeling upset about the test (mindfully aware of how they were feeling), not being alone in finding the test difficult (common humanity), and encouraging the students not to be too hard on themselves (self-kindness). The second group instead heard a more fixed mindset statement, that they must be intelligent in the first place to have been accepted to the university. All of the students were then given the chance to take another vocabulary test, and this time they could opt to review the words for as long as they wanted to in advance. The students who had been in the self-compassion group studied for significantly longer than those in the more fixed mindset group, displaying the increased focus on learning that Dweck highlights as a key characteristic of a growth mindset.

The reasons for this impact of self-compassion on our mindset are not entirely clear. Perhaps treating ourselves with compassion lessens our self-judgement and need for approval. The reduced rumination, increased optimism and quietened voice of self-criticism that result from self-compassion might permit us to more clearly see opportunities and possibilities for our growth and development, rather than just obstacles.

Self-compassion benefits leaders as individuals, and is a useful practice for compassion more widely. Leaders with a growth mindset are more likely to notice the performance of teams and individuals, and to give the balanced, constructive feedback from which the roots of more growth mindsets can grow. A canopy of compassion and self-compassion provides the ideal conditions for a compassionate, growth mindset organisation to flourish.

(ii) Improved social connectedness

Self-compassion can make us live longer. That may seem like a bold claim, but consider the impact of self-compassion on social connectedness. Social connectedness is included in this cognitive section as it can develop either spontaneously or through conscious understanding and practice.

Social connectedness, as we have seen, is our subjective sense of close, positive social relationships with others – in other words, our belonging and relatedness. Lack of social connection may be perceived simply as 'loneliness', but its impact is serious. We all have powerful, subjective experiences of belonging - or otherwise. Remember, poor social connectedness is more detrimental to our health than excessive weight, increased blood pressure or smoking.

Self-compassion meditations, even when practiced for only a few minutes at a time, have been shown to improve social connectedness (Hutcherson et al. 2008). This improvement results in a myriad of benefits. Strong social connectedness prompts higher levels of trust and cooperation, and even increases our self-esteem. With strong social connectedness, we improve our skills of emotional and social regulation. Our immune systems are strengthened, and we recover from illness more quickly.

Longevity, then, is a beneficial side-effect of self-compassion and its association with social connectedness.

Emotional

Self-compassion also positively impacts us emotionally. We will now explore two of the main emotional benefits: mood regulation and stress moderation.

(i) Regulating our moods

The impact of self-compassion in moderating our moods to within an acceptable range is significant. Calmness and optimism are two side-effects of self-compassion; when we are calm and optimistic, we can more easily manage our emotional intelligence and make better decisions. Kristin Neff and her colleagues (2007) found strong positive correlations between self-compassion and agreeableness, conscientiousness, optimism and wisdom, as well as a significant negative association with neuroticism or susceptibility to stress. Some of these areas, notably conscientiousness, agreeableness, and neuroticism, belong to the 'Big Five' factors of personality alongside extraversion and openness. Neff found that self-compassion practices could predict positive psychological health beyond what was attributable to personality alone. For example, even if we typically have high neuroticism – the unpalatable word psychologists use to describe susceptibility to stress – we can moderate this to a significant extent through self-compassion. Compassion supports us in processing, rather than suppressing, our emotions.

Self-compassion increases positive affect, and reduces negative affect (Berking and Whitley 2014; Neff 2003). In other words, it increases the likelihood that we experience the world positively rather than negatively. Possible explanations for this outcome include mood stabilisation which helps us to regulate our emotions and responses, an improved ability to take an external perspective on oneself and the evolutionary, survival benefits of emotional regulation (Dahl et al. 2015; Gilbert 2009). Whilst reasons for this effect of self-compassion are not yet conclusive, neuroimaging studies indicate that compassion meditations increase activity in the insula and amygdala, areas of the brain involved in emotional detection and processing (Hoffmann et al. 2011; Lutz et al. 2009). Hence, self-compassion might facilitate improved detection and regulation of emotion in the brain, and so contribute to our improved emotional intelligence. Such emotional regulation is, of course, an important resource for compassionate leaders.

Preliminary findings from neuroendocrine research further suggest that compassion meditations may reduce our subjective distress and associated adverse immune responses (Hoffman et al. 2011). Our immune systems are suppressed when we are stressed, making us more susceptible to illness and burnout. We are able, through compassion, to see the world more calmly and with a greater sense of ease. Our immune systems, as well as our colleagues, are grateful for this perspective, as we develop our reserves of inner tranquility through our practice of self-compassion.

Another study by Iranian psychologists Gh. Samaie and Hojjat Farahani (2011) concluded that self-compassion significantly moderates the relationship between rumination and stress, offering us a psychological and physiological buffer in stressful situations. Self-compassion lowers our levels of defensiveness and lessens the emotional distress that interferes with our ability to self-regulate our moods and emotions.

(ii) Moderating stress, anxiety and depression

Stress impacts individual leadership functioning as well as both the mental health and psychological resources of those we work with. As leaders impact the psychological resources of their colleagues and teams through their own stress, they are simultaneously depleting the ability of others to be compassionate. This is why, in our new construct of compassion, the appraisal of role and resources is so important.

In life, in the workplace, and in leadership, reducing our anxiety levels is useful. Anxiety-driven thinking leads to more errors, a focus on difficulties over opportunities, and an under-estimation of the amount of support we have available to us. Anxiety can put us in a lonely, difficult place from which we may struggle to either perform or to lead others.

Compassion for ourselves is increasingly regarded as an effective means to reduce the frequency and severity of both anxiety and depression. Self-compassion is a key component in Mindfulness Based Cognitive Therapy (MBCT). MBCT research which tracks participants over a number of years has shown that an increase in levels of self-compassion results in a decrease in the mind-wandering associated with depression. Harvard Professor Jonathan Greenberg and colleagues (2018) have shown that higher levels of self-compassion significantly predict improvements in depression. It may be that self-compassion is more effective than more common reappraisal techniques of managing depression because it interrupts repetitive rumination patterns. Box 7.2 offers an evidence-based approach to managing stress, anxiety and depression in leaders through self-compassion.

Box 7.2 Self-compassion and Leaders

A leader's positive emotions predict the performance of their entire group.

(Fredrickson 2003: 172)

The benefits noted above apply to those in leadership positions as much as anyone else, yet the effects of self-compassion specifically on leaders is a largely under-researched area. Still, there are specific areas where self-compassion approaches are of particular use to leaders. Research on self-esteem, servant leadership, and kindness in leadership are related concepts which have received more focus and provide useful context, although results in these areas are sometimes mixed. Self-esteem does not correlate with leadership ratings by subordinates (Chemers et al. 2000) although leadership kindness does appear to correlate with increased prosocial behaviours (Haskins et al. 2018). Even servant leadership, combining a motivation to lead with a desire to serve others, is sometimes considered a less effective approach than personality-driven transformational leadership (Choudhary et al. 2013; Burns 1978).

Addressing this gap in the research, I conducted a study into the impacts of self-compassion on the self-reported wellbeing levels of leaders. This extended the self-compassion research beyond predominantly undergraduate and clinical settings, and widened leadership research beyond studies of self-esteem, kindness, and servant leadership. The study recruited leaders with an average age of 46, based predominantly in European countries, with significant levels of organisational responsibility. These leaders were employed across a broad selection of sectors including financial services, manufacturing, FMCG and the armed forces. Unlike many compassion-focused studies, which often have predominantly female participants, the gender split in this research was more balanced at 55% male and 45% female.

The participants in this study were allocated to one of four groups, as summarised in Table 7.1. Their individual ratings of self-compassion, stress, anxiety and depression were measured at the start and end of a month-long period. During this month, participants were asked to follow one of four interventions, all of which are available in full later in this chapter:

Table 7.1: OC – AC Research Conditions.

Auditory	Both	Control	Description
Participants listened to a short self-compassion meditation daily,	Participants received both the audio file meditation and the descriptions	Participants received no interventions	Participants were given a brief outline of the definition and typical constructs of compassion and self-compassion

The results of this research showed that, apart from the Control group, all others had a statistically significant improvement in their self-reported wellbeing measures of stress, anxiety and depression. Interestingly, these improvements were visible irrespective of which intervention the participants had used. This may indicate that, as leaders, we can choose which approach we take to self-compassion; there is no 'one way' to be more compassionate towards ourselves. Regardless of the approach you prefer, just a few minutes each day can have a significant, positive impact on your feelings of stress, anxiety or depression.

Behavioural

Self-compassion not only impacts what we think and feel, it also changes how we behave. Let us now examine what self-compassion does for our ability to perform at our best and to improve our resilience.

(i) Performing at our best

In the workplace, as well as more generally, self-compassion can be viewed as a source of empowerment, learning, and inner strength. It reduces stress and aids our peace of mind, as well as enhancing our overall psychological wellbeing.

Being compassionate towards ourselves moves us from the 'fight or flight' sympathetic nervous system to engaging our prefrontal cortex (PFC). The PFC plays a central role in our executive functions such as complex planning, decision-making, focusing our attention, inhibiting our impulses, and improving our cognitive flexibility. All of these, of course, allow us to perform at our best in a leadership context. Self-compassion, much more than self-criticism, enables us to perform to the best of our ability, even in a fast-paced, complex environment.

When we fail to live up to our own expectations, self-compassion can be useful as a motivator for personal change. The study by Juliana Breines and Serena Chen (2012) mentioned earlier found that people who treated themselves with self-compassion after mistakes were more motivated to improve upon their personal weaknesses, worked harder in order to improve test scores and were more determined to atone for their moral transgressions. None of us are perfect; self-compassion frees us from being trapped by our mistakes.

(ii) Improved resilience

Resilience is our ability to recover, adapt to, or bounce back from setbacks. Football manager Iain Dowie famously coined the term 'bouncebackability' when describing how his team, Crystal Palace, went from almost being relegated to developing a resilience which resulted in their promotion to the Premier League within six months.

In sport and elsewhere, this ability to recover quickly is the subject of much discourse and desire. For those who like to compete, either on the sports field or in the boardroom, quick recovery from setback matters. Navigating obstacles and uncertainty, alongside moving forward purposefully and calmly are more preferable outcomes than rumination and 'stuckness'.

An organisational example of the power of self-compassion and resilience is briefly outlined in Box 7.3.

Box 7.3: Self-compassion and Resilience

Sometimes the smallest nudges can have the biggest results. Mark (not his real name) had just delivered his presentation to the whole company. An experienced and natural presenter, Mark usually enjoyed these meetings almost as much as he enjoyed the praise afterwards. This time, however, things had gone wrong. His slides kept glitching and, while presenting, he spotted two errors which he knew the CEO would have noticed. His voice began to sound more nervous and less resonant than usual, and his attempts at humour fell flat.

Mark was not the type to apply self-compassion. At least, not knowingly. One of his colleagues, though, made a few simple observations during a quick post-meeting coffee chat:

"It wasn't that bad, Mark. I thought it went well. Don't be so tough on yourself." (self-kindness)

"Remember my presentation last month? It was awful! We've all been there." (common humanity)

"I see you're feeling down. That's normal. The presentation wasn't the end of the world, just a bump in the road." (mindfulness)

Later, as Mark thought about these comments, he began to apply some self-compassion. Through being gentle and understanding with himself, remembering that he was not alone in his difficulty, and not becoming overwhelmed by his feelings, Mark soon regrouped. He chalked the presentation up to experience and was soon able to focus his renewed attention more productively.

Football managers and other leaders would do well to consider self-compassion as a means to develop resilience. Studies have shown that self-compassion not only improves psychological resilience, but also results in improved performance after failure. So, if we want to learn from our mistakes and quickly move on, we should try self-compassion. Being compassionate with ourselves is a more effective approach then mentally beating ourselves up. In short, self-compassion increases our bouncebackability.

Actions to build self-compassion

We have explored the differences between self-compassion and self-criticism, self-pity and self-esteem. Through cognitive, emotional and behavioural lenses, we can truly begin to understand the power of self-compassion, particularly for leaders.

Chapters 8 and 9 contain a wealth of resources for developing compassionate leadership and compassionate organisations. The rest of this chapter is dedicated to providing short, research-based, practical ways to measure, practice and develop your own levels of self-compassion.

Benchmarking your self-compassion

It may be useful to measure your current level of self-compassion before you apply any of the recommended interventions. This will provide you with information to reflect upon, and also gives you a benchmark, should you decide to track your own progress.

A word of warning: if you suffer from extreme levels of self-criticism, some of these exercises and approaches may prove extremely challenging for you, and you might want to do them in conjunction with other support.

Self-compassion scale

Dr Kristen Neff has developed a particularly useful self-compassion scale, which asks the respondent to rate between 1–5 how closely their experience relates to 26 statements. Neff later developed a shortened form of the scale, which has 12 statements, yet almost perfect correlation with the longer scale; this can be found in the 'Further Resources' section of this book.

In both of Neff's scales, all of the statements are aligned to one of the three areas of self-compassion outlined above, such as those shown in Figure 7.2.

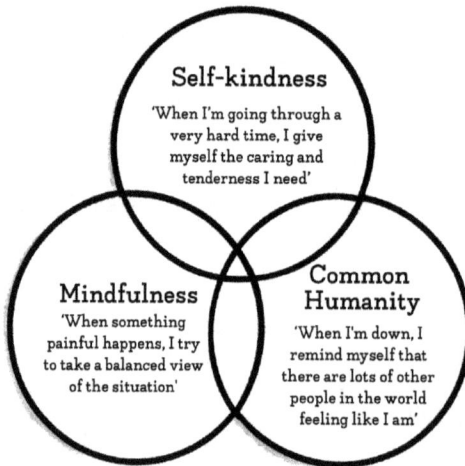

Figure 7.2: Self-compassion with example statements (adapted from Neff 2003).

Once you have established your own self-compassion benchmark, there are a number of research-based methods you can adopt in order to enhance your levels of self-compassion. As my research into the effects of self-compassion on leaders noted, there is no single 'best' way to build our self-compassion. Even minor interventions over a short period of time can have a significant effect on our levels of stress and our emotional wellbeing.

Leadership research into self-compassion interventions

These are the interventions used in my research mentioned above, which looked at the impact of self-compassion interventions on levels of stress, anxiety and depression in leaders.

The first intervention was simply awareness and understanding of the traditional (Figure 1.1) and new constructs of compassion (Figure 2.1) and Neff's definition of self-compassion (Figure 7.1). It is important to note that just knowing about these, and being able to use them as a frame for issues that arise, is in itself a useful compassionate intervention.

To ensure participants had read the slides, and to check their understanding, they then took a short quiz. The questions are below, for you to check your own under-standing, and to embed your learning:

Q1: How is compassion typically defined?
    a) Feeling sorry for someone
    b) Noticing pain, feeling a response, taking action
    c) Wanting to help everyone
    d) Noticing pain and taking action

Q2: What additional step is included in the new construct of compassion?
    a) Judging
    b) Waiting
    c) Appraisal

Q3: What does the appraisal step involve? (select all that apply)
    a) Appraising your role and resources
    b) Considering your patterns of behaviour
    c) Appraising for safety and intention
    d) Feeling sympathy

Q4: What are the three elements of self-compassion? (select all that apply)
    a) Mindfulness
    b) Self-kindness
    c) Judgement
    d) Common humanity

The second intervention in my research was a short, approximately 3.5 minute long self-compassion meditation. This was sent to participants as a voice file to be saved onto a mobile phone. The meditation is reproduced below, and it can either be read out aloud or you can record your own version:

Welcome to your daily self-compassion meditation.

Sit in a comfortable position, close your eyes, and take three, deep, relaxing breaths.

Open your awareness to the sounds in your environment. Stay in the present moment by simply becoming aware of whatever you notice.

Form an image of yourself sitting in the chair. Notice your posture as if you were seeing yourself from the outside.

Next, bring your awareness inside your body and note the world of sensations occurring there in this very moment.

Now feel your breathing wherever it's most obvious to you. Pay special attention to every out-breath.

With each out breath, repeat these self-compassion phrases silently to yourself, after me:

> May I be safe
> May I be peaceful
> May I be kind to myself
> May I accept myself just as I am
> (Repeat three times)

Now, slowly letting go of this meditation, allow yourself to be exactly as you are in this moment.

And when you're ready, slowly and gently open your eyes.

(Adapted from Neff and Germer 2018)

Simply repeat or listen to the meditation once a day, at a time that suits you – as long as you are not driving or similarly need to be concentrating, and are unlikely to be disturbed by others. Many participants listened to the meditation before going to sleep at night, while others chose a quiet moment in their office. One army officer participant even told me that the only way he had peace to do his meditation without interruption or being questioned about what he was doing was to disappear to the bathroom for a few minutes to listen to his meditation!

Adjusting self-talk

As mentioned above, we often speak to ourselves in a way that we would never speak to someone else, and which we certainly would not appreciate someone else speaking to us. The first step towards adjusting our self-talk is to become more aware of the words and patterns we use, and consider the messages these send to ourselves.

In order to do this, here are some questions for you to consider:
- What do you criticise yourself for?
- What do you say?

- What do you say often?
- How do you say the words?
- Who, if anyone, does the inner critic sound like or remind you of?
- Would you say these words in this way to a friend?

Once you have a sense of your self-talk patterns, consider how you can make your words more compassionate. This is often the hardest stage to begin with, but is worth gentle perseverance. Some suggestions include:
- Move your words away from catastrophizing
  If we make a mistake at work, catastrophising can take us from simply 'I made a mistake' to a personal attack 'I'm such an idiot' to an extreme scenario such as 'I'm going to be found out, then I'll be fired and I'll never find another job, and I'll lose my home . . .'. As well as increasing anxiety levels, this sort of catastrophising self-talk can be paralysing. Self-compassion allows us to recover more quickly and to take positive action.
- Avoid generalisations from one incident
  When things sometimes go wrong, as they will, avoid self-talk such as 'this always happens to me' or 'I never get this right'. When you notice such generalisations – often obvious when the words 'always' or 'never' are used – remember to look for exceptions to the generalisations.
- Stop labelling yourself
  We may do something unfortunate or embarrassing sometimes, but we are not 'a failure'. We are all more than our occasional actions.
- Beware the tyranny of 'shoulds'
  If your self-talk includes lots of 'shoulds' (such as 'I should keep everyone happy' or 'I should volunteer to do the extra work'), ask yourself whether the 'should' is currently valid or not. Is this the Parent from Transactional Analysis talking? Whose rules are you living by?

The good thing about self-talk is that it is typically in our heads, so we can practice adjusting it without anyone else noticing. Just like the compassion model itself, the first step is awareness. From such awareness, change is possible.

Self-compassion mirror

In a fascinating, yet remarkably simple, study, Nicola Petrocchi and colleagues (2016) asked participants to write down four phrases that they would use when speaking to a friend who was suffering misfortune, yet was being self-critical. Once these phrases were written down, participants were assigned to one of three groups: the first group repeated the phrases out loud, whilst looking at themselves in a mirror. The second group repeated the phrases without the mirror, and the third group looked at themselves in the mirror without saying anything.

The results of this study showed that the group who said the phrases out loud whilst looking at their own reflection in the mirror had significantly lower levels of self-criticism and higher levels of soothing positive affect than either of the other groups. What is not yet clear is why this was the case. Maybe looking at our reflection in a mirror allows us a view that others might have of us – slightly removed, more objective, and literally seeing what others see.

This self-compassion intervention, then, is to do exactly what the participants in this study did. Start by imagining a friend who is distressed by an unfortunate incident or mistake they have made, and who is being self-critical about their role in this. Write down four phrases you might say to them. Then, take a little time to look at yourself in the mirror and notice if self-criticism rears its head. When you are ready, say the four phrases to your reflection, taking your time and saying them with feeling. You can say them more than once, of course.

This is a deceptively simple self-compassion intervention which will leave you feeling more positive and being less critical of yourself.

Self-compassion letter

This intervention is designed to support the process of substituting a self-critical voice with a more self-compassionate one.

> This is my letter to the world
> That never wrote to me.
> (Emily Dickinson)

I used this letter writing exercise a number of years ago as part of a weekend retreat workshop for recent MBA graduates. Many of them told me afterwards that they had dreaded this exercise, as they thought it was going to be 'fluffy', yet in reality it was one of the most impactful sessions of the weekend, with long-lasting effects. One of the participants, a Scandinavian physician, wrote to me afterwards:

> Your workshop was life changing . . . I just re-read the letter to myself. I thought it would now feel embarrassing, but it did not . . . I have had a tendency, like many others, to have slight depression-like symptoms related to polar-night period when there is so little sunlight . . . I felt so strongly that the room I left was so dark as I wrote the letter, and that I now feel that there is so much more light around me. (personal correspondence, 2018, with permission)

I include this not for reasons of my own self-esteem; I am well aware of the dangers that presents. I include it, rather, to reassure my reader. Writing a letter to ourselves can feel distinctly unfamiliar and uncomfortable at first. Discomfort, however, often indicates growth. This is an incredibly powerful exercise which can bring long-lasting rewards.

Remember the research by Juliana Breines and Serena Chen in which participants were significantly more motivated to improve their perceived personal weaknesses and make amends for moral transgressions? One of the exercises in this study was to write a self-compassion letter. None of us are perfect, yet all of us can move forward. This letter writing exercise can support our self-development, ability to change and desire to atone for our mistakes.

Steps for the letter writing exercise:

No-one else need see the letter you write, so you can be completely honest and open in this exercise.

To begin, bring to mind something about yourself which makes you feel ashamed, embarrassed or not good enough. It can be anything – something you have done, a relationship problem, part of your personality, anything.

Spend a few minutes considering how this makes you feel. Angry? Ashamed? Sad? Upset?

Now focus on writing a letter to yourself which acknowledges these feelings, seeks to understand rather than judge them, and expresses compassion. Start your letter with 'Dear <your name>. . .'. If you get stuck, here are some suggestions to help your writing:

Acknowledge the feelings you have about this issue, and name them without becoming overwhelmed.

Remind yourself of the 'common humanity' aspect of self-compassion, that no one is perfect, and everyone suffers.

Without judging or blaming, consider how external factors such as family or childhood may have contributed.

Consider how a 'previous you' may have done things in the past that you are now not proud of. Be kind to that former you, while still taking responsibility for yourself.

Consider what you would say to a friend, or what a friend might say to you. Keeping in mind the action orientation of compassion, focus on what small steps you might want to take in order to feel better about the issue.

How you finish your letter is your choice. One of the MBA workshop participants told me that he simply signed "love, Allan". Then he realised that is exactly what he need to do – to love himself.

When you have finished your letter, read it, then put it to one side and re-read it at a later stage. It is entirely your discretion whether to keep it. If you do so, reading it when you are feeling low about the issue you tackled can be a useful, self-compassionate exercise that will allow you to recover from difficulty more quickly.

Thank and release the inner critic

Acceptance and Commitment Therapy (ACT) is a psychotherapeutic approach which encourages us to accept, rather than fight, difficult feelings and emotions. In a way, the more we wrestle and fight with something, the stronger we are inadvertently making our adversary. It may be useful, then, to accept that the inner critic exists and will never be entirely silenced. Noticing and labelling the inner critic's voice helps to distinguish and categorise their input, in order to keep it distinct from more positive, useful and balanced thoughts.

When your inner critic begins a mournful soliloquy, do not try to completely silence them, lest you hear their muffled screams. The inner critic almost undoubtedly has a good intention to protect you or prevent you from making a dangerous mistake. However, in their hyper-vigilant state, they may not be aware that tigers are not about to pounce, or that you have learned how to cope with adversity over the years.

So, when your inner critic begins to talk, label their input, silently thank them for caring about you and reassure them that you are ok. Release them, and you, from their distress.

Compassion imagery

In Rockliff's research noted earlier in this chapter, participants lowered their cortisol levels simply by imagining being the recipient of compassion. A variation of the imagery exercise they used is included in this self-compassion section, as it is a self-directed exercise.

Compassion is a response to suffering, so you may find it useful to consider some of your own suffering before you do this exercise. Keep yourself safe. The suffering can be a mistake you made, something you did but now regret, or experiences which have left an invisible bruise.

> Sit somewhere comfortable where you are unlikely to be disturbed. Take three deep breaths. Then, for a little over five minutes, imagine compassion being directed at you from an external source. This external source can be human or otherwise; it is the feeling of compassion that the source generates which matters. If it is useful, create a mental picture of this compassionate other.

> In the Rockliff experiment, a researcher prompted every minute or so with comments like "allow yourself to feel that you are the recipient of great compassion" or "allow yourself to feel the loving kindness that is there for you". When doing this exercise alone, you can simply remind yourself of these comments whenever suits you best.

Like many of the self-compassion exercises outlined above, this exercise is deceptively simple yet potent in its effects.

New compassion construct and self-compassion

The new compassion construct can as easily be applied to self-compassion as it can to other-focused compassion, as illustrated in Figure 7.3. As we become more aware of our own suffering and of our inner critic, we can choose how to respond. We know that acceptance and understanding are more useful than attempts to silence critical voices. When we feel an emotional response to our own suffering, the mindfulness of self-compassion allows us to notice this without becoming overwhelmed. As we consider the appraisal step, we have evidence-based practices designed to develop our own compassionate resources. And, as we respond to our own suffering, we can do this with the same thoughtful care and compassion that we would use with another.

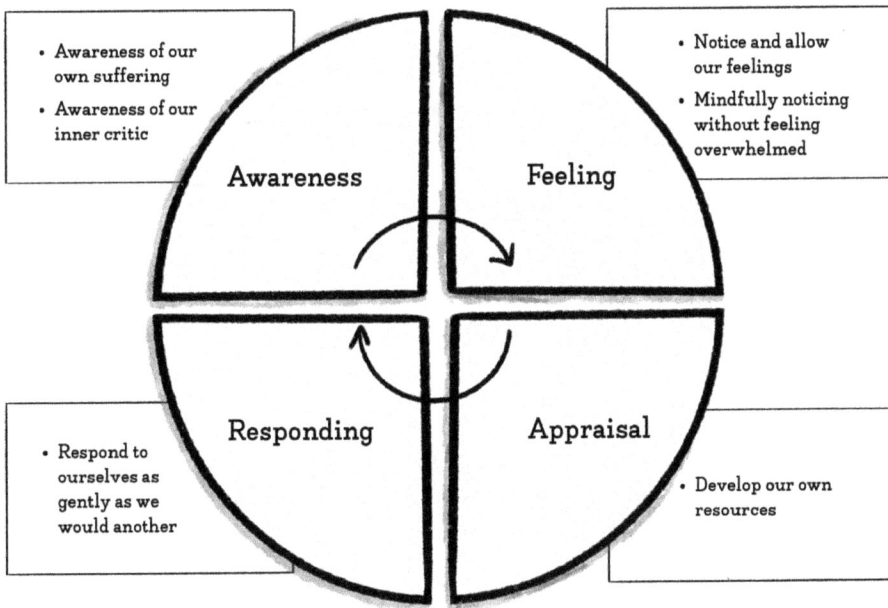

Figure 7.3: Self-compassion and the New Compassion Construct.

Self-compassion is clearly highly beneficial to leaders. It makes us less stressed or anxious, mentally healthier and more able to recover from adversity. Through self-compassion, we can find ourselves more willing to change for the better and more regulated in our moods. Our social connectedness will improve, which brings a plethora of mental and physical benefits. And, with self-compassion outcomes including a growth mindset and improved resilience, we will be able to perform at our very best. By applying self-compassion practices, we are able to more fully develop our compassionate leadership and so to build more compassionate organisations.

Key Chapter Points

- Self-compassion is comprised of three elements: mindfulness, self-kindness and common humanity.
- Self-compassion is not navel gazing, self-esteem, self-pity or self-criticism.
- There are numerous physiological and psychological benefits of practicing self-compassion. Self-compassion benefits for leaders include reduced stress and increased resilience.
- Being our own toughest critic is less beneficial psychologically and physically than being self-compassionate.
- Self-compassion can be quickly learned, and has fast results. This chapter has outlined a number of ways – derived from contemporary research – to increase your self-compassion.

Chapter 8
Developing compassionate leadership

Our history has always been the sum total of the choices made and the actions taken by each individual man and woman. It has always been up to us.   (Barak Obama)

There's a difference between knowing the path and walking the path.   (Morpheus, The Matrix)

Compassion as a leadership choice

Neuroscientist Richard Davidson has noted that we are neurologically equipped for compassion in a similar way as we are for language. However, for either of these to flourish we must nurture our biological predispositions with experience. We are all born with an ability to recognise and respond to the suffering of others; our choice is where to focus our energy and what aspects of our selves to nurture. In other words, we can choose to be compassionate leaders.

> We who lived in concentration camps can remember the men who walked through huts comforting others, giving away their last piece of bread. They may have been few in number, but they offer sufficient proof that everything can be taken from a man but one thing: the last of the human freedoms – to choose one's attitude in any given set of circumstances, to choose one's own way.   (Frankl 1959/2004: 75)

Yet, as we have seen, compassion is conspicuous by its absence from most management theory and practice. This omission is even more intriguing when we consider that our capacity for compassion is increasingly considered to be innate. Babies prefer puppets who act with compassion, and toddlers spontaneously reward fairness (Ziv et al. 2021). Yes, humans can be dogmatic, overly self-confident and sometimes think that others deserve their fates, but we are also sometimes seemingly more concerned by others' pain than our own, we act in prosocial ways even towards strangers, and we can overcome trauma to become even more inclined to support others (Crockett et al. 2014; Chancellor et al. 2018; Lim and DeSteno 2016). As a species, we seem to have an inherent basic goodness and generally prefer prosocial actions from an early age. Our capacity for compassion will be impacted by our personality traits, social environments, and a host of other conscious and unconscious factors, but it remains intact.

Tired of reading research about the more negative aspects of human behaviour, Scott Barry Kaufman and colleagues (2019) developed a 'light triad' of behaviours: humanism, kind treatment of others without the need for reciprocity and our faith in humanity. In doing this, Kaufman was seeking to address the balance where the 'dark triad' of narcissism, Machiavellianism and psychopathy received so much more research attention than the more positive side of our personalities. Kaufman's research

https://doi.org/10.1515/9783110763126-008

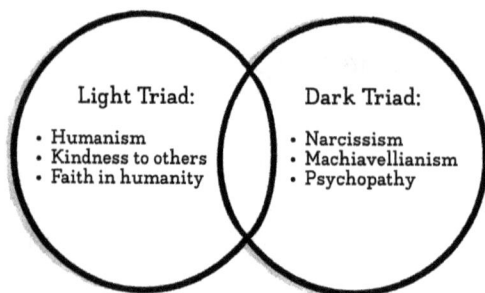

Figure 8.1: Light and dark triads.

to date supports the view that we each have both lighter and darker aspects of our personalities, as illustrated in Figure 8.1. His work suggests that we are more likely than not to be on the light side in our everyday thoughts, emotions and behaviours. To find out your dark – light balance, Kaufman's tests are available online, with more detail on where to find these in the Further Resources section.

This chapter is focused on supporting a compassionate leadership choice. As we develop our compassionate leadership capability through this chapter, we will discover more nuance in the new compassion construct. Our ability to bolster our resources is enhanced with each practice. We can appraise situations with greater proficiency, incorporating our own feelings whilst simultaneously taking a step back from our individual judgements, perspectives and biases. This enables us to have a clearer, wider view from which we can choose an appropriately useful response, rather than one which puts us or others in physical or psychological jeopardy. Our ability to stay in compassion, rather than to slide into empathy or lurch into altruism, is beneficial both to ourselves as leaders and to those we lead.

Why choose compassionate leadership?

Compassion is a leadership strength. As well as the psychological and physiological benefits available to all, compassionate leaders improve accountability and build long term psychological safety in their organisations. They deal with conflict in such a way that it does not derail individual or team effort. They foster a culture of openness and innovation, and even develop the relational reserves which could mean the difference between organisational survival or extinction. Contrary to popular criticism, compassionate leadership is both strong and flexible, rather than weak and brittle:

> One of the criticisms I've faced over the years is that I'm not aggressive enough or assertive enough . . . . it means I'm weak. I totally rebel against that. I refuse to believe that you cannot be both compassionate and strong. (Jacinda Ardern, quoted in Dowd 2018)

Compassion can be a positive force for individual leaders, and for the people, organisations or countries they serve. The notion of autocratic 'great man' direction has passed its use-by date and a time of more humane leadership is finally within reach. In a way, our leadership is not about us as leaders; it is about the consequences of our acts and intentions. Even John F. Kennedy Jr., son of President Kennedy and Jacqueline Onassis, hinted at this possibility: "People often tell me I could be a great man. I'd rather be a good man" (attrib.). Tough decisions can be taken in humane and decent ways. It is as much how we do something as what we do that matters.

So, will developing compassionate leadership lead to the demise of effective management, a weakening of the organisation and those who work within it? From the research to date, the answer appears to be a resounding 'no'. On the contrary, compassionate leadership is a morally sound, practical approach which results in increased levels of organisational commitment, competence and compliance. As you read this chapter, reflect on your own experiences of compassionate leadership (Box 8.1) and consider how these might be informing your own actions.

Box 8.1: Reflection: Compassion List

Firstly, make a note of the three people who have been most compassionate towards you. What was the situation? What did they do? What impact did their actions have on you, at the time and even now?

Next, consider whose list you might be on, and why. Was this second list easier or harder to do? Remember, we have different preferences for giving and receiving compassion.

Do you extend your compassion widely or narrowly? Who are you judging and why? How accepting are you (really) of your own or others' suffering?

How does this impact your work? What steps can you take to deepen or widen your compassion?

Compassionate leadership and organisational outcomes

A book on compassionate leadership is bound to extol the virtues of compassion. That said, organisations have the busy business of customers, clients and shareholders to attend to, and compassion might feel like a footnote to these more important, rational activities. However, there is increasing evidence that compassionate leadership is inextricably linked to organisational outcomes.

We have already seen the results of my own research into Organisational Compassion (OC) and Affective Commitment (AC), and noted the positive outcomes associated with higher AC in organisations. We have seen from other studies that compassion results in outcomes such as lower stress and anxiety, increased prosocial behaviours, improved employee engagement and performance, and higher job satisfaction, all of which lead to improved outcomes for both the organisation and the individuals within it.

Amplification of leadership also has an effect on organisational outcomes. A leaders' words reverberate more loudly and their silences can be deafening. A leader's behaviours are magnified and their actions, or lack thereof, are felt more keenly. Compassionate leaders can use this understanding to their advantage, creating ripples of compassion which, when they reach the edge of the cultural reservoir, can ripple back inwardly again to support everyone in the organisation.

Professor David DeSteno (2018) argues that a key role of leaders is to instil 'grit and grace' in their teams. By grit, he means perseverance and resilience in the face of adversity. Grace is what he considers to be the outcome of decency, respect and generosity; these qualities, he argues, are the hallmarks of effective cooperation. DeSteno notes that grace is fostered through the cultivation of gratitude, pride and compassion. These qualities matter because they enable the development of social bonds and make us more inclined to support the people around us. Even more tangibly from an organisational outcomes perspective, DeSteno has found that people who experience pride or compassion continue to work on difficult tasks for over 30% longer than those feeling other upbeat emotions, such as joy or happiness.

Organisational elevation

Compassionate leadership may also contribute to Vianello and colleagues' (2010) notion of organisational 'elevation': an uplifting, prosocial response to witnessing moral excellence in leadership. Such moral leadership is most noticeable when leaders have to contend with difficult practical or ethical issues, or when they are responding with compassion to individual or collective pain.

This research found that leaders who are visibly dedicated to positive collective outcomes, and who treat people especially well, prompt such 'elevation' in their organisations. Similar to much of the research we have already examined, they note that this elevation is strongly associated with increases in interpersonal consideration, employee compliance and Affective Commitment. It could even be that such benefits and employee behaviours reduce the likelihood of morally questionable actions which make for an uneasy reading of front page headlines (Figure 8.2):

**Like the Titanic:
Enron 20 Years On**

**World Class Scandal
at WorldCom**

**Dieselgate: British Car
Buyers' Claim Against
VW Reaches High Court**

Figure 8.2: Newspaper headlines (adapted from Davies 2021; Hancock 2002; Hofmann 2021).

Organisational culture is, in many ways, a deep reservoir which reflects the ethics and behaviours of its leadership. Embedding and developing compassionate leadership into an organisation can prevent the depths from becoming murky.

We will now explore how to develop our compassionate leadership capability, using the new compassion construct as a frame.

Developing our compassionate leadership

Using the new compassion construct is in itself a practice of compassionate leadership. Awareness of what compassion is and what it is not, alongside the unique 'appraisal' step of the new approach, are themselves useful interventions. Understanding these allows us to move our leadership focus away from empathy or altruism, towards more nourishing, sustainable compassion. Keeping the new compassion construct (Figure 2.1) and 'compassion maths model' (Figure 2.4) close to hand can serve as gentle reminders to incorporate these into your normal daily practices. Figure 8.3 summarises the areas we will now explore in relation to developing our compassionate leadership with the new compassion construct.

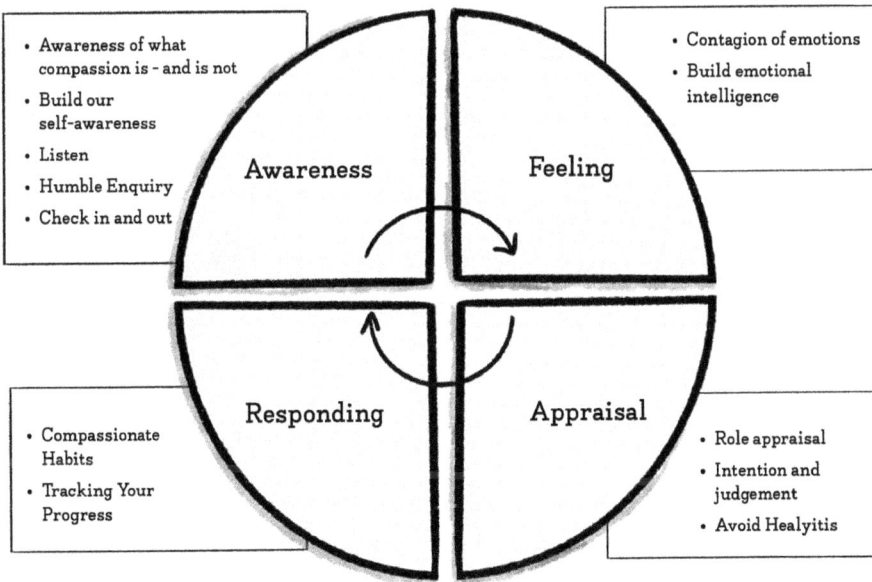

Figure 8.3: Developing compassionate leadership with the New Compassion Construct.

We are all leaders, just in different ways. Leadership is less an organisational role or job title, more an approach. The compassionate path of leadership is made through walking along its course. Therefore, the practices which follow are offered as practical ways of developing our compassionate leadership as we choose to take this route.

As the aphorism remind us, all models are wrong but some are useful. As you practice developing your compassionate leadership, try not to latch onto any particular practice as being an 'answer'. Instead, consider these as different lenses or focuses for your attention. Some of the compassion practices may seem unusual or a little uncomfortable at first, but that discomfort may be the beginning of fresh understanding and development.

Psychiatrist and Rabbi Abraham Twerski memorably talked about such discomfort in his YouTube video on what lobsters have to teach us about stress. The Rabbi begins by pointing out that lobsters are initially confined by their shells as they try to grow. When their discomfort becomes too much, the lobster takes refuge under a rock, casts off its shell and grows a new one. As Twerski emphasises in his video, "the stimulus for the lobster to be able to grow is that it feels uncomfortable". Humans, just like lobsters, he argues, "can grow through adversity" (one assumes he means psychologically, rather than physically).

Rather than retreating under a rock, adopting a micro-experiment method is a more beneficial approach to your compassionate leadership development. Again, rather than seeking an 'answer', be content to curiously explore. See what works for you and what does not, and whether the results vary by context. Keep adapting, trying different approaches and reflecting. Remember that micro experiments require us to have self-compassion when things go wrong. Even in the worst-case scenarios, reflection will allow learning to be gleaned from any experience, regardless of the outcome, and self-compassion will allow us to regroup and move forwards.

Awareness

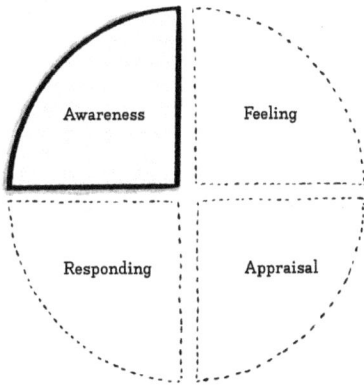

a) Building awareness

The first step of the new compassion construct is awareness. Simple awareness. Without this, we remain oblivious to others, and such ignorance is neither blissful nor useful. Awareness of suffering is necessary before the other steps of compassion can occur.

Building our self-awareness

Of course, as well as becoming aware of the suffering of others, we also need increase our capacity for self-awareness; noticing our own judgements and biases, and assessing our capacity for compassion. Blind spots distort our view, and such distortion is particularly prevalent when we have experienced success. Being vigilant to the blind spots we do not yet know about can be an uncomfortable exercise in humility.

Some of this self-awareness is in-the-moment, a fleeting observation, useful even if only to modify our immediate behaviours. Awareness can also be developed in a deeper, more considered way. Harvard's Implicit Association Tests (IAT) are a useful resource in this regard. Measuring an individual's beliefs and attitudes, these test results are particularly interesting as they often offer awareness of a previously unrecognised implicit belief. Tests are updated regularly, and include a wide range of areas such as gender, sexuality, age, religion, disability and skin tone. A link to these can be found in the Further Resources section.

Psychologist Robert Kegan notes that the accumulation of knowledge alone is insufficient for adult development and meaningful growth. Any transformation to 'higher' development requires us to not just learn new things, mindlessly collecting knowledge to add to other piles of knowledge. Rather, it requires careful self-reflection in order to uncover unconscious beliefs and allow changes in our perspectives. Kegan refers to this as the subject-object dance, where the subject is our unexamined beliefs and viewpoints – things which we are subjected to – while the objects are things we can critically evaluate, question and ultimately change. Our growth occurs as we transform more aspects of our unexamined subjects to become objects where examination, challenge and ultimately change become possible.

Kegan (1983) proposed six stages of development from the incorporative self and impulsive mind of early childhood through to the autonomous, inter-individual orientation, as illustrated in Figure 8.4.

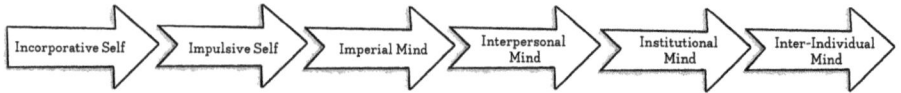

Figure 8.4: Theory of Adult Development (adapted from Kegan 1983).

Kegan considered these stages to be sequential, and argued that we could only make progress once we became aware of each successive stage. More recently, others have argued that these stages are not fixed, there is scant evidence that they are as sequential as we might hope, and we most likely move between them depending on changing contexts and interactions. Development, as ever, is not a straight line in an upward trajectory; applying the Kegan development phases most usefully involves noticing which stage we find ourselves in, and then deliberately transforming subjects to objects through critical reflection. Wherever we think we are, it is worth keeping in mind that we are probably at a lower stage than we might hope. The Blind Spot Bias and Superiority Illusion of Chapter 6 are useful reminders which may serve to keep us humble about our development. Indeed, Kegan suggests that less than 1% of the adult population will ever achieve the final stage. This last stage of the ever-evolving self, characterised by the willingness to question ourselves, to accept our changing multiple identities, and openness to multiple perspectives rather than seeking 'truth', is more an aspiration than a destination.

Regardless of our developmental stage, Kegan encourages us to critically self-reflect in order that we may grow and develop as adults. Awareness of the multifaceted nature and malleability of our concept of self can be a lifelong, liberating journey. Critical self-reflection can reveal our previously unseen biases and patterns of behaviour, and allow us to make more conscious choices. Reflection can make us more aware of our in- and out-groups; such awareness allows us to develop our compassion to be even more encompassing.

Such self-awareness is a fundamental part of metacognition: thinking about how we think and considering our typical thinking patterns. Cognitive neuroscientist Stephen M. Fleming argues that improving our self-awareness has a number of valuable leadership benefits; it improves our decision-making, makes us more alert to fake news and enables us to think more clearly when under pressure. "Just as a good conductor can make the difference between a routine rehearsal and a world-class performance, the subtle influence of metacognition can make the difference between failure and success in many aspects of life" (Fleming 2021, no page). Such nuance brings a greater level of understanding to leadership in the awareness step of the new compassion construct.

Building awareness through meditation

We can also build our self-awareness through meditation. According to Stephen M. Fleming (2022), it is through meditation that we develop our ability to focus on ourselves without distraction. This gives us more awareness of our own emotional and mental states, and can therefore make us more adept at understanding and managing ourselves. Such self-awareness allows us to recognise our own patterns, assumptions and distortions. This understanding has been shown to have tangible benefits including significantly improved exam results and having a more compassionate response to ourselves and to others.

Many different forms of meditation are available, from teacher-led approaches, readily available meditation apps, and even simply taking time each day to sit quietly and observe our breathing. Others, such as the loving-kindness meditation, have already been shared in Chapter 3. Trying out different approaches will help you to find whatever works best for you.

Building awareness through reflective and reflexive practices

Reflection is a useful leadership practice which enhances our self-awareness, self-care and personal growth. It is reflective practice which turns knowledge into wisdom. There is no one way to reflect, and development of reflective practice is very individual. Broadly, there are three main areas where reflection can focus:

1. Content reflection:
   What happened? What did I learn, either about myself or something else? What will I do differently as a result of this understanding?
2. Self-reflection:
   How am I showing up today? What am I choosing to keep hidden? How are my professional relationships, and why?
3. Assumption reflection:
   What biases, assumptions or judgements am I making? What do others notice about me, that I may not notice myself?

These three areas are not discrete, and reflective practice often alternates between them. Nor are they hierarchical. We do not move from content to self to assumption, and thus find that we have 'arrived'. Neurosurgeon Paul Kalanithi summed up this approach to reflective practice rather beautifully when, in the last few months of his life, he wrote: "you can't ever reach perfection, but you can believe in an asymptote towards which you are ceaselessly striving" (2016: 115). In addition to being a practice rather than a destination, these broad areas are all of equal importance; there is little benefit in examining our assumptions if we neither consider how they impact the content of our professional lives, nor how they change over time.

Methods of reflection can include discussion with others, potentially with some element of supervision, or regular reflective writing. The latter is often considered a particularly strong approach. The act of writing slows us down a little, so that we can explore more deeply than superficial, fleeting thoughts. A resulting written record can then provide further material upon which to reflect. Indeed, for some experts, "reflective writing *is* the reflective process, rather than just recording what has been thought" (Bolton 2014: 115, author's emphasis). To Bolton's mind, the process of reflective writing reveals not just the 'what' and 'how' of an event but also, crucially, the 'why'. This encourages reflection on beliefs and assumptions, rather than just experienced events.

Reflective practice can be as simple or complex, superficial or deep as we choose. Overall, its primary purpose is simply to make us curious about ourselves, and take time to consider possible answers from multiple perspectives – even, perhaps especially, uncomfortable ones. Questions and enquiry are more valuable and enduring than any definitive answers. Replacing judgement with curiosity will help us to move more subjects to objects, while examining our beliefs through reflection can help us to understand the rationale or events which lie behind them.

There is, however, a danger that introspection can lead to excessive rumination. To avoid this, as we explored in Chapter 2, it often helps to frame questions as 'what' rather than 'why' enquiries. This supports our reflection becoming a tangible action rather than aimless introspective musings and potentially harmful ruminations. Some examples of 'what' reflection questions might be:

> What do I dislike about my role? What am I missing as a leader? What would I think of me if I met me for the first time today? What assumptions do I hold about myself or others? What makes it hard for me to be compassionate? What stops me from taking action? What if I'm wrong?

Ultimately, although reflection can be difficult or uncomfortable, it allows us to know, connect with and develop ourselves in order that we might more effectively lead others.

> Mastering others is strength. Mastering yourself is true power.   (Lao Tzu)

Reflexive practice is also useful to build our awareness. It is the continual noticing, questioning and adaptation of occurrences in the moment, rather than after the fact. Reflexive practice requires us to question ourselves and the ways in which we impact and create the situations we find ourselves in. As well as supporting our understanding about the complexity of intertwined roles and relationships, reflexivity can increase our awareness of what has previously been unknown to us: how our attitudes, assumptions and actions impact others, and how they might have unwittingly helped create the cultural practices we claim to abhor. Such understanding moves us from being passive victims to becoming critical, active architects of more compassionate cultural systems.

Reflection takes the boat out of the water, checks it for damage and undertakes necessary, visible repairs. By contrast, reflexive practice is an awareness of broader current conditions, their impact, and our role in creating our context; it is more akin to critically assessing our own sailing ability whilst simultaneously adjusting to the prevailing winds. Neither reflection nor reflexivity is intrinsically better or more useful. They are equally necessary, and our ability to practice them both is a source of leadership strength and of personal growth.

b) Listening

Awareness requires us to listen to what is said and also to what is unsaid. If we can truly listen to both spoken and silent, then we can start to influence what is emerging, instead of only responding to what has already emerged.

Paying attention seems to be increasingly difficult as screens dominate our lives and keep us focused on doing rather than being. Nancy Kline (1999) defines listening as the quality of our attention for each other. Rather than giving commands or answers, she encourages us to support others in their thinking by listening to them, then listening more and then listening even more. When the other person claims that they cannot think of anything else to say about a subject, simply ask 'what else do you think about this?' and then listen again. Kline's premise is that the brain which holds the problem most likely also contains the solution, and that such skilful listening will enable the other person to explore this more deeply than any external 'solution' would. In a complex world, the leader of an organisation is almost the least likely to have the technical, detailed knowledge required to provide solutions. Instead, Kline's work encourages leaders to create an environment of deep listening and profoundly considered action.

Such listening has echoes in Thich Nhat Hanh's approach: 'deep listening is the kind of listening that can help relieve the suffering of another person. You can call it compassionate listening. You listen with only one purpose: to help him or her to empty his heart'.

Kline further reminds us that the expression on our face will convey to the other person our level of genuine interest. She notes, "your face matters. It can determine where people dare venture . . . remember that unconscious rigid nicey-nice is just as inhibiting of a person's thinking as unconscious rigid concern or impatience. The point is to be interested and show it. And not to be artificial. Be yourself, your truly interested, respectful, fascinated self" (1999: 44). To Kline's advice, we might add that when the other person is suffering, we can be our authentically compassionate self and allow that to be visible too.

Humble Enquiry

MIT Professor Edgar Schein (2013) encourages us to do less telling, more asking and to listen more fully. He calls this approach 'Humble Enquiry'. Showing an interest in the other person and their perspective, with humility and a genuine attitude of curiosity, will reap more relational benefits than a culture of 'do and tell'. Schein's advice for developing an attitude of humble enquiry is similar to some of the approaches to compassionate leadership: increased awareness of ourselves and others, appropriate pace and mindful awareness, developing a practice of self-reflection, and recognising the interconnected rather than hierarchical nature of our working cultures.

> It really boils down to this: that all life is interrelated. We are all caught in an inescapable network of mutuality, tied into a single garment of destiny. Whatever affects one directly, affects all indirectly.
> (Dr Martin Luther King Jr, Massey Lecture number 5, 'Christmas Sermon on Peace', Dec 1967)

Martin Luther King's speech was alluding to his approach of peace and non-violent protest, yet his words are equally applicable to compassionate leadership. Our world and the organisations we lead are increasingly uncertain and complex. Not only is change rapid and unpredictable, but in a globalised world there are an almost infinite number of interconnected and constantly changing factors at play. As organisations become more networked in response to these changes, our interconnectedness becomes increasingly apparent. As Psychoanalyst Erik Ericson noted, "Life doesn't make any sense without interdependence. We need each other, and the sooner we learn that, the better for us all" (in Goleman 1988).

Schein's approach of Humble Enquiry is especially useful in our interconnected world, particularly when we find ourselves caught up in conflict or suffering. The approach is deceptively simple: Find time and a neutral place to talk and, more importantly, to listen. The purpose is not for the other person to apologise, or accept that they are wrong and you are right, or for them to necessarily change their behaviour as a result of your feedback. The purpose is simply to understand a little more. Conflict is often down to difference in interpretation, and so understanding the other person's perspective can be a useful antidote. Seek to understand rather than to be understood. Keep your enquiry genuine and humble.

Checking in and checking out

Simple steps towards building our awareness through listening can be as simple as checking in and out of meetings. These are so effective that they have become a mainstay of elite sports teams and even some special forces units.

Too many meetings are focused entirely on task. If someone is struggling, they are unlikely to be able to concentrate on producing their best work. Focusing on task over people is a short-lived strategy doomed to failure. Focusing on people first makes it more likely that the work will follow.

A simple, effective approach to checking in and out is as follows:
- Take a few moments to silently check in on ourselves first. Consider: what am I bringing, what would I like others to know today?
- Then begin the check-in process:
  - Everyone speaks without interruption or comment
  - This is not group therapy, although it can be emotional; keep safe boundaries for yourself and others
  - Check-in does not have to be positive, it just has to be true. Remember that the leader will set the tone, so once the check-in routine is established within a team, it is therefore useful if leader checks in last
  - 'Fine' is not a feeling
- Check-ins may feel like a waste of time in a busy schedule, but people who feel seen, heard and understood are more likely to be able to focus, and more willing to engage. They help to build psychological safety, as trauma can occur when we

are neither seen nor known. The time taken to check in is quickly recompensed through high levels of team engagement and focus.

- Leaders may hear new information in check-ins, or notice what has been hinted at but not explicitly expressed. This awareness allows them to follow up on specifics afterwards.

- Checkouts at the end of a meeting are similar to check-ins, and they allow people to express feelings as a meeting draws to a close. This can be done in the same way as a check-in, or can be more rapid 'one word check outs'. Again, 'fine' is not allowed. Instead hopeful, concerned, overwhelmed, inspired ... these words and many others are far more useful in check-outs. And again, an adept leader will listen to the words used in check-outs, notice the way things are said or omitted, and will follow up where needed.

Feeling

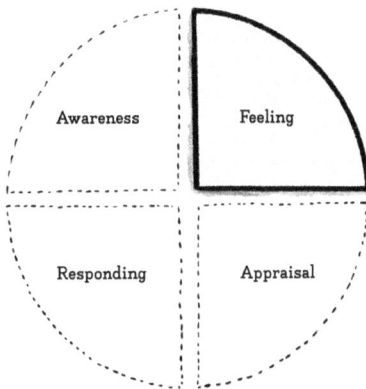

a) Emotions and contagion

The second stage of the new compassion construct is the feeling of an emotional response to suffering. Emotions are a crucial, often overlooked, area of leadership. To some, such emotions and feelings have no place in the modern organisation, lest they become a bleeding-heart liability. However, emotions are not something to be ignored or avoided, rather they should be noticed, allowed and respected.

We should accept that emotions can sometimes be painful. Procrastination, deflection, distraction, blame and even constant self-improvement are common ways in which people try to escape from their emotions. Indeed, Paul Gilbert suggest that the fear of receiving compassion from others is strongly associated with self-criticism, depression, anxiety and stress. It is unlikely that such fears are limited to the therapist's couch; they will also be present in the workplace.

Researchers such as Thomas Sy and colleagues (2005) have demonstrated that the emotions of leaders transfer to others in the organisation. This is true regardless of whether the emotions are positive or negative. In many ways, this is not entirely unexpected. As social beings, it may have been useful to transmit emotions even before the emergence of language. In modern-day organisations, this infectious 'emotional contagion' of leaders impacts the effort and subsequent performance of their teams. Put simply, colleagues either 'catch' their leader's positive emotions, which results in better team cohesion and improved outcomes, or pick up on negative emotions which has a detrimental effect on individual wellbeing and organisational outcomes. The power of a leader is not just in what they say or do, it is also transmitted in how they feel.

Ultimately, the emotions we emit as leaders involve choices and intentions. However, even if we choose a compassionate intention, things will still go wrong. We will sometimes become overwhelmed, miss signals, be misunderstood, judge or respond in anger. Uncritically following a compassionate path could blind us to our own misplaced but well-intentioned blunders. It remains easier to see the faults in others, so we must remain wary of virtue. Writer and philosopher Alan Watts, in his wonderfully titled lecture 'The Road to Hell is Paved with Good Intentions' (no date) noted that "we can look back on those people and see how evil that was, but we can't see it in ourselves . . . so therefore, beware of virtue".

b) Building emotional intelligence

Emotional Intelligence (EI or EQ), Daniel Goleman's (1996) popular approach to recognising, evaluating and managing emotions, divides critics. Some argue that it is an ill-defined, unmeasurable construct (Davies et al. 1998). Some measures of EI which examine self-perception of personality traits are often reliant on well-established psychometrics, leading to other criticisms that the EI Emperor has simply draped his garments over less easily digestible, well-established personality assessments (Harms and Crede 2010).

Regardless, an overwhelming body of evidence shows that such actions as developing leadership awareness, self-management and management of others are important for the wellbeing of individuals and health of organisations. Indeed, a recent meta-analysis has shown that so-called EI may be twice as important than general mental ability for entrepreneurs to be successful (Allen et al. 2021).

We have already explored a number of ways in which leaders can build this emotional intelligence. Meditation allows us to become more aware of ourselves and to assess how we are showing up. Checking in with ourselves frequently, even silently, brings more awareness to what we might be transmitting to others. Self-compassion practice enhances our positive, contagious emotions and improves our emotional regulation. Such regulation supports our recovery from adversity, helps us to manage our emotions, and is a key skill in managing ourselves and others.

Appraisal

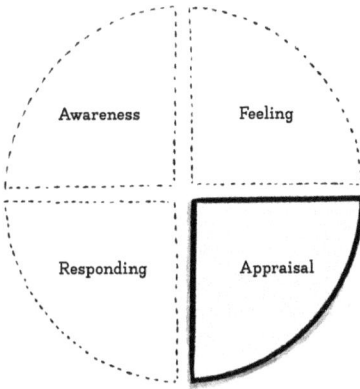

a) Role appraisal

Lead on compassionate responses

The new compassion construct encourages an appraisal of your role as leader. Keeping in mind Schultz's handling of the Starbucks shootings (Box 2.7), remember that you must lead when your organisation experiences suffering. Take advice from those around you – lawyers, PR, and others – by all means, but you simply cannot delegate an effective compassionate response. When a leader fails to lead on compassion, they create a vacuum in which the silence can become deafening.

Schultz tailored his responses to the tragedy, finding out what was most useful to those in need, rather than presuming to know or adopting a one-size-fits-all approach. When leading on a compassionate response, hold the appraisal step in mind. Remember that this step contains an appraisal of four parts: the situation to ensure a safe, appropriate, and well-intentioned response, your patterns of behaviour, your role in order that you lead most effectively, and your resources in order that you do not languish in empathy or tip into altruism.

Look for themes

When we begin to notice the need for compassion, it can become overwhelming. In your role as leader it is impossible for you to be everywhere at once.

Therefore, your compassion needs a strategic approach so that you can effectively address common themes which require a compassionate response. Look for patterns: are there particular roles or teams where suffering seems more prevalent? Are there periods in a calendar year or business cycle which seem more difficult than others? It is important to look for what is not said or what is stifled. A team who feels psychologically safe may be more open in sharing their troubles than a team where fear of retribution is the norm, so do not take results at face value. Another important consideration is where teams have significant issues, we should not leap to judgement and retribution. The leader of a struggling team may themselves be suffering, and a compassionate approach which seeks to understand their challenges may yield better results than one which favours blame and reckoning.

b) Intention and judgement

The dangers of healyitis

Be mindful that an understanding of compassion and its power may result in a bad case of 'healyitis'. The condition is fictitious but its symptoms are not. They include a strong belief that some understanding and a noble intention bestow upon us the right to intervene. This condition is a dangerous one, and the best immediate remedy is to remind ourselves of Karpman's Drama Triangle within the compassion appraisal step. Beware the allure of the rescuer role.

For longer term treatment, the best medicine is to continue to work on yourself more than on anyone else. Include self-compassion in your practice, not just that which is focused on others. Remember that the three elements of self-compassion – mindfulness, common humanity and self-kindness – are the foundation for this practice. Use self-compassion meditations to develop this understanding further, as well as reducing stress and anxiety. Continue building your self-awareness and seeking out dissent. Hope, without expectation of results, that your practice will develop into a compassionate role model in the image of Schultz, Ardern or Weiner.

Carl R Rogers, founder of the humanistic psychology movement and person-centred therapy, provides a useful perspective lest we think that a bout of healyitis means that we can now 'fix' people. Rogers believed that people are best placed to understand themselves and fulfil their own potential, rather than have expertise bestowed upon them by another. To Rogers, everyone has a natural inclination towards personal growth, and this can be facilitated through compassion and, as already discussed, Unconditional Positive Regard. People do not require to be fixed or improved. Instead, psychologically holding someone with compassion and without judgement allows them to do their own inner work, should they choose to:

> People are just as wonderful as sunsets if I can let them be. In fact, perhaps the reason we can truly appreciate a sunset is that we cannot control it. When I look at a sunset . . . I don't find myself saying, 'Soften the orange a little on the right hand corner, and put a bit more purple along the base, and use a little more pink in the cloud colour'. I don't do that. I don't try to control a sunset. I watch with awe as it unfolds. (Rogers 1980: 22)

Even our best intentions can be dangerous. As Alan Watts noted, "the reason you want to be better is the reason why you aren't" (no date). Much like the pursuit of happiness can lead to increased levels of frustration and angst, an endless pursuit of self-development can be the very thing which gets in the way of our personal growth.

Similarly, an intense focus on compassionate leadership might easily tip into excessive altruism, or may become forced or inauthentic. Watts's warning serves to remind us that our desire to leave a compassionate legacy might be precisely what gets in the way of us doing so. We should hold our intentions both consciously and lightly. Our desire to be a compassionate leader should not distract us from practicing compassionate leadership.

Still, whilst remembering Watts's advice, the intention to be compassionate can be a powerful one. We can intentionally select a motivation to relieve suffering, and through deliberate practice we can impact our brain's functioning and our subsequent behaviours. Our daily decision-making is manipulated by a myriad of internal and external, intentional and passive influences. We may never entirely escape from these, but we can choose a compassionate intention as a consistent backdrop to the acts on our daily stage. Such a staging can provide us with the space in more difficult moments to choose how we respond, rather than to react.

Responding

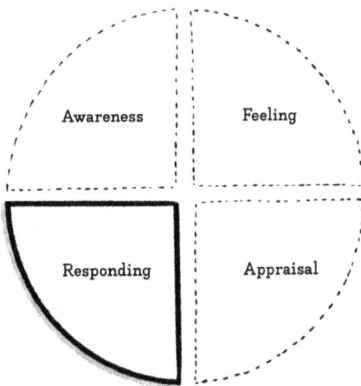

a) Compassionate habits

Refining our approach in all of the areas above will support with the last step in the new compassion construct: responding. Awareness of ourselves and of suffering, keeping the contagion of emotions in mind, and choosing well-resourced appropriate responses will take us a long way on the path towards compassionate leadership.

Sometimes, though, we could do with a little help. BJ Fogg (2020) in his 'Tiny Habits' approach recommends building new habits onto existing ones, rather than just trying to add more into your already busy schedule. For example, if you want to do more sit-ups each day, build these onto an established habit and so do them every time you brush your teeth. Similarly, build compassion into what is already in your existing schedule, in whatever way this works for you. This can be as simple as establishing check in and check outs into current regular meetings, deliberately spending more time each week noticing and responding to suffering, including compassion in regular senior discussions, or consciously building compassion into the existing employee lifecycle.

Building compassion into routines will not only make them easier to practice, it will result in a consistency which will promote trust. No organisation or leader can simply decide that they are now compassionate, and thus make it so. Compassion, like trust, is millions of small actions and moments, and – also like trust – is easily shattered.

b) Tracking your progress

The phrase 'what gets measured gets done' is overused, and not entirely accurate, but it serves as a useful prompt. Compassionate leadership is not always easy. Sometimes, it can feel frustratingly futile, akin to arriving at the aftermath of a volcanic eruption holding only a dustpan and brush. Our impact or progress can be impossible to see. Remember, although our impact may never be visible to us, how it feels for others is perhaps a more important outcome.

This is where the measurement of compassionate leadership is useful. Establishing a benchmark allows us to draw a mark in the volcanic ash near the beginning of our journey. Measuring our progress can build momentum and keep us sustained during difficult periods.

In the next chapter, we will explore the measurement of organisational compassion, designed to give an understanding of what issues there are and where support is needed most. In this chapter, we will briefly mention some of the measures useful for developing our own compassionate leadership.

Remember, resulting scores are not a compassion badge to wear ('I'm a 3.6 on compassion for others'), but rather provide benchmark information and prompt further consideration. A wider view which includes a general trajectory of progress is more useful than a narrow focus on absolute scores. The questions contained within the measures serve as a useful impetus for reflection, to consider what is easier or more difficult for you.

The scales outlined below are all designed to measure aspects of compassion, and all have strong validity and reliability.

a) Self-compassion Scale
(Raes et al. 2011)
There are short and long versions of Neff's Self-Compassion scale, both of which measure how we typically treat ourselves in times of difficulty. The user answers either twelve or twenty-six questions on a 5-point scale from 'almost never' to 'almost always'. Questions are based on the three aspects of self-compassion: self-kindness, mindfulness and common humanity.

b) **Compassionate Engagement and Action Scale**
(Gilbert et al. 2017)
Gilbert offers three scales which together measure self-compassion, compassion for others and compassion from others. Again, a numerical scale is used to answer thirty-nine statements about how we typically feel and behave in difficult situations.

c) **Fears of Compassion Scale**
(Gilbert et al. 2011)
This scale looks at aversion or fear of compassion, including giving compassion or being a recipient of it. Comprised of thirty-eight short statements, again the user simply notes their answer on a 5-point scale.

d) **Compassionate Love for Humanity Scale**
(Sprecher and Fehr 2005)
The twenty-one questions in this scale are designed to measure compassion for wider humanity, not just those known to or close to us. Questions are necessarily wide-ranging and include aspects of our feelings, thoughts and behaviours towards others. If time is of the essence, a shortened version of this scale is available, the Santa Clara Brief Compassion Scale (Hwang et al. 2008).

e) **Friendship Compassion and Self-Image Goals Scale**
(Crocker and Canevello 2008)
This fascinating scale examines compassionate and self-image orientations; the former is concerned for others and enhance relationships, while the latter construct our image and can be detrimental to relations with others. We might want to be compassionate, yet most of us also care about how we are perceived and how we therefore present ourselves to the outside world. High self-image scores are associated with more seeking of validation from others and defensive reactions to conflict. Higher compassion scores, by contrast, are associated with increased levels of self-compassion and a more growth-orientated mindset.

There are many other scales which may be useful associated areas for consideration, such as the Social Safeness and Pleasure Scale (Gilbert et al. 2009) and the Perceived Stress Scale (Cohen et al. 1983). Of course, in all of these scores, there is no 'right' or 'wrong'; there is simply difference. Being curious about our results and what they might indicate is a more useful approach than that which focuses on a numerical result.

Compassionate leadership results

In many ways, there is no truly visible 'result' from compassionate leadership. There are positive side effects and there may be unintended consequences for both individuals and organisations. Most of all, though, the process of compassionate leadership, even more so than its incidental positive side-effects, is perhaps its own reward.

The key to progress is to start small. Get comfortable in the water, then learn how to swim before you leap into the deep end. Remain wary of ever thinking you have mastered compassion. Remember the warning in Chapter 4 about leadership propensity for hubris? Stay humble instead. The Zen Buddhism concept of *Shoshin*, or 'beginner's mind', is a useful antidote to the arrogant closed-mindedness of anything approaching expertise.

Leadership in the firing line

Being compassionate to people who we care about is typically easier to do than finding compassion for those who annoy or upset us. Even Einstein acknowledged this difficulty, noting that we tend to reserve our care for those closest to us, yet imploring that we should challenge ourselves to extend our compassion to all living things. In some ways, we should be grateful to those who upset and offend us, as they are offering an opportunity to practice our compassion. If we only ever experienced a world of kindness and joy, and somehow managed to avoid all anger and hurt, we would be limited in our capacity for empathy, that ability to stand in another's shoes which is the crucial building block for compassion. As we saw in Chapter 6, some of the most well-known compassionate role models experienced significant adversity in their earlier years. Indeed, some emerging research even suggests that trauma in childhood can lead to higher levels of compassion in adulthood (Greenberg et al. 2018).

Our imperfections are an important source of our shared humanity and our capacity for compassion. The practice of feeling compassion for someone even when they will not, or cannot, share their pain with us is simultaneously useful and humane. Sunsets during a tempest are just as beautiful as those reflected in millpond seas.

Feeling compassion for those who hurt us or who are angry with us, though, is easier said than done. As leaders, we will often feel the brunt of frustrations when the organisation cannot or will not meet individual expectations. Pay rises. Restructures. Career progression. Even with the best intentions (remember those dangerous things?) these are just some of the areas prone to subjectivity and frustration in any organisation.

What can a compassionate leader do in such circumstances?

Calmness: notice your own physiological responses when the amygdala hijack occurs. This typically includes anger and an increase in heart and breathing rates. Our bodies are getting themselves ready to escape from a tiger; we need to reassure ourselves that there is no such predator. When the amygdala starts taking control, breathe deeply a few times. If needs be, remove yourself from the situation until you regain your composure and until your prefrontal cortex (PFC) is back in the driving seat of your brain. As well as being the area of the brain associated with complex planning and decision-making, the PFC also allows us to moderate our impulses and control our behaviour. Having your PFC in control will allow you to choose an appropriate response, rather than react in fear or anger.

Curiosity: Curiosity and connection are more useful responses than animosity and anger. Yet our curiosity can shut down when someone upsets us or we feel under attack. Once we have our prefrontal cortex back in control, we can allow ourselves to be curious. What is happening in the other person's life which is influencing their current behaviour? Is this a pattern of behaviour or an isolated incident? None of this means that people have a carte blanche to behave in whatever way they want to, nor does it mean that you have to excuse everything just because you have a curious, compassionate perspective. What it does mean is that you are less likely to fan the flames of anger, and that you can meet the behaviour with calm curiosity rather than anger or judgement. Such cognitive empathy allows us to consider another perspective, rather than insist that we are 'right' and the other is 'wrong'.

Emotional empathy is also a useful response. This allows us to treat the other person as a human, not as a human embodiment of whatever annoys us. This does not require us to psychoanalyse them or to create hypotheses about their early life. It simply requires us to consider that they may be under pressure or that they might be having a bad day. Everyone suffers, it is just when, how and why that differ.

Reflection on ourselves is often a good place to start when we find ourselves in difficult circumstances. Why do we react the way we do? What is it about the other person's behaviour that we find bothersome, when others might find it less irksome? Is it that we do not want to be challenged? Or that we find their approach too similar to that of someone we prefer to avoid?

What lies beneath: Underneath anger there is often fear. In their memorable 2011 'Life Story' advert, UK children's charity Barnardo's showed a retrospective on a happy young man, Michael. Flashback snapshots of his life story show him as an angry teen, a frustrated tween, and a confused child. As the advert finishes, the youngest iteration of Michael looks directly into the camera and whispers "I'm scared". Compassion for those in the grip of anger may allow a deeper exploration or release from the reason for their behaviour; the presenting issue is never the issue. The Barnardo's strapline on this advert was that "it doesn't have to end like it began". Compassionate responses to suffering can make this hope a reality.

Same Yet Different
Take a moment to consider what you notice about the coins shown in Figure 8.5.

Figure 8.5: Two coins.

Did you notice that they are the same denomination? Or that they are facing in different directions? We can choose to focus on our differences or on our similarities. The things we dislike in others are often what we reluctantly see in ourselves. We are more similar than we might like to admit. If we find someone to be annoying or rude, they might equally consider us to be the same way. Find some common ground, even if it is that your clash stems from the same roots of frustration or exhaustion.

Searching for similarity, rather than for difference, is especially useful when faced with in-group bias or conflict. Awareness of in- and out-groups, and remembering that the other people also suffer, reminds the compassionate leader of the interconnectedness and inevitable suffering contained in the human existence.

Finding similarities is easier to do before discord erupts. A simple ice-breaker which has been successfully used in many corporate and volunteering organisations is to ask pairs of people to find three things in common with each other. The only rule is that it cannot be 'we are both at this event today' or 'we work in the same building' or similar. Answers have ranged from birth order in families, favourite TV shows, a shared, intense dislike of peanut butter, and many more. Despite our disagreements, no-one is entirely right or wrong, good or bad. Sorting for similarity can help us to remember to see people more fully when differences of opinion inevitably occur. We always have more in common than we might realise.

Our compassionate leadership legacy

Much as our camera phones have portrait, panorama or close-up settings, we can adapt our practical understanding of compassion to suit a specific context. As leadership moves away from notions of 'individual great man' leadership into more networked, less hierarchical organisational and cultural systems, we can co-create our future through our collective and individual actions and intentions. A hundred small compassionate acts may be more impactful and sustainable than an occasional grand deed. Leaders need to be clear on what they are seeding their interconnected, networked organisational systems with. The actions we take today support the change of tomorrow. Compassionate leadership can move our organisations forward to a more sustainable future for all.

If all this seems like hard work, consider this. The purpose of leadership is not necessarily to be powerful. Perhaps instead, it is to be good rather than great. To be compassionate, to know yourself sufficiently to be able to make a positive difference to the suffering of others, whilst accepting that you will most likely never really understand your impact.

When it comes to compassionate leadership, practice does not make perfect. Even if there was such thing as a perfectly compassionate human, the weight of such unbearable virtue would be crippling. It is feasibly more useful to "accept oneself as a stream of becoming, not a finished product" (Rogers 1961: 122).

Instead, an aspiring compassionate leader might do well to remember the adage, 'there is no way to compassion, compassion is the way'. Conscious, intentional, yet lightly held practice of compassion is more effective and enduring than any attempt at reaching a compassionate destination. Buddhist monk Shunryu Suzuki had a useful perspective on practice, advising that it should be entirely inclusive and encompassing. This echoes the call made above to widen our in-groups as much as possible: "real practice has no purpose or direction, so it can include everything that comes" (Suzuki, attrib.). Such a lack of 'purpose or direction' does not necessarily mean have no intent, but rather to widen our view beyond what is familiar and obvious, and to allow room for all that we experience. All the experiences we can open ourselves to – even, nay particularly, the difficult or painful ones – are useful. They provide rich material for reflection, and thus for our integration and personal growth. From such richness, our compassionate leadership can grow and thrive.

Key Chapter Points
- Compassionate leadership impacts organisations in many different ways. Grounded in evidence-based research from psychology, behavioural change and other disciplines, the key to this chapter is practice.
- Compassion is innate, yet can become obscured. We can increase our awareness, unlearn some unhealthy habits and refocus our efforts on human-centred leadership.
- Leadership intention and choice are of significant importance due to the contagion of emotions and the disproportionate power of leadership.
- A compassionate approach integrates other skills, models and experience of leadership and development – some of these are discussed in more detail, including Theory of Adult Development, Humble Enquiry, Time to Think and Rogers' person-centred approach.
- Leadership and organisational performance are inextricably linked. Developing compassionate leadership is impactful for the individual leader, their employees and the organisational bottom line.
- We also explored some of the benefits of compassion to leadership when in the firing line. These included the ability to stay calm and curious, seeking to understand more fully and accepting difference.

Chapter 9
Designing a compassionate organisation

Managing compassionately is not just a better way to build a team, it's a better way to build a company.
(Jeff Weiner, CEO, LinkedIn)

True compassion is more than flinging a coin to a beggar; it comes to see that an edifice which produces beggars needs restructuring.
(Dr Martin Luther King Jr)

Greater than the sum of parts

As we saw in the previous chapter, there is much a compassionate leader can do in terms of their considered, intentional practice and response to suffering. Research clearly shows us that compassionate leaders reap individual psychological and physiological benefits, as well as bringing these to the people they work with.

However, an organisation cannot be truly compassionate on the actions of its leaders alone. Such an unsupported structure would teeter from over-reliance on these individuals, neither supporting nor augmenting their efforts. An organisation which is designed for compassion supports its leaders in their practice and allows compassion to be clearly experienced and amplified.

Back in 1983, Philosophy Professor and medical ethics expert Gregory Pence wrote about the teaching of compassion. He noted that the shape of an organisational system and the environment or culture it supports are more important to the development of compassion than any one individual:

> Compassion can indeed be taught if systems of medical education reward this virtue alongside other medical virtues such as diagnostic skill and factual command, but merely to rely on the efforts of a few individuals to transmit compassion – however prestigious and tireless they may be – is to forsake compassion as a characteristic of excellence. (Pence 1983: 191)

With this in mind, this chapter focuses on practical, evidence-based ways to create and develop a compassionate organisation. Creating such a structure simultaneously supports the efforts of leaders to be compassionate and reinforces their individual compassionate practice. In this way, compassion relies less on a handful of compassionate leaders, and is instead an integral part of organisational structure and systems.

The approaches to create a compassionate organisation are clustered into four main areas: strategic, structural, cultural and behavioural, with subsections as illustrated in Figure 9.1. Once we have explored these in some detail, we will briefly discuss the measurement of compassion in organisations.

https://doi.org/10.1515/9783110763126-009

Strategic	Structural	Behavioural	Cultural
Moral Psychology Q: Is IQ valued more than EQ? A: Compassion explicitly incorporated into ESG	**HR Policies & Employee Lifecycle** Q: Where is compassion integrated well, and how can this be widened? A: Ensure compassion included in formal policies	**Behavioural Change & Nudges** Q: What possible unintended consequences might nudges produce and what will you do? A: Use nudges, create more, and enable volunteering	**Psychological Safety & Trust** Q: What undermines safety? A: Seek out and thank dissenting voices
Building Commitment Q: What in & out groups exist, and how can these be integrated? A: Conscious, consistent appreciation	**Responses, Resources & Reward** Q: How to best reward compassion in a sensitive manner? A: Use the compassion blueprints to frame leadership discussion	**Leadership Opportunities for All** Q: Where would formalised training reap most benefit? A: Extend basic, opt-in compassion training to all employees	**Culture** Q: Does your organisation reward resonant or dissonant leadership? A: Ensure leaders are clear on compassionate expectations and role modelling

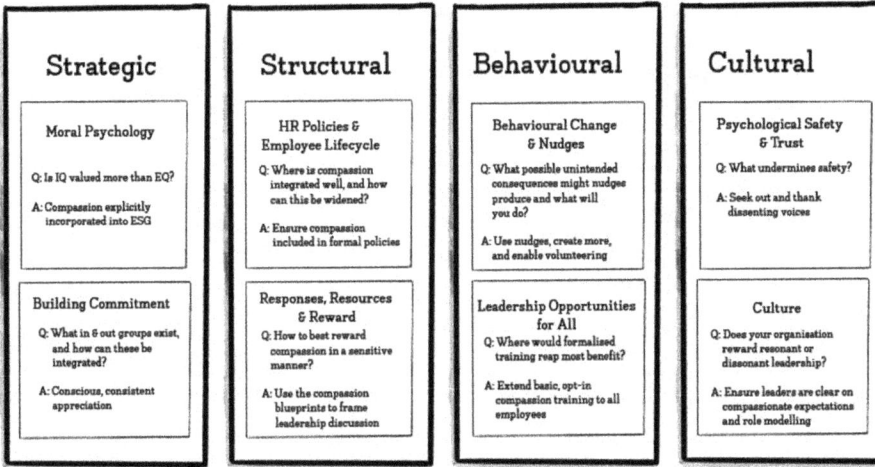

Figure 9.1: Areas for consideration in designing a compassionate organisation, with some questions (Q) and actions (A).

As we explore these areas, it is useful to keep in mind some lessons from improv theatre. Fully formed solutions stop progress, whereas numerous different, small contributions are more useful and so should be actively encouraged. Multiple, tiny, individual acts allow the emergence of something collaboratively formed and durable. In creating a compassionate organisation, it is not only for leaders to set the tone and direction, it is also for each individual to actively participate. As the improv mantra urges us: bring a brick, not a cathedral.

Strategic

The moral psychology of business

In Chapter 4, the importance of compassion in Adam Smith's *Theory of Moral Sentiments* was noted, although Smith is better known amongst economics students for his praise of free enterprise. Smith never overtly related his approach to morals with his foundation stone of capitalism, so it is not surprising that these often remain as distant cousins, sometimes barely on speaking terms. Philosopher and business ethicist Robert C. Solomon, in his 1998 essay 'The Moral Psychology of Business: Care and Compassion in the Corporation' noted that the issue with such estrangement was that it allows organisations to operate without either emotional engagement or consideration of the wider world. Solomon, and many others since, have argued the case for a clear-eyed assessment of business ethics, in order that organisations are responsible for what they do and how they do it.

Nowadays, consumers and Governments are increasingly holding organisations to account. Environmental, Social and Governance (ESG) frameworks are no longer a tick-box exercise; they are integral to how organisations operate and how brands are perceived. The general consensus amongst investment analysts is that well-established ESG factors lead to improved returns. Indeed, McKinsey (2019) have argued that ESG not only improves organisational top line growth, it also reduces costs and expensive legal interventions, increases employee productivity and optimises investments. Robert Solomon died in 2007, but he would likely be encouraged by the increasing scrutiny of business ethics and the continued movement of social enterprises and ESG measures from the periphery to the mainstream of many modern-day economies. Organisations can no longer consider moral sentiments as academic or irrelevant. Compassion needs to be an integral part of a well-considered ESG strategy.

It is interesting to note that Solomon considered compassion to be an essential pre-requisite of management, despite pervasive rhetoric about leadership toughness. He noted that whilst being efficient and effective are, of course, important skills for management, without compassion there will likely be a distinct lack of loyalty or enthusiasm from employees. Indeed, Solomon went so far as to say that "compassion without intelligence is no virtue, but intelligence without compassion is not good management" (1998: 530).

Building commitment through compassion

Earlier, in Chapter 5, I outlined my research on Organisational Compassion (OC) and Affective Commitment (AC) and noted why these matter to organisations. We shall now examine how can we enhance both.

Developing OC, as we will see in this chapter, permeates everything from leadership behaviours to formal policies and psychological safety. According to research by Christian Grund and Krystina Titz (2022), AC can be enhanced through an increase in available training and perceived support for employee personal development. This could partly be explained with reference to Social Exchange Theory, where we essentially do a conscious or unconscious cost-benefit analysis before deciding whether or not to continue with an association. Examples of such social exchange assessments could be of friendships where one person works harder to maintain the relationship, or of colleagues where the downsides of difficult behaviour are considered bearable in light of individual contribution. Under Social Exchange Theory, an organisation which invests in its people is effectively making a deposit into the 'goodwill fund' which can be drawn on at a later stage, if required.

Such goodwill is also fostered through appreciation. This can be as simple and informal as leaders thanking people for their efforts; recognising effort more than outcome is a useful nuance which encourages a growth mind-set approach. The more specific the thanks, the more it will resonate with the recipient and the clearer you will be about desired future behaviours: there is a world of difference between a generic 'thank you for all your efforts' and 'thank you, Anna, for all your efforts in engaging the stakeholders about this proposed change. A number of them mentioned to me that you listened well, took their concerns into consideration, and followed up with resolutions'.

Appreciation can be embedded in a networked way throughout an organisation, not just through leadership recognition. Teams who regularly practice 'shout-outs' of recognising individual impact amongst their peers report high levels of AC and engagement. More formal recognition can be enhanced via virtual or physical 'shout-out' boards, as well as though employee recognition programmes and awards.

Recognition, either from leaders or colleagues, and whether formal or informal, increases AC and is considered to be a major factor in self-reported happiness at work. Do not be fooled by the apparent simplicity of recognition. The consistency, specificity and personalisation of recognising compassionate acts all determine the impact of appreciation. Sometimes the smallest things have the greatest resonance. Recognition of suffering is an important consideration for organisational AC; we have already discussed this with reference to Employee Assistance Programmes in Chapter 5.

Leaders need to ensure their commitment-building efforts include all employees. Therefore, another strategic priority which requires a compassionate lens includes those designed to improve Inclusion and Diversity (I&D). I&D policies and practices are both strategic and operational; they are not something to be left to chance. McKinsey reported in 2020 that 39% of respondents had declined an offer of employment because they thought that the organisation lacked a truly inclusive environment. This figure rose to 44% of women, 45% of ethnic minorities and 50% of LGBTQ+ respondents.

The very core of I&D requires our empathic ability to put ourselves in the shoes of another, plus compassionate action to alleviate suffering and avoid exclusion. Of course, organisations require a robust I&D approach, aligned with clear policies and demonstrable action. They also need employees to understand their own biases and judgements, and how these might be contributing to issues of inclusivity.

As outlined in Chapter 6, compassionate leaders need to become more aware of their biases and their in- and out-groups, so that they can truly start to understand suffering from another perspective. Such introspection and understanding is, however, not limited to those in leadership positions. Everyone in an organisation should be supported to examine their judgements and biases, ideally though careful, facilitated exploration. Only when such understanding becomes commonplace will true progress be made to match lofty I&D rhetoric. As LinkedIn's former CEO Jeff Weiner said to a Wharton graduating class (2018):

> By breaking free of our own tribes, even if only for a moment, and seeing things through the lens of people unlike ourselves, we can begin to close the gaps, whether they be socio-economic, racial, gender, political or otherwise.

Structural

HR policies and the employee lifecycle

Policies and practices can be thought of as the formal and informal ways, respectively, in which an organisation operates. Policies refer to the more formal structures and processes in an organisation, whilst practices are defined here as the more informal occurrences which include communication, informal interactions and management flexibility around formal policies. Bringing these together gives a balance of structure and flexibility, so that managers are supported yet have more discretion than they do red tape.

Policies, as the more formal expressions of and approaches to compassion, need to be clearly articulated and available to all; that everyone knows that they exist and can access them is in itself an important foundation of a compassionate structure. Ideally HR policies should be accessible without anyone having to ask for them, such as on an internal organisational web page. Everyone suffers, but not everyone will be forthcoming about this. Widely available compassionate policies will allow people to find the support they need in the way that best suits them and without forcing disclosure.

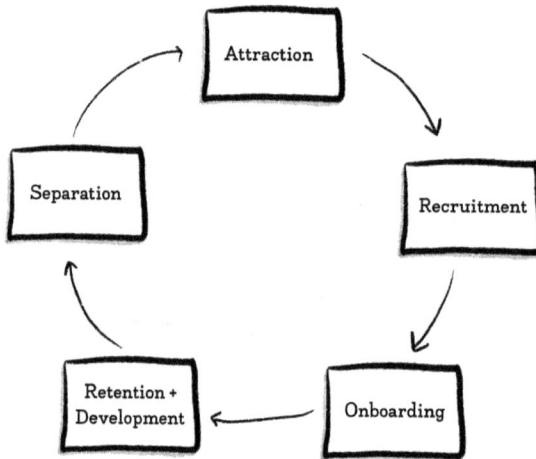

Figure 9.2: Employee lifecycle.

There are obvious occasions when compassion is an appropriate response to suffering, such as when an employee experiences the death of a close family member. Compassionate policies, however, should be available for less extreme situations and are ideally implemented throughout the employee lifecycle, shown in Figure 9.2. During job design, advertising and recruitment, the compassionate aims of the organisation can be stated, roles can include explicit responsibility for the wellbeing of self and others, and candidates who are unsuccessful can be treated with dignity. Time is precious, yet giving feedback to such candidates may make a significant difference to the disappointed individual, as well as reflecting well on the organisation.

For appointed candidates on-boarding is a crucial time to set a compassionate tone and expectations, as well as for the organisation to hear fresh perspectives and ideas. During my OC/AC research interviews, one of the respondents commented favourably on the post-hire policy within his organisation. This included conversations each quarter for the first year with HR, focusing on his opinions about the organisation, any area he was struggling with and offering suggestions for improvements. Becoming aware of issues in this structured way was a first step towards compassion and change.

Personal development is, as we have already seen, an important precursor for Affective Commitment (AC). Such development can include formalised compassion training, as explored later in this chapter, both for line managers and others. In organisations where such interventions take place, AC levels increase and employees often report that the new compassion construct and common language around compassion make potentially difficult conversations easier to handle.

If we want to retain employees, we need to notice when they are struggling or disengaged at work. Compassionate leaders can support individuals, understand underlying issues and simultaneously notice repeating patterns. Formal structures for support, for escalation and even for whistleblowing all provide necessary signposts that lead to compassionate action and employee retention.

Varying circumstances of departure from an organisation, whether voluntary or not, positive or otherwise, will necessitate different approaches. Even a difficult exit is best treated with compassion, as both the person leaving and those staying all fare better when departures are handled well. Exit interviews – alongside more proactive 'stay interviews' – are useful. Beginnings and endings require close attendance, so when an employee is leaving an organisation, whether through their own volition or otherwise, taking the time to hear their concerns is a useful individual and organisational investment. Compassion is a commercial approach even at this stage in the employee lifecycle, as engaged, positive organisational alumni can be a useful source of future talent, recommendation and opportunity.

Within the employee lifecycle, compassionate leave is increasingly common in organisations, and can be a useful 'catch all' policy for a myriad of situations. The need to recognise and address suffering has recently resulted in the introduction of compassionate policies covering shared parental leave, adoptions and miscarriages. Previously taboo subjects such as the physical and psychological impacts of the menopause have yet to become mainstream policies, but the tide is moving in that direction. If this suite of policies feels too difficult, too costly or too time consuming for an organisation, it is worth remembering the research which demonstrates that people who feel compassionately cared for in a time of need will generally recover more quickly (Post 2011). Furthermore, they will likely return with a renewed and improved sense of engagement and positive inclination towards the compassionate organisation. As noted by one of the participants in my OC/AC research:

Compassion can get people through issues more quickly, so it's a commercial decision to be compassionate.

The appraisal step in the new compassion construct is particularly useful when discussing organisational responses to difficulties within an employee lifecycle. Regardless of the source of the problems, an organisation can consider its role in the alleviation of suffering, whether or not to support and what the nature and extent of that support might be. Karpman's Drama Triangle is a useful consideration, in order that the organisation is not cast in the role of either prosecutor or rescuer, and that the employee is not treated as a victim. A thoughtful, compassionate response which is contextually appropriate and in the best interests of the suffering individual, whilst avoiding the Drama Triangle trap, is a more appropriate balance to seek.

Compassionate organisational responses, resources and reward

Desmond Tutu is widely attributed to have said 'There comes a point where we need to stop just pulling people out of the river. We need to go upstream and find out why they're falling in.' In this way, organisations need to create and maintain sufficient life-rafts, whilst also looking for patterns of suffering which can be addressed at their origin.

Monica Worline and Jane Dutton (2017) provide blueprints for designing such organisational compassion architecture. Their detailed plans encourage organisations to participate in self-rating and to have associated discussions across a number of compassionate capability areas. Working through these blueprints enables organisations to assess and improve their compassionate competence, leveraging their organisational strengths and addressing their compassionate gaps. A summary of Worline and Dutton's blueprints is outlined in Table 9.1, as a frame for senior leadership discussion and development of a compassionate organisation.

Discussing these areas, understanding where and why different perspectives exist, and examining both organisational strengths to be leveraged and gaps to be addressed are all useful considerations for senior leadership. Understanding these organisational attributes will allow for appropriate, timely compassionate responses when the need arises, rather than a rabbit-in-the-headlights reaction from a standing start. Such blueprint-facilitated discussions also serve as a leadership reminder about compassionate role modelling.

Rewarding compassionate action shows which behaviours are valued in an organisation. In this respect, reward does not necessarily imply a financial payment. Compassionate rewards can be as simple as a leader who has heard about a specific compassionate incident seeking out and thanking the person who took action to alleviate suffering. If this seems a rather basic leadership action, remember that this can have a disproportionate impact. In Adam Grant and Francesca Gino's studies (2010) on the behavioural impact of gratitude, employees whose leaders acknowledged and thanked them for their efforts saw a significant increase in the quantity and outcome of subsequent fundraising calls. Gratitude and reward will pay back handsomely.

Table 9.1: Compassionate Organisation Blueprints (adapted from Worline and Dutton 2017).

Capability	Area	Aim
Competence of Response	Speed	Quick to hear about and respond to suffering, and adapts response as needed over time
	Scope	Providing useful, targeted resources which can alleviate a broad array of suffering
	Magnitude	Has sufficient available resources to alleviate suffering of many kinds
	Customisation	Considering each individual person and situation in the response, rather than 'one size fits all'
Social Architecture	Networks	Many, networked clusters of people with high quality relationships
	Culture	Espoused and enacted values place an emphasis on the importance of people, not just profit
	Roles	People have autonomy, belonging, competence, and also share responsibility for looking after themselves and others
	Routines	Care about people is paramount in the way decisions are made
	Leadership	Leaders publicly value and role model compassion as a core competence in the organisation
	Stories	People hear and can easily recall stories of compassion it the organisation

Of course, rewarding compassion needs to be handled sensitively. What this means will vary by individual circumstance and preference, and should therefore allow for the discretion of practices. Not everyone wants their compassionate acts publicly lauded, and the person whose suffering prompted the action must be kept safe.

Again, compassionate leaders need to find balance. This time the balance is between remembering to seek out and reward or acknowledge compassionate acts, but without this practice becoming rigid or forced. Remember that authenticity, consistency and ownership are paramount when it comes to compassion. Do not become the leader who rewards compassionate acts at 3 pm every Friday afternoon because there is a reminder in your diary to do so, or one whose assistant emails a standard thank you note on your behalf.

Behavioural

Compassion, behavioural change and nudges

No matter what we say or do as leaders, people are more likely to remember how we made them feel. And people who feel supported and psychologically safe will perform better, work harder and stay with us for longer. Another truism of leadership is that others generally do not do what you tell them to, instead they do what they see you doing. Creating a compassionate context, role modelling the new compassion construct and seeding organisational systems with compassion through training, communication and reward will bring about the compassionate organisations we seek.

Such behavioural change can be further bolstered through applying nudges. Economist Richard Thayler and Legal Professor Cass Sunstein (2008) proposed that nudges are more likely to result in behavioural change than would education, coercion or requirement. Nudges were defined as the positioning of alternatives, framed in such a way that this would result in people making predictable choices without them feeling coerced. Thayler and Sunstein suggested that to be considered a 'nudge' any intervention would have to be both cheap and require minimal involvement from others.

Behavioural nudges are often considered more effective than cognitive rationale because choosing to do something will often be more impactful than being told what to do. A word of caution, though: although a recent meta-study found a strong relationship between nudges and behaviour overall, it also found that c.15% of nudges backfire, and inadvertently result in a reversal or reduction of the desired behaviour (Mertens et al. 2021). The most famous, if apocryphal, example of this is probably the Cobra Effect which took place in Delhi under British rule. Concerned about the prevalence of cobras, the British offered a financial reward for every dead cobra. It did not take long, however, for enterprising locals to consequently start breeding and then killing the snakes as a source of income. When the British realised this, they stopped the payments, and so the entrepreneurs released their now-worthless reptiles. Needless to say, the cobra population quickly became much larger than it had been originally. The moral of this story: nudges are useful, but remain vigilant to unintended consequences.

We can apply Thayler and Sunstein's nudge principles to building compassionate organisations. Five examples are listed below, yet the possibilities are endless. Be creative, develop more nudges for your organisation, and remember the guidelines: low cost and minimal intervention.

Compassion nudge 1: Bias & judgement

Bayeté Ross-Smith is an American artist whose work encourages us to consider our own judgements and preconceived notions about each other. One of his most famous series, *Our Kind of People* seeks to explore how gender, skin tone, race, ethnicity and even clothing impact our judgements about someone's character. The series shows a number of different people, with each person shown in six different outfits from their own wardrobe. Looking through the series prompts interesting feelings and questions about our own responses.

Ross-Smith's series can be used as a basis for conversation within an organisational workshop setting; please credit him as the artist. Choosing any one of the subjects, give each workshop participant a single photo from the six, without allowing anyone to see what the others have. Ask everyone to note down their observations about the person in their photo, what they would think if they met them at work and what they would think if this was the new partner of a close friend. After a minute or so, pair people up to compare their observations. Of course, at this point, they notice that the people are the same; only the clothing is different. The discussion to encourage is not about shame or blame, rather it is to encourage an exploration about what influences our perceptions – even something as simple as clothing – and what the implications of this might be. Noticing our preconceptions in this way is an opportunity to widen our circles of compassion.

Compassion nudge 2: Public commitments

As a leader, what are your commitments to compassion? Write them in your own messy, scrawled, flawed handwriting and make them visible, similarly to that shown in Figure 9.3. Doing this not only forces us to consider what compassionate actions we will take, but also gives clear permission for people to hold us accountable. We typically like to live up to our public declarations.

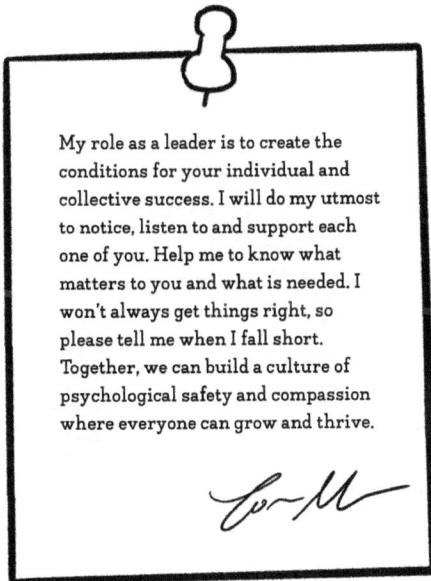

My role as a leader is to create the conditions for your individual and collective success. I will do my utmost to notice, listen to and support each one of you. Help me to know what matters to you and what is needed. I won't always get things right, so please tell me when I fall short. Together, we can build a culture of psychological safety and compassion where everyone can grow and thrive.

Figure 9.3: Public compassion commitment.

Compassion nudge 3: Inclusion

Particularly in the days of open plan offices and increased flexible working patterns, providing some large dining areas allows people to connect informally. Consider providing a 'conversation & connection' table for those who either do not know many people, or who would like to be introduced to new perspectives. Allow for both formal and informal gatherings so that people can share and be seen, and suffering might be more easily noticed and responded to.

Other nudges include operating a 'buddy' system for new starters, outside of their functional teams. Nudges can also include personalisation of diversity reporting through use of real-life individual stories and photographs alongside high level quantitative metrics; this will counteract our propensity for psychic numbing (Chapter 4) resulting in more understanding and positive action.

Compassion nudge 4: Belonging and connecting

Our deepest human need is to belong. Belonging is a basic emotional necessity, as we want to be accepted by others and to feel connected as social creatures.

Research on Dutch schoolchildren (Van den Berg and Cillessen 2015) found that pupils who sat in close proximity were more positive about each other, and that even animosity was somewhat neutralised by such daily physical closeness. These classroom learnings can be applied to the workplace, breaking down unconscious avoidances and encouraging more cross-collaboration. Other nudges which can support more connection and belonging are randomised coffee chats, which can be facilitated by simple online randomisers. Even choosing to sit at different desks or in unfamiliar open plan areas can support the expanding of connections and networks. Proximity fosters understanding and reduces out-groups.

Compassion nudge 5: Access

One of the most impressive CEOs I have ever worked with was one of the most accessible. Of course, like all CEOs, his day was crammed full of meetings, shareholder demands and unexpected problems. But every morning that he was in the office, he could be found in the staff canteen, drinking coffee and nonchalantly scanning a newspaper. Despite being the CEO of a telecoms company, his phone was nowhere in sight. Reading the newspaper was not strictly work, so people felt that they could interrupt him. Those who just wanted to say hello could do so as they walked past, and others who wanted a more in-depth discussion could sit with him and would be listened to. Not only did his employees feel seen and heard, they also knew that they had regular access to their CEO without having to seek this formally. Feeling seen increases our chances of pro-social behaviour and improves our sense of belonging. From the CEO's perspective, this was time well spent. Not only did he create a loyal, trusting workforce, but he also heard about concerns, issues and successes that he may otherwise not have been privy to, and could integrate these into his work. By keeping communication open in this simple way, he had established a pathway which could be easily accessed in times of suffering. Sometimes the simplest of actions reaps the greatest rewards.

Compassionate leadership opportunities for all

Compassionate leadership opportunities should not be restricted to those with the most senior job titles. A truly compassionate organisation will create a compassionate structure and opportunities for all. Some of the practices mentioned in the previous chapter, focused on leaders, can be adapted and disseminated more widely through-out an organisation.

Compassion training is useful in order to ensure that compassionate management is a cornerstone of the employee experience. A compassionate approach to perfor-mance issues will allow for less judgement, greater understanding and a more satis-factory resolution for all involved. Major life events and the impacts these have on people also require a compassionate approach.

Below are a selection of approaches to compassion training. Some are individual, others simple to implement organisationally, and lastly there are those which are more formalised.

Understand compassion and self-compassion constructs

The new construct of compassion (Chapter 2) and Neff's definition of self-compassion (Chapter 7) are cornerstones of this book. Referring back to these constructs, and practicing the exercises which help to strengthen them, is the simplest, yet most ef-fective, compassion training that organisations can provide. Through the understand-ing and lenses that these models offer, everyone in an organisation can actively consider their role in building organisational compassion, and can reflectively learn from their experiences.

Elke Smeets and colleagues (2014) ran an experiment where they held a short meeting once a week for only three weeks during which they taught an under-standing of what self-compassion is and how to improve it, much as outlined in Chapter 7. Their experiment found that this intervention produced significant in-creases in the self-efficacy, wellbeing and optimism of participants. Valuable out-comes for any organisation, and yet this intervention requires minimal time commitment for impressive results.

Training everyone in organisations about these constructs of compassion and self-compassion establishes a common language to facilitate conversation, and will help espouse the compassionate values which organisation wants to be held accountable for. Importantly, such training should introduce the models as a means for change. An organisation which wants to be truly compassionate needs to understand the gap between its espoused and enacted values, and plan its ac-tions accordingly.

Our Most Compassionate Friend

Some of the most powerful compassion training opportunities can occur when things go wrong, when we make mistakes, and when we fail to live up to our own standards. In these moments, rather than distracting ourselves, trying to bolster our self-esteem or blaming others, we will improve our personal and organisational outcomes if we can learn to treat ourselves the way that a friend would. The best friends do not necessarily always agree with you, but in times of need they will most likely show us more compassion than we typically show ourselves. This intervention involves a pause in order to ask ourselves what that compassionate friend might say to us. By encouraging our critical inner voice to have a more compassionate perspective, we are training our minds to practice self-compassion.

Compassion meditations

My research outlined earlier in this book showed the impact of self-compassion on leaders, resulting in reduced levels of depression, stress and anxiety. The simple meditation used in this study is available in Chapter 7. Making such resources available across organisations allows people to adopt as much or as little of these evidence-based interventions as they find useful.

In addition to self-compassion, Buddhist compassion meditations have also been shown to be impactful. Participants in a study by Helen Weng and colleagues (2013) used the phrase 'May you be free from suffering, may you have joy and ease' as they thought about other people. A control group were taught a positive cognitive reappraisal technique. Both groups listened to online guided instructions for around 30 minutes every day for two weeks. Afterwards, the researchers found two crucial differences between the groups. Firstly, the group trained in compassion were more financially generous to other people in need, including strangers, than the reappraisal group were. Secondly, when comparing fMRI scans done before and after the training, the researchers found that for the compassion group participants, there was increased activity in the brain regions associated with emotional regulation, positive emotions and understanding towards others. Again, this study highlights how a small investment of time offers a beneficial return to individuals and organisations.

Meditations can be short and easily integrated into busy days. Their impact is significant: reducing stress, allowing us to control our emotions, helping us to feel better and increasing our consideration for others. Such results are durable. Leah Shapira and Myriam Mongrain (2010) found that the impact of on-line self-compassion exercises continued to show a significant increase in happiness even after six months, alongside a significant reduction in depression which was sustained for up to three months after the training.

Much of the training noted above is self-directed and experiential in nature. Such self-directed change can be particularly formidable if supported by some of semi-formal interventions, such as ensuring a common understanding of what compassion is.

Formalised compassion training

In addition to the practices noted above, there are an increasing number of more formalised compassion training approaches available. Learning and development opportunities are increasingly valued by succeeding generations, and we have already noted the Affective Commitment benefits of offering training to employees. Luckily, compassionate leadership and training does not typically require silent retreats to mountain summits, and can have a fairly rapid impact. As we have already seen, even brief compassion interventions have impressive results in a short amount of time.

Some of the more formalised training available includes Compassion Cultivation Training, an eight-week general programme developed by Stanford University and Thupten Jinpa, and Cognitively-Based Compassion Training, developed by Emory University. Also useful, and freely available, are the Harvard Implicit Association Tests already mentioned in Chapter 8. Again, the sometimes-unexpected results and reflections these tests reveal are important, so ensure that there is time and space for these to be discussed. This can be as simple as informal lunchtime discussions or action learning sets where employees uncover practical, compassionate actions to address specific, complex organisational issues.

Volunteering for eudaimonic happiness

Volunteering allows employees to have impact beyond the organisation, to develop their leadership skills in a new context and to bring back valuable skills and perspectives to their workplace. Volunteering can reduce notions of 'them and us', thus fostering greater empathy, compassion and understanding, while also reducing out-groups.

Employees who volunteer enjoy a greater sense of belonging and achievement, improved job satisfaction and more positive wellbeing when compared with non-volunteers (Rodell et al. 2016). Doing something for others helps employees to recover from the demands of work, as such compassionate acts enhance individual positive emotions. There are clear organisational benefits, as employees who volunteer perform better at work and are more likely to display pro-citizenship behaviours towards their colleagues.

Box 9.1 encourages reflection and practical steps to enhance eudaimonic happiness in organisations.

> **Box 9.1**
> Practice eudaimonic happiness: volunteer, do something for others without expectation of reward, participate in random acts of kindness. What opportunities can you make available in your organisation?

In Chapter 5 we explored the notion of eudaimonic happiness, which was beneficial both psychologically and physiologically. Offering organisation-led opportunities for volunteering, such as team days doing something for others, or book drives for local schools, can make volunteering easy to opt into. Allowing employees time off to participate in their own preferred forms of volunteering will also result in the associated benefits. Be creative in your approach to compassion, and everyone in the organisation will reap the rewards of eudaimonic happiness.

Cultural

Psychological safety and trust

Understanding what psychological safety is and how it can be built allows leaders to effectively apply it across many different situations. The psychological safety required for dissent and to allow mistakes to be made without fear of reprisal are crucial for individual wellbeing and for organisational survival. One of the most famous examples of what can happen when such safety is missing is that of NASA and the space shuttle Colombia disaster of 2003. On take-off, a small piece of the shuttle broke off and hit the wing. NASA engineers discussed the likely impacts and requested to Mission Control that the wing tiles be assessed. They were not listened to, their concerns were disregarded, and many later reported that they did not feel that such dissenting voices were welcome. During re-entry two weeks later, the shuttle disintegrated, killing all seven astronauts on board. An investigation later found that the damaged wing was the most likely cause. Had the engineers' concerns been listened to and acted upon, disaster could have been avoided. Of course, poor psychological safety does not always have such dramatic or high-profile impacts. Yet corporate scandals such as Volkswagen Dieselgate, the fraudulent practices of Enron or the infamous lack of ethics at Lehman Brothers all illustrate the danger of silencing dissenting voices.

There are many ways to build psychological safety; mostly it is built over time and informally through a multitude of small actions and responses. Methods of developing psychological safety align closely with our new approach to compassionate leadership:

- When someone questions your actions, points out a mistake or offers challenging feedback, be thankful and appreciative that they are offering you a perspective on a potential blind spot. If you respond defensively or with anger, people will stop being open with you. At the very least, thank them for speaking up.
- Embrace a culture of compassionate candidness, respect and openness.
- Remember Unconditional Positive Regard. We all suffer, and it is a rare person who comes to work deliberately trying to do a bad job.
- Be clear and consistent in your expectations of others, both in terms of outputs and behaviours.
- Be open about your imperfections and mistakes, in order that these are openly role modelled for others in the organisation.
- Demonstrating self-compassion when you make mistakes is a worthwhile behaviour which improves resilience and reduces stress.

Trust and psychological safety are inextricably linked, although the former is predominantly between individuals while the latter is a group construct. Psychological safety makes it safe to raise concerns and make mistakes without fear of retribution. Stephen Covey asserts that ". . . trust is the hidden variable that affects everything" (2006: 239). He notes that is it not sufficient for leaders to have personal integrity and relational trust; they also have a responsibility to ". . . create, deploy, and maintain systems that promote an environment of high trust" (2006: 238). This notion of creating such a trusting, safe context is crucial for the development of organisational compassion. All personal and organisational development is contingent upon trust and psychological safety.

Compassion increases our willingness to trust, and the human brain is especially sensitive to trustworthiness. One study (Bartram and Casimir 2007) focused on trust and outcomes in an Australian call-centre. Researchers found that job performance was mediated by self-reported levels of trust in the organisation leadership. Quite simply, higher levels of trust in leadership significantly improved employee job performance. When a senior leader lacks compassion, people will hide suffering from them. The trust which results from resonant, compassionate leadership results in improved employee performance.

People need to be trusted to perform in their roles. This can be seen as strongly relating to the Self-Determination Theory of personal motivation, illustrated in Figure 9.4. Richard Ryan and Edward Deci (2000) outlined the three innate psychological needs of autonomy, development of competence, and a culture of belonging and relatedness. Trust is a key aspect of autonomy, where we are trusted to do our job without surveillance:

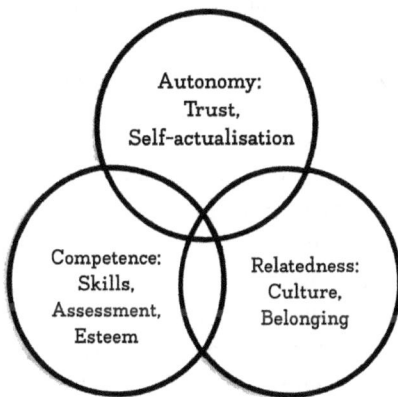

Figure 9.4: Self-Determination Theory, adapted from Ryan and Deci, 2000.

All three of these needs must be met in order to enhance individual motivation, wellbeing and self-regulation. Building compassionate leadership results in an improvement of individual employee motivation, as well as heightening organisational trust and psychological safety.

Leadership creation and reinforcement of culture

Satya Nadella, CEO of Microsoft, has been lauded for his compassionate leadership style. As we discussed in Chapter 4, this style is in stark contrast to that of his immediate predecessor. Under Nadella's leadership, the prevailing organisational culture has changed from 'know-it-alls' to 'learn-it-alls', and he has openly credited empathy as being the bedrock of Microsoft's recent successful innovations. He has acknowledged his son, Zain, who was born with special needs, as being his greatest teacher in this respect. Nadella notes that Zain developed his father's ". . . personal passion for and philosophy of connecting new ideas to empathy for others" and states that this drive is why he is "deeply committed to pushing the bounds on what love and compassion combined with human ingenuity and passion to have impact can accomplish" (Nadella 2017). The results of this decidedly human approach are clear: substantially increased company earnings and share value, successful innovation in accessibility and AI, and a new-found ability for Microsoft to collaborate with competitors.

The case of Nadella will make for interesting debates between business school students for many years to come. But does leadership really make much of a difference to individuals? A fascinating study by Boyatzis and colleagues (2012) revealed via fMRI scans that different neural mechanisms are involved when recalling memories of positive, resonant leaders versus dissonant leaders. The areas involved when recalling resonant leaders are those associated with positive affect, emotional processing and decision-making despite uncertainty. Conversely, the areas of the brain recruited when recalling a dissonant leader are related to constricted attention, avoidance, negative emotions and a reduction in compassion. Simply put, our brains respond more positively, improving our decision-making and emotional regulation, when we experience resonant leadership. So, yes. Compassionate leadership makes an enormous difference for the performance of individuals and for organisational culture.

Leaders must to be clear in their compassionate expectations if these are to become embedded into the cultural fabric of the organisation. Ideally, compassionate leaders will overtly share their aspirations and practices, much as Nadella did. Demonstrating self-compassion when they get things wrong, and being open to reverse-mentoring in order to uncover blind-spots are approaches which will benefit the leader as much as anyone. Sensitive communication and celebration of compassionate acts are effective approaches. This should not be done in order to cheerlead, but rather to recognise compassion, where appropriate and with permission. This way, compassionate acts, big and small, become normalised as a behaviour, and become part of the organisational cultural narrative.

What gets measured (sometimes) gets done

If, then, compassion is an important part of the modern-day organisation, it is important to consider exactly what organisational compassion might be, how to measure and influence it, and how it can be integrated it into organisational structures.

An organisation is more than a collection of individuals, albeit ones who typically share a common purpose. Therefore, a compassionate organisation is greater than all the individual propensity for compassion combined. Organisational culture will reflect the prevalent, senior behaviours and leadership's inclination or otherwise towards compassion. Some of this is measurable, yet how people actually *feel* is also critical to consider.

Have you ever felt happiness? Hopefully. Can you define it? Possibly. Would our definitions of happiness be exactly the same? Unlikely. Although we can all experience something we might call happiness, the term itself may mean different things to different people. The same is true of words such as 'engagement' or 'compassion'. In my own research on AC and OC, the participants were not aware of what the survey was measuring and they may not have been able to define what 'compassion' meant to them. What mattered was the individual experience or perception of compassion; whether they felt heard, seen and supported in times of need. Just like 'happiness' or 'engagement' at work might mean slightly different things depending on our upbringing, life experiences or even first language, it is the experience of compassion that matters more than the precise definition. This is similar to Solomon's concern in his moral psychology essay, discussed earlier in this chapter, where he notes that practical application is more important than precise definitions.

So, similarly to the individual compassion measures in the previous chapter, it is important to keep in mind some health warnings about these organisational compassion measures. Firstly, measures are primarily useful for establishing a benchmark and then assessing subsequent progress. Secondly, the conversations, reflections and actions that these measures prompt are equally, if not more, valuable than any scores they produce. Regardless of the measure used, an organisational compassion score is in itself fairly meaningless. An understanding the reasons for the score matters more, along with tangible actions and genuine commitment to improvement. Thirdly, whilst quantitative scores are useful, qualitative evidence is also worthwhile in order to provide colour and depth to the findings. By and large, the measurement of compassion, whether for ourselves as individuals or for a whole organisation, should be taken as a directional guide rather than a definitive answer.

Part of the reason for noting these provisos is simply that there is no agreed consensus on how to measure the compassion of an organisation. A number of psychology and psychiatry researchers from across the UK and the US completed a meta-review of this question (Strauss et al. 2016). They found, unsurprisingly, a lack of consensus on both the definition of compassion and how this should be measured. Nor is there agreement on measuring organisational happiness, wellbeing or even culture, but that does not mean we should not try. Not all that matters can be measured; not all that can be measured matters.

The simplest measure of an organisational outcome is the bottom line. Compassionate leadership affects this too. A Gallup survey (2002) of US employees in the immediate aftermath of the 9/11 attacks asked whether organisations had responded to the attacks in a compassionate way. This included making financial philanthropic donations, giving employees compassionate leave where needed, and addressing employee issues or concerns following the attacks. Where the compassionate response was considered to be excellent, 48% of employees were engaged while only 6% were actively disengaged. By comparison, when the compassionate response was considered to be poor, only 11% were engaged while a staggering 39% were actively disengaged. For comparative purposes, in pre-9/11 engagement research, Gallup had found that a 19% active disengagement level was responsible for a loss of around $300 billion in productivity to the US economy. Lack of compassion hurts people and hurts organisations; in Gallup's words, "When compassion is called for, know that your bottom line is at stake".

Key approaches to measuring organisational compassion

There are three main approaches to assessing organisational compassion:

1. Organisational Compassion Quiz

The Compassion Lab at University of Michigan Ross School of Business has partnered with Berkeley's Greater Good Science Center (GGSC) to produce a Compassionate Organisation Quiz. The questions can be easily accessed and tracked via the GGSC website, a link to which is included in the Further Resources section. Questions in this quiz are answered on a 5-point Likert scale, and are predominantly focused on behavioural norms within an organisation, such as:

> When someone in my organisation expresses that they are having a hard time, most people believe they deserve a caring response.
> Or
> In my organisation, everyone is too busy to pay attention to whether someone is suffering or not.

This quiz is easy to understand, and the GGSC website provides recommendations for action based on the results. As before, the results are useful as a benchmark from which to begin a compassionate journey, and to assess progress.

2. Multiplied Individual Compassion

As organisations are collections of individuals, we can use an individual measure of compassion, such as those outlined in Chapter 8, and create a compassion index by collating all of the responses. This approach is most often used in measuring subjective, largely unquantifiable, yet important concepts such as happiness. The overall compassion trends of an organisation can then be assessed, and action taken to improve the overall trajectory.

Organisational compassion, however, is most likely more than a sum of individual parts. Cultural impacts, professional and personal relational networks, and leadership behaviours all impact organisational systems, so keep this in mind if adopting this approach.

3. Indirect Measures of Compassion

The indirect approach was taken by Ace Simpson and Ben Farr-Wharton (2017) through their assessment of organisational compassion in relation to the more established Perceived Organisational Support (POS), Organizational Citizenship Behaviour (OCB), and employee wellbeing measures. POS assesses the extent to which employees believe that the organisation cares for them and values their contribution, while OCB measures discretionary pro-social employee behaviours. By the same token, measuring Affective Commitment could give an indirect insight into the levels of organisational compassion. Simpson and Farr-Wharton found POS to precede compassion, as well as strong associations between OCB and wellbeing. As a result of their work, they have created the NEAR (Noticing, Empathising, Assessing, Responding) Organisational Compassion Scale.

As with individual measures of compassion outlined in Chapter 8, there is no one size which fits all. Work with what suits your organisation best, adapt question wording to reflect your cultural norms, experiment with nudges and reflect upon your results.

Organisational compassion is a blend of individual perceptions and actions alongside group processes and beliefs, each impacting the other in a constantly adjusting interplay. Developing a compassionate organisation is therefore both art and science, designing supporting structures whilst also enabling flex and adjusting to specific organisational needs. It requires us to simultaneously understand that compassion impacts the bottom line and yet is most usefully measured directionally rather than in absolute terms. The work required to build and maintain such a compassionate organisation is never finished. Stepping back in order to see structural issues, alongside constant upkeep and care, will keep such a compassionate organisation from falling into disrepair. Sustainably compassionate organisations require leaders who reflect on their own intentions, whose multitude of small actions create and maintain psychological safety, and who can handle the 'not knowing' of directional compassionate results. Such leaders will deliver benefits which will be expressed through the performance results, employee engagement levels and even the survival of their organisations.

Key Chapter Points

- Building a compassionate organisation embeds compassion more fully into the culture, and makes the presence of compassion less reliant on a small handful of leaders. Compassionate leadership is most effective when integrated into an organisational structure which supports and amplifies compassion.
- Practical approaches to creating more compassionate organisations are clustered into four main areas:
  - Strategic
  - Structural
  - Behavioural
  - Cultural
- Through these areas, we explored compassionate business ethics, building employee commitment, and the importance of organisational responses to suffering. Also included were the employee lifecycle and formal policies, as well as behavioural nudges and reinforcing a compassionate culture. The importance of psychological safety and trust was emphasised in the context of organisational compassion.
- Measuring the progress – or otherwise – of an aspiring compassionate organisation is also discussed. Three main approaches to such measurement are included, alongside some words of caution. Remember that OC measures are best thought of as directional rather than absolute. Not all that matters can be measured.

Chapter 10
The future of compassionate leadership

Compassion is the radicalism of our time.   (His Holiness the Dalai Lama XIV)

The future depends on what we do in the present.   (Mahatma Ghandi)

The power of compassion

The time has come to reintegrate Adam Smith's seemingly disparate areas of focus in the modern organisation: capitalism and compassion are bed fellows, not adversaries. Despite years of prevailing management theory which has viewed compassion with suspicion, the evidence for its gentle power is clear and compelling. Compassion benefits our own individual mental and physical wellbeing, alongside those of our employees and customers, and allows us greater resilience in the face of stress and anxiety. It improves our social connectedness, which brings a plethora of psychological and physiological benefits to each of us. Cellular inflammation levels are reduced through compassionate action, and our organisations can benefit from improved levels of trust and psychological safety created by compassionate leaders. Conflict is resolved more effectively through a compassionate lens, and the people who work in compassionate organisations want to stay, to deliver in their roles and to care for each other.

Compassion is fundamental to the future of leadership. Back in the late 1990s, Robert Solomon argued that with compassion as an ethical and organisational virtue, not a sentimental weakness or irrational incompetence, an organisation will reap the rewards of strength through psychological safety and embedded commitment. Increasingly, contemporary research is proving him right. Compassionate leadership needs to be reintegrated into organisations and, indeed, into everyday life.

We do not need to establish Departments for Compassion. Instead, compassion will be most effective as an integral part of any organisational culture. We need to build compassion into the structure of our organisations and to weave it into the fabric of everyday organisational life. This is not a 'knit your own granola' brand of leadership for people who cannot handle the pressure of modern organisations. Quite the opposite:

> The caring corporation is not just a hotbed of sentimentality and 'bleeding hearts', with no competitive sense whatever. Indeed . . . a caring corporation cultivates the most basic strength of any organization, mutual dedication and a sense of security rather than defensive self-interest.
>
> (Solomon 1998: 518)

A truly compassionate leader does not sacrifice themselves on the pyre of organisational suffering. Instead, by recalling the appraisal step in the new compassion construct, they

https://doi.org/10.1515/9783110763126-010

are able to both resource themselves sufficiently and to notice when 'compassion' is actually empathy or altruism in disguise. A leader whose compassion is entirely other-focused is missing a key aspect of sustainable leadership: self-compassion. Compassion which does not include ourselves is likely to be incomplete at best, detrimental at worst. Equally, if our compassion only includes those we like or consider to be members of our in-group, then it is favouritism rather than compassion. Compassion which is reserved for members of our own in-groups is both incomplete and unethical. Conversely, if we can find compassion for those who have wronged us, those who we regard as our professional or personal adversaries, and even those who we do not know, then we will likely take a step closer to becoming truly compassionate leaders. As we recall Einstein's plea to constantly widen our circles of compassion, we can recognise that while this may not be easy, it is an increasingly necessary, even urgent, aspect of modern leadership.

Humane leadership

As we have seen, humane leadership has remained oddly absent from traditional management theory. In the words of Jason Kanov and colleagues, "the study of organisations tends to engage our minds but fails to engage our hearts" (2004: 810). How strange that humans seem so quick to disregard their own beautiful, fragile humanity – the very thing that makes us human.

Outdated stifling hierarchies, command and control, fear and reprisal appear to be on their organisational deathbeds. New approaches are emerging, creating psychological safety across networked, often remote, organisations, guided by leaders whose espoused ethics are clearly visible in their actions. This is not a mere change in organisational frameworks, but rather a more fundamental shift to a form of leadership with humanity as an integral element. We are on the cusp of a shift in global systemic consciousness. People care less about how much money you have, more about how you earned it and what you will do with it. Increasingly, people are less interested in your job title than they are in the impact you have. Compassion affects us all on a cellular, individual, organisational and societal level. Most of all, compassionate leadership is about remembering what it is to be utterly human.

Integrating compassion into contemporary leadership theory can be viewed either as an advance, or as a return to what we have forgotten. Much like human development more generally, our innate capacity for compassion requires gentle attention in order to flourish. Compassion is less something we need to learn, rather it is something for us to remember and to rekindle. For our innate propensity for compassion to be expressed, those seeds of compassion need to be tenderly nourished. Compassion does not fall from the sky; it grows from the seeds we plant and nourish.

Ironically, as we have learned, it is those who most studiously avoid compassion who can disproportionately benefit from it. The people most likely to benefit from reading this book might actively avoid even picking it up. We cannot force people to adopt a compassionate approach. What we can do is lead by example, role model what we value, and support others on their first, faltering compassionate steps. Each chapter of this book includes practical suggestions for developing practice. Nudges and a compassionate cultural context will provide the most fertile ground in which compassion can grow and thrive, even for those who might fear it.

Intention, choice and practice

As a leader, a combination of your consciously compassionate intention, choices and practice makes for a devastating combination. This book provides you with guiding principles, clear models and practical suggestions for developing your leadership and organisations. Remember, there will always be exceptions and surprises, especially where wonderfully messy, non-linear, emotional humans are concerned. Be self-compassionate when you do not live up to your own expectations, and stay compassionate when others fall short of theirs too.

As we discovered in Chapter 7, the Organisational Design concept of 'self as an instrument' acknowledges the incredible impact we can have as leaders. We have seen throughout this book how this is certainly the case with compassion, as we influence ourselves and each other every time we choose a compassionate response to suffering. The inner work we do on ourselves as leaders increasingly makes such outer work possible. Appraising our own behavioural patterns and rules of belonging allows us to question whether they continue to serve us well or whether we would prefer to choose another path. Understanding that such patterns are often unconscious and created by a myriad of historical and personal factors enables us to see each other more fully and with less judgement.

When faced with anger or resentment, we can stay calm and curious about what is hidden behind such emotions, knowing that presenting issues are rarely the real problem. Pain wears many masks. Deepening our reflective and reflexive practice means that we can start to live an examined life, and to skilfully make in-the-moment adjustments to changing, challenging circumstances. Do not underestimate the power of this individual fine tuning. A multitude of subtle inner shifts will create more durable and impactful leadership than any dramatic grandstand positioning ever will.

Our capacity for genuine compassion and care might be what makes the greatest difference to suffering, even if the other person never tells you this. Compassionate leadership expects no reward.

Through reading this book, you will have developed a robust understanding about compassion. You will know what it is and is not, why it matters in leadership and its benefits for those working in organisations. A delicate balancing act is now required, where you can apply your knowledge, set your compassionate intention . . . and then let it go. Hold your compassion lightly. Simply being fully present with suffering is one of the most useful things any leader can do. When faced with suffering, put models, research and your phone to one side, and give your undivided attention to those who will benefit from your capacity for compassionate wisdom. The power of such a seemingly simple practice should not be understated:

> . . . what really counts is that in moments of pain and suffering someone stays with us. More important than any particular action or word of advice is the simple presence of someone who cares . . . In a time so filled with methods and techniques designed to change people, to influence their behaviour, and to make them do new things and think new thoughts, we have lost the simple but difficult gift of being present to each other. We have lost this gift because we have been led to believe that presence must be useful . . . we have forgotten that it is often in 'useless', unpretentious, humble presence to each other that we feel consolation and comfort. Simply being with someone is difficult because it asks of us that we share in the other's vulnerability, enter with him or her into the experience of weakness and powerlessness, become part of uncertainty, and give up control and self-determination. And still, whenever this happens, new strength and new hope is being born . . . For this reason, [those who sit with us] are the ones who bring new hope and help us discover new directions . . .   (Nouwen et al. 1983: 11–12)

Such simplicity in the face of suffering should not be underestimated. Statistically speaking, most of us will (hopefully) never have to risk the dangers inherent in rescuing another person from a blazing inferno. Our compassionate acts will mostly be small and are unlikely to appear on the evening news. Such acts will, however, matter. Even the smallest compassionate action might have a disproportionate impact for the recipient. Even without racing into a blazing building, you might just save a life.

The future of compassionate leadership

Compassionate leadership demonstrates that a more people-centred approach is both possible and commercially astute. Overwhelming evidence has shown that we can deliver organisational results in a humane way, and that such humanity might be the very thing that protects our organisations during crisis. Compassionate leadership is not an excuse to be a sob story agony aunt or uncle. It is simultaneously an intensely human and a strategically commercial act. How many millions of pounds could have been saved in legal fees, pay-offs, severance pay or new hire recruitment if listening with compassion had been at the heart of difficult conversations or moments of suffering?

Taking the time and space people need to be seen and heard might sometimes feel like a burden, but the personal and organisational rewards of such leadership actions are – as we have explored throughout this book – both bountiful and increasingly necessary.

More so than ever before, our world needs leaders who can notice and respond to suffering. Organisational challenges in our fragile world include the balancing of profit, people and planet, alongside delicate encounters with stress, depression and other mental health issues. We need leaders who understand the impacts of their responses to suffering, and who can design and seed organisations which have compassion at their heart.

Above all, we need leaders who appreciate that compassion matters. It matters quite simply because when it is properly understood and applied, compassion makes a world of difference – and it may even be the difference our world needs.

Further resources

1. Kirstie Drummond Papworth's TeDx Talk on Compassion (2019) https://www.ted.com/talks/kirstie_drummond_papworth_compassion_gets_a_tough_time
2. Kaufman Light-Dark Triad Scale https://scottbarrykaufman.com/lighttriadscale/
3. Harvard Implicit Association Tests https://implicit.harvard.edu/implicit/
4. Compassionate Organisations Quiz Created by the Greater Good Science Center at the University of Berkeley https://greatergood.berkeley.edu/quizzes/take_quiz/compassionate_organizations
5. Neff's Self-compassion Scale https://self-compassion.org/self-compassion-scales-for-researchers/

https://doi.org/10.1515/9783110763126-011

References

Adami, C. and Hintze, A. (2013). Evolutionary Instability of Zero-determinant Strategies Demonstrates that Winning Is Not Everything. *Nature Communications, 4*: 2193.

Adams, T. (2021). How Joshua Coombes Became Hairdresser to the Homeless and Example to Us All. Available at: https://www.theguardian.com/society/2021/aug/01/how-joshua-coombes-became-hairdresser-to-the-homeless-and-example-to-us-all

Allen, J.S., Stevenson, R.M., O'Boyle, E.H. and Seibert, S. (2021). What Matters More for Entrepreneurship Success? A Meta-analysis Comparing General Mental Ability and Emotional Intelligence in Entrepreneurial Settings. *Strategic Entrepreneurship Journal, 15*(3): 352–376.

Anderson, C., Sharps, D.L., Soto, C. and John, O.P. (2020). People with Disagreeable Personalities (Selfish, Combative and Manipulative) Do Not Have an Advantage in Pursuing Power at Work, *PNAS, 117*(37): 22780–22786.

Annor, I. (2018). Black Men Arrested in US Coffee Shop to Meet Company CEO. *Africa News.* Available at: https://www.africanews.com/2018/04/16/black-men-arrested-in-us-coffee-shop-to-meet-company-ceo//

Babiak, P. and Hare, R.D. (2007). *Snakes in Suits: When Psychopaths Go to Work.* New York: Harper Business.

Barnard, L.K. and Curry, J.F. (2011). Self-Compassion: Conceptualizations, Correlates, & Interventions. *Review of General Psychology, 15*(4): 1–15.

Barsade, S.G. and O'Neill, O.A. (2014). What's Love Got to Do with It? A Longitudinal Study of the Culture of Companionate Love and Employee and Client Outcomes in a Long-term Care Setting. *Administrative Science Quarterly, 59*(4): 551–598.

Bartram, T. and Casimir, G. (2007). The Relationship Between Leadership and Follower In-role Performance and Satisfaction with the Leader: The Mediating Effects of Empowerment and Trust in the Leader. *Leadership & Organization Development Journal, 28*(1): 4–19.

Battilana, J. and Casciaro, T. (2021). *Power, for All: How It Really Works and Why It's Everyone's Business.* London: Simon and Schuster.

Barnett, A. (2020). Aviation Safety: A Whole New World? *Transportation Science 54*(1): 84–96.

Bennett, A. (1908). *How to Live on Twenty-four Hours a Day.* Amazon.

Berne, E. (1964). *Games People Play: The Psychology of Human Relationships.* London: Penguin.

Berking, M. and Whitley, B. (2014). *Affect Regulation Training: A Practitioner's Manual.* London: Springer.

Bodanis, D. (2021). Can You Succeed Without Being a Terrible Person? *Financial Times.* Available at: https://www.ft.com/content/5056e19d-7d90-4a64-a437-8a047deb383b

Bolton, G. (2014). *Reflective Practice: Writing and Professional Development (4th ed.).* London: Sage.

Boyatzis, R.E., Passarelli, A.M., Koenig, K., Lowe, M., Mathew, B., Stoller, J.K. and Phillips, M. (2012). Examination of the Neural Substrates Activated in Memories of Experiences with Resonant and Dissonant Leaders. *The Leadership Quarterly, 23,* 259–272.

Bowlby, J. (1969). *Attachment and Loss: Vol. 1.* New York: Basic Books.

Breines J.G. and Chen, S. (2012). Self-Compassion Increases Self-Improvement Motivation. *Personality and Social Psychology Bulletin, 38*(9): 1133–1143.

Brown, B. (2008). *I Thought It Was Just Me: Women Reclaiming Power and Courage in a Culture of Shame.* New York: Penguin Random House.

Brown, D.J. (2018). In the Minds of Followers: Follower-centric Approaches to Leadership. In Antonakis, J. and Day, D.V. (eds.). *The Nature of Leadership* (pp. 82–108). Sage Publications, Inc.

Brown, S.L., Nesse, R.M., Vinokur, A.D. and Smith, D.M. (2003). Providing Social Support May Be More Beneficial Than Receiving It: Results from a Prospective Study of Mortality. *Psychological Science, 14*(4): 320–327.

Buckels, E.E., Trapnell, P.D. and Paulhus, D.L. (2014). *Trolls Just Want to Have Fun. Personality and Individual Differences, 67,* 97–102. https://www.sciencedirect.com/science/article/pii/S0191886914000324

Burns, J.M. (1978). *Leadership.* New York: Harper & Row.

https://doi.org/10.1515/9783110763126-012

Carson, J.W., Keefe, F.J., Lynch, T.R., Carson, K.M., Goli, V., Fras, A.M. and Thorp, S.R. (2005). Loving-Kindness Meditation for Chronic Low Back Pain: Results from a Pilot Trial. *Journal of Holistic Nursing*, *23*(3): 287–304.

Chancellor, J., Margolis, S.J., Bao, K. and Lyubomirsky, S. (2018). Everyday Prosociality in the Workplace: The Reinforcing Benefits of Giving, Getting, and Glimpsing. *Emotion*, *18*(4): 507–517.

Chemers, M.M., Watson, C.B. and May, S.T. (2000). Dispositional Affect and Leadership Effectiveness: A Comparison of Self-esteem, Optimism, and Efficacy. *Personality and Social Psychology Bulletin*, *26*(3): 267–277.

Cheung-Judge, M.Y. (2001). The Self as an Instrument. *OD Practitioner*, *44*(2): 42–47.

Chödrön, P. (2004). *The Places That Scare You: A Guide to Fearlessness in Difficult Times*. London, Harper NonFiction.

Choudhary, A.I., Akhtar, S.A. and Zaheer, A. (2013). Impact of Transformational and Servant Leadership on Organizational Performance: A Comparative Analysis. *Journal of Business Ethics*, *116*, 433–440.

Cohen, A. (1996). On the Discriminant Validity of the Meyer and Allen Measure of Organiza-tional Commitment: How Does it Fit with the Commitment Construct? *Educational and Psychological Measurement*, *56*, 494–503.

Cohen, S., Kamarck, T. and Mermelstein, R. (1983). A Global Measure of Perceived Stress. *Journal of Health and Social Behavior*, *24*, 386–396.

Coleman, P. (2021). Embrace Complexity to Overcome Polarization? Available at: https://fluentknowledge.com/shows/the-purple-principle/the-way-out

Costa, P.T. and McCrae, R.R. (2006). *NEO Revised NEO Personality Inventory (NEO PI-R)*. Oxford: Hogrefe.

Costa, P.T. and McCrae, R.R. (1990) Personality: Another 'Hidden Factor' Is Stress Research. *Psychological Inquiry*, *1*(1): 22–24.

Covey, S.M.R. (2006). *The Speed of Trust: The One Thing that Changes Everything*. London: Simon and Schuster.

Crocker, J. and Canevello, A. (2008). Creating and Undermining Social Support in Communal Relationships: The Role of Compassionate and Self-image Goals. *Journal of Personality and Social Psychology*, *95*, 555–575.

Crockett, M., Kurth-Nelson, Z., Siegel, J., Dayan, P. and Dolan, R. (2014). Harm to Others Outweighs Harm to Self in Moral Decision Making. *Proceedings of the National Academy of Sciences*, *111*(48), 17320–5.

Culpepper, R. (2000). A Test of Revised Scales for the Meyer and Allen Three-Component Commitment Construct. *Educational and Psychological Measurement*, *60*(4): 604–616.

Dahl, C.J., Lutz, A. and Davidson, R.J. (2015). Reconstructing and Deconstructing the Self: Cognitive Mechanisms in Meditation pPractice. *Trends in Cognitive Sciences*, *19*(9): 515–523.

Dalai Lama, (2001). *The Power of Compassion*. London: Thorsons.

Darley, J.M. and Latané (1968). Bystander Intervention in Emergencies: Diffusion of Responsibility. *Journal of Personality and Social Psychology*, *8*(4): 377–383.

Davies, M., Stankov, L. and Roberts, R.D. (1998). Emotional Intelligence: In Search of an Elusive Construct. *Journal of Personality and Social Psychology*, *75*(4): 989–1015.

Davies, R. (2021). Dieselgate: British Car Buyers' Claim Against VW Reaches High Court. https://www.theguardian.com/business/2021/dec/05/dieselgate-british-car-buyers-claim-vw-reaches-high-court

Davies, S. (2018). Life Is Complicated and that Is Good. Available at: https://www.aier.org/article/life-is-complicated-and-that-is-good/

Department of Health. (2013). The Handbook to the NHS Constitution Available at www.gov.uk/government/publications/the-nhs-constitution-for-england

DeSteno, D. (2018). How to Cultivate Gratitude, Compassion, and Pride in Your Team. Available at: https://hbr.org/2018/02/how-to-cultivate-gratitude-compassion-and-pride-on-your-team

Divakaruni, C.B. (2019) The Forest of Enchantments. Gurugram: Harper Collins.

Dizikes, P. (2020). Commercial Air Travel Is Safer than Ever. Available at: https://news.mit.edu/2020/study-commercial-flights-safer-ever-0124

Dowd, M. (2018) Lady of the Rings: Jacinda Rules https://www.nytimes.com/2018/09/08/opinion/sunday/jacinda-ardern-new-zealand-prime-minister.html

Dutton, J.E., Workman, K.M. and Hardin, A.E. (2014). Compassion at Work. *The Annual Review of Organizational Psychology and Organizational Behavior*, 1, 277–304.

Dweck, C. (2017). *Mindset: Changing the Way You Think to Fulfil Your Potential*. New York: Random House.

Edmondson, A. (2018). *The Fearless Organisation: Creating Psychological Safety in the Workplace for Learning, Innovation and Growth*. Chichester: Wiley.

Einstein, A. (1950). *Letter to Norman Salit*. Jerusalem: Hebrew University of Jerusalem.

Ekman, P. and Ekman. E. (2017). Is Global Compassion Achievable? In Seppala, E., Simon-Thomas, E., Brown, S.L., Worline, M.C., Cameron, C.D. and Doty, J.R. (eds.). *The Oxford Handbook of Compassion Science*. Oxford University Press.

Eldor, L. (2017). Public Service Sector: The Compassionate Workplace – The Effect of Compassion and Stress on Employee Engagement, Burnout, and Performance. *Journal of Public Administration Research and Theory, Vol 28, Issue 1*, 1–18.

Eurich, T. (2018). What Self-Awareness Really Is (And How to Cultivate It). Available at: https://hbr.org/2018/01/what-self-awareness-really-is-and-how-to-cultivate-it

Financial Times. (2020). Jacinda Ardern's Victory for Compassionate Competence. 20 October 2020: https://www.ft.com/content/04e59098-7dc5-4ec3-a543-7cb6f4eb6716

Financial Times. (no date). The FT Guide to Compassion https://www.ft.com/content/e53d6c5b-0ae7-4eef-b397-ce110c8d7b2b

Fisher, R. (1981). Preventing Nuclear War. *Bulletin of the Atomic Scientists*, 37(3): 11–17.

Fleming, S.M. (2022). *Know Thyself: The New Science of Self-Awareness*. London: John Murray.

Fleming, S. (2021). How to Boost Your Self-awareness and Make Better Decisions. Available at: https://www.newscientist.com/article/mg25033332-300-how-to-boost-your-self-awareness-and-make-better-decisions/#ixzz7Ko2SQCm7

Fogarty, L.A., Curbow, B.A., Wingard, J.R., McDonnell, K. and Somerfield, M.R. (1999). Can 40 Seconds of Compassion Reduce Patient Anxiety? *Journal of Clinical Oncology*, 17(1): 371–379.

Fogg, B.J. (2020). *Tiny Habits: Why Starting Small Makes Lasting Change*. London: Penguin.

Forbes . (2021). 14 Ways Leaders Can Boost Empathy in the Workplace. Available at: https://www.forbes.com/sites/forbesbusinesscouncil/2021/08/23/14-ways-leaders-can-boost-empathy-in-the-workplace/?sh=153355bf4731

Foroohar, R. (2019). What I Want for Xmas – More Empathy. https://accounts.ft.com/login?location=https%3A%2F%2Fwww.ft.com%2Fcontent%2Ff3a9400e-2369-11ea-92da-f0c92e957a96

Frankl, V.E. (1959/2004). *Man's Search for Meaning*. London: Rider.

Fredrickson, B.L. (2003). Positive Emotions and Upward Spirals in Organizations. In Cameron, K.S., Dutton, J.E. and Quinn, R.E. (eds.). *Positive Organizational Scholarship: Foundations of a New Discipline*. San Francisco: Berrett–Kochler.

Fredrickson, B.L. (2013). Positive Emotions Broaden and Build. In P. Devine and A. Plant (eds.). *Advances in Experimental Social Psychology* (Vol. 47, pp. 1–53). Burlington: Academic Press.

Frost, P.J., Dutton, J.E., Maitlis, S., Lilius, J.M., Kanov, J.M. and Worline, M. (2013). Seeing Organizations Differently: Three Lenses on Compassion. In Clegg, S.R., Hardy, C., Lawrence, T.B. and Nord, W.R. (eds.). *The Sage Handbook of Organization Studies (2nd edition)*. London: Sage.

Furnham, A. (2003). Belief in a Just World: Research Progress over the Past Decade. *Personality and Individual Differences*, 34(5): 795–817.

Gallo, A. (2021) Managers: Compassion and Accountability Aren't Mutually Exclusive. Available at: https://hbr.org/2021/08/managers-compassion-and-accountability-arent-mutually-exclusive

Gallup. (2002). Who Cared? Available at: https://news.gallup.com/businessjournal/427/who-cared.aspx

Gallup. (2021). US Employee Engagement Data Holds Steady in First Half of 2021. Available at: https://www.gallup.com/workplace/352949/employee-engagement-holds-steady-first-half-2021.aspx

Gayle, D. (2018). Arrests of Two Black Men at Starbucks for 'Trespassing' Sparks Protests. Available at: https://www.theguardian.com/us-news/2018/apr/16/arrest-of-two-black-men-at-starbucks-for-trespassing-sparks-protests

GGSC. Greater Good Science Centre. Available at: https://greatergood.berkeley.edu

Gilbert, P. (2009). *The Compassionate Mind*. London: Robinson.

Gilbert, P., Catarino, F. and Duarte, C. (2017). The Development of Compassionate Engagement and Action Scales for Self and Others. *Journal of Compassionate Health Care, 4*, 4.

Gilbert P. (2019). Explorations into the Nature and Function of Compassion. *Current Opinion in Psychology, 28*, 108–114.

Gilbert, P., McEwan, K., Mitra, R., Richter, A., Franks, L., Mills, A. and Gale, C. (2009). An Exploration of Different Types of Positive Affect in Students and Patients with a Bipolar Disorder. *Clinical Neuropsychiatry, 6*(4): 135–143.

Gilbert, P., McEwan, K., Matos, M. and Rivis, A. (2011). Fears of Compassion: Development of Three Self-report Measures. *Psychology and Psychotherapy: Theory, Research and Practice, 84*, 239–255.

Gittell, J.H., Cameron, K., Lim, S. and Rivas, V. (2006). Relationships, Layoffs, and Organizational Resilience: Airline Industry Responses to September 11. *The Journal of Applied Behavioral Science, 42*(3): 300–329.

Goetz, J.L., Keltner, D. and Simon-Thomas, E. (2010). Compassion: An Evolutionary Analysis and Empirical Review. *Psychological Bulletin, 136*(3): 351–374.

Goleman, D. (1988). Erikson, in His Own Old Age, Expands His View of Life. *New York Times*. Available at: https://archive.nytimes.com/www.nytimes.com/books/99/08/22/specials/erikson-old.html

Goleman, D. (1996). *Emotional Intelligence*. London: Bloomsbury.

Goleman, D. (2008) Hot to Help: When Can Empathy Move Us to Action? Available at: https://greatergood.berkeley.edu/article/item/hot_to_help

Gopinath, M., Nair, A. and Thangaraj, V. Espoused and Enacted Values in an Organization: Workforce Implications. *Management and Labour Studies, 43*(4): 277–293. doi:10.1177/0258042X18797757

Grant, A.M., Dutton, J.E. and Rosso, B.D. (2008). Giving Commitment: Employee Support Programs and the Prosocial Sensemaking Process. *Academy of Management Journal, 51*(5), 898–918.

Grant, A.M. and Gino, F. (2010). A Little Thanks Goes a Long Way: Explaining Why Gratitude Expressions Motivate Prosocial Behavior. *Journal of Personality and Social Psychology, 98*(6): 946–955.

Greater Good Science Centre. (no date). Empathy Quiz. Available at: https://greatergood.berkeley.edu/quizzes/take_%E2%80%8Bquiz/empathy

Greenberg, J., Datta, T., Shapero, B.J., Sevinc, G., Mischoulon, D. and Lazar, S.W. (2018). Compassionate Hearts Protect Against Wandering Minds: Self-compassion Moderates the Effect of Mind-wandering on Depression. *Spirituality in Clinical Practice, 5*(3): 155–169.

Grund, C. and Titz, K. (2022). Affective Commitment Through Further Training: The Roles of Firm Provision and Employee Participation. *Review of Managerial Science, 16*(4): 1195–1226.

Hafenbrack, A.C., LaPalme, M.L. and Solal, I. (2022). Mindfulness Meditation Reduces Guilt and Prosocial Reparation. *Journal of Personality and Social Psychology, 123*(1): 28–54.

Hamlin, J.K., Wynn, K. and Bloom, P. (2010). Three-month-olds Show a Negativity Bias in Their Social Evaluations. *Developmental Science 13*(6): 923–929.

Hancock, D. (2002). 'World Class Scandal at WorldCom' https://www.cbsnews.com/news/world-class-scandal-at-worldcom/

Harms, P.D. and Credé, M. (2010) Emotional Intelligence and Transformational and Transactional Leadership: A Meta-Analysis. *Journal of Leadership & Organizational Studies, 17*(1): 5–17.

Harris, T.A. (1973). *I'm OK – You're OK*. London: Random House.

Harvard Health. (2020). Understanding Acute and Chronic Inflammation. Available at: https://www.health.harvard.edu/staying-healthy/understanding-acute-and-chronic-inflammation

Haskins, G., Thomas, M. and Johri, L. (2018). Kindness in Leadership. Abingdon: Routledge.

Hellemans, C., Dal Cason, D. and Casini, A. (2017). Bystander Helping Behaviour in Response to Workplace Bullying. *Swiss Journal of Psychology*, 76(4): 135–144.

Henson, J. (2005). *It's Not Easy Being Green: And Other Things to Consider*. New York: Hyperion.

Hickson, G.B., Clayton, E.W., Entman, S.S., Miller, C.S., Githens, P.B., Whetten-Goldstein, K. and Sloan, F.A. (1994). Obstetricians' Prior Malpractice Experience and Patients' Satisfaction with Care. *JAMA: Journal of the American Medical Association*, 272(20), 1583–1587.

His Holiness the Dalai Lama. (1999). *The Art of Happiness: A Handbook for Living*. London: Hodder.

Hofmann, J. (2021). 'Like the Titanic: Enron 20 Years On' https://www.investorschronicle.co.uk/news/2021/09/02/like-the-titanic-enron-20-years-on/

Hoffmann, S.G., Grossman, P. and Hinton, D.E. (2011). Loving-kindness and Compassion Meditation: Potential for Psychological Interventions. *Clinical Psychology Review*, 31, 1126–1132.

Holt-Lunstad, J., Smith, T.B. and Layton, J.B. (2010). Social Relationships and Mortality Risk: A Meta-analytic Review. *PLOS Medicine* 7(7).

Hume, David. (1740/1985). *A Treatise of Human Nature: Book 3*. London: Penguin Classics.

Hutcherson, C.A., Seppala, E.M. and Gross, J.J. (2008). Loving-kindness Meditation Increases Social Connectedness. *Emotion*, 8(5): 720–724.

Hwang, J.Y., Plante, T. and Lackey, K. (2008). The Development of the Santa Clara Brief Compassion Scale: An Abbreviation of Sprecher and Fehr's Compassionate Love Scale. In *Pastoral Psychology*.

Inagaki, T.K. and Ross, L.P. (2018). Neural Correlates of Giving Social Support: Differences Between Giving Targeted Versus Untargeted Support. *Psychosomatic Medicine*, 80(8): 724–732.

Jung, C.G. (1938). Psychology and Religion. In Jung, C.G., *Collected Works 11: Psychology and Religion: West and East*. Princeton: Princeton University Press.

Kahneman, D. (2011). *Thinking, Fast and Slow*. London: Penguin.

Kalanithi, P. (2016). *When Breath Becomes Air*. London: Random House.

Kanov, J.M., Maitlis, S., Worline, M.C., Dutton, J.E., Frost, P.J. and Lulius, J.M. (2004) Compassion in Organizational Life. *The American Behavioural Scientist*, 47(6), 808–827.

Kant, I. (1785/1996). *Kant: The Metaphysics of Morals*. Cambridge: Cambridge University Press.

Kanungo, R.N. and Conger, J.A. (1993). Promoting Altruism as a Corporate Goal. *The Academy of Management Executive (1993–2005)*, 7(3): 37–48.

Karpman, S. (1968). Fairy Tales and Script Drama Analysis. *Transactional Analysis Bulletin*, 7(26), 39–43.

Kaufman, S.B., Yaden, D.B., Hyde, E. and Tsukayama, E. (2019). The Light vs. Dark Triad of Personality: Contrasting Two Very Different Profiles of Human Nature. *Frontiers in Psychology 10*, 467.

Kaurin, A., Schönfelder, S. and Wessa, M. (2018). Self-compassion Buffers the Link Between Self-criticism and Depression in Trauma-exposed Firefighters. *Journal of Counseling Psychology*, 65(4): 453–462.

Kearney, D.J., Malte, C.A., McManus, C., Martinez, M.E., Felleman, B. and Simpson, T.L. (2013). Loving-kindness Meditation for Posttraumatic Stress Disorder: A Pilot Study. *Journal of Traumatic Stress*, 26(4): 426–434.

Kegan, R. (1983). *The Evolving Self: Problem and Process in Human Development*. Harvard University Press.

Keysers, C. and Gazzola, V. (2009). Expanding the Mirror: Vicarious Activity for Actions, Emotions, and Sensations. *Current Opinion in Neurobiology*, 19(6): 666–671.

Kierein, N.M. and Gold, M.A. (2000). Pygmalion in Work Organizations: A Meta-analysis. *Journal of Organizational Behavior*, 21(8): 913–928.

Kini, P., Wong, J., McInnis, S., Gabana, N. and Brown, J.W. (2016). The Effects of Gratitude Expression on Neural Activity. *NeuroImage*, 128, 1–10.

Klimecki, O.M., Leiberg, S., Ricard, M. and Singer, T. (2014). Differential Pattern of Functional Brain Plasticity after Compassion and Empathy Training. *Social Cognitive and Affective Neuroscience*, 9(6): 873–879.

Klimecki, O. and Singer, T. (2011). *Empathic Distress Fatigue Rather than Compassion Fatigue? Integrating Findings from Empathy Research in Psychology and Social Neuroscience*. In Oakley, B., Knafo, A., Madhavan, G. and Wilson, D.S. pp. (368–383). Pathological Altruism, Oxford University Press.

Kline, N. (1999). *Time to Think: Listening to Ignite the Human Mind*. London: Cassell.

Knobloch-Westerwick, S., Liu, L., Hino, A., Westerwick, A. and Johnson, B.K. (2019). Context Impacts on Confirmation Bias: Evidence from the 2017 Japanese Snap Election Compared with American and German Findings. *Human Communication Research, 45*(4): 427–449.

Kohut, H. (2011). *The Search for the Self: Selected Writings of Heinz Kohut 1978–1981: Volume 3*. Edited by Paul H. Ornstein. Routledge, London.

Kruger, J. and Gilovich, T. (1999) 'Naïve Cynicism' in Everyday Theories of Responsibility Assessment: on Biased Assumptions of Bias. *Journal of Personality and Social Psychology, 76* (5): 743.

Kundera, M. (1984). *The Unbearable Lightness of Being*. London: Faber & Faber.

Lamothe M., Boujut E., Zenasni F. and Sultan S. (2014). To Be or Not to Be Empathic: The Combined Role of Empathic Concern and Perspective Taking in Understanding Burnout in General Practice. *BMC Family Practice, 23*(15): 15.

Langer, E. (1990). *Mindfulness*. Cambridge, MA: Perseus Books.

Lee, R., Draper, M. and Lee, Sujin. (2001). Social Connectedness, Dysfunctional Interpersonal Behaviours, and Psychological Distress: Testing a Mediator Model. *Journal of Counselling Psychology. 48*, 310–318.

Lerner, M.J. and Miller, D.T. (1978). Just World Research and the Attribution Process: Looking Back and Ahead. *Psychological Bulletin, 85*(5): 1030–1051. https://psycnet.apa.org/doi/10.1037/0033-2909.85.5.1030

Leung, M.K., Chan, C.C.H., Yin, J., Lee, C.F., So, K.F. and Lee, T.M.C. (2013). Increased Gray Matter Volume in the Right Angular and Posterior Parahippocampal Gyri in Loving-kindness Meditators. *Social Cognitive and Affective Neuroscience, 8*(1): 34–39.

Lilius, J.M., Worline, M.C., Dutton, J.E., Kanov, J., Frost, P.J. and Maitlis, S. (unpublished). *What Good Is Compassion at Work?*

Lilius, J.M., Worline, M.C., Maitlis, S., Kanov, J., Dutton, J.E. and Frost, P.J. (2008). The Contours and Consequences of Compassion at Work. *Journal of Organizational Behavior, 29*, 193–218.

Lilius, J.M., Worline, M.C., Dutton, J.E., Kanov, J.M and Maitlis, S. (2011). Understanding Compassion Capability. *Human Relations, 64*(7): 873–899.

Lim, D. and DeSteno, D. (2016). Suffering and Compassion: The Links Among Adverse Life Experiences, Empathy, Compassion, and Prosocial Behavior. *Emotion 16*(2), 175–182.

Lutz, A. Brefczynski-Lewis, J., Johnstone, T. and Davidson, R.J. (2008). Regulation of the Neural Circuitry of Emotion by Compassion Meditation: Effects of Meditative Expertise. *PLoS ONE; 3*(3): e1897

Lutz, A., Slagter, H.A., Rawlings, N.B., Francis, A.D., Greischar, L.L. and Davidson, R.J. (2009). Mental Training Enhances Attentional Stability: Neural and Behavioural Evidence. *Journal of Neuroscience, 29*(42): 13418–13427.

Madden, L.T., Duchon, D., Madden, T.M., and Plowman, D.A. (2012). Emergent Organizational Capacity for Compassion. *Academy of Management Review, 37*(4): 689–708.

Martin, D., Seppälä, E., Heineberg, Y., Rossomando, T., Doty, J., Zimbardo, P., Shiue, T., Berger, R. and Zhou, Y. (2015). Multiple Facets of Compassion: The Impact of Social Dominance Orientation and Economic Systems Justification. *Journal of Business Ethics, 129*, 237–249.

Matos, M., McEwan, K., Kanovský, M., Halamová, J., Steindl, SR., Ferreira, N., et al. (2021). Fears of Compassion Magnify the Harmful Effects of Threat of COVID-19 on Mental Health and Social Safeness across 21 Countries. *Clinical Psychology & Psychotherapy, 28*(6): 1317–1333.

Mayer, J.D. (2014). *Personal Intelligence*. New York: Scientific American.

McKinsey. (2019). McKinsey Quarterly: Five Ways that ESG Creates Value. Witold Henisz, Tim Koller and Robin Nuttall. https://www.mckinsey.com/~/media/McKinsey/Business%20Functions/Strategy%20and %20Corporate%20Finance/Our%20Insights/Five%20ways%20that%20ESG%20creates%20value/Five-ways-that-ESG-creates-value.ashx

Melwani, S., Mueller, J.S. and Overbeck, J.R. (2012). Looking Down: The Influence of Contempt and Compassion on Emergent Leadership Categorizations. *Journal of Applied Psychology*, 97(6), 1171–1185.

Mercadillo, R.E., Díaz, J.L., Pasaye, E.H. and Barrios, F.A. (2011). Perception of Suffering and Compassion Experience: Brain Gender Disparities. *Brain and Cognition*. Available at http://www.joseluisdiaz.org/wp-content/uploads/2011/04/PerceptionSuffering_MenWomen_Mercadillo2011.pdf

Mencken, H.L. (1920/2010). *Prejudices: Second Series*. Cornell University Library.

Mertens, S., Herberz, M., Hahnel, U.J.J. and Brosch, T. (2021). The Effectiveness of Nudging: A Meta-analysis of Choice Architecture Interventions Across Behavioural Domains. *PNAS 119*(1).

Meyer, J.P. and Allen, N.J. (1990). The Measurement and Antecedents of Affective, Continuance and Normative Commitment to the Organization. *Journal of Occupational Psychology*, 63, 1–18.

Meyer, J. P., Stanley, D. J., Herscovitch, L. and Topolnytsky, L. (2002). Affective, Continuance, and Normative Commitment to the Organization: A Meta-analysis of Antecedents, Correlates, and Consequences. *Journal of Vocational Behavior*, 61(1): 20–52.

Michigan State University. (2013). News Release: 'Evolution Will Punish You if You're Selfish and Mean' Available at: https://www.eurekalert.org/news-releases/637864

Molenberghs, P. (2013). The Neuroscience of In-group Bias. *Neuroscience & Biobehavioral Reviews*, 37(8): 1530–1536.

Nadella, S. (2017). The Moment That Forever Changed Our Lives. https://blogs.microsoft.com/accessibility/satya-nadella-the-moment-that-forever-changed-our-lives/

Neff, K.D. (2003). Self-Compassion: An Alternative Conceptualization of a Healthy Attitude Toward Oneself. *Self and Identity*, 2(2): 85–101.

Neff, K.D. (2011). Self-compassion, Self-esteem and Well-being. *Social and Personality Psychology Compass*, 5(1): 1–12.

Neff, K.D. and Germer, C.K. (2018). *The Mindful Self-Compassion Workbook*. London: The Guilford Press.

Neff, K.D., Kirkpatrick, K.L. and Rude, S.S. (2007). Self-compassion and Adaptive Psychological Functioning. *Journal of Research in Personality*, 41, 139–154.

Nietzsche, F. (1881/1997). Book II. In Clark, M. and Leiter, B. (eds.). *Nietzsche: Daybreak: Thoughts on the Prejudices of Morality* (Cambridge Texts in the History of Philosophy, pp. 57–94). Cambridge: Cambridge University Press.

Nietzsche, F. (1887/2013). *On the Genealogy of Morals*. London: Penguin.

Nin, A. (1961). *Seduction of the Minotaur*. Athens, Ohio: The Swallow Press.

Nouwen, H.J.M., McNeill, D. and Morrison, D. (1983). *Compassion: A Reflection on the Christian Life*. London: Doubleday.

Nussbaum, M. (1994). Pity and Mercy: Nietzsche's Stoicism. In Schacht, R. (eds.). *Nietzsche, Genealogy, Morality: Essays on Nietzsche's Genealogy of Morals* pp. (139–167, 139). Berkeley: University of California Press.

Nussbaum, M.C. (2001). *Upheavals of Thought: The Intelligence of Emotions*. Cambridge University Press.

Obama, B. (2009). Public Papers of the Presidents of the United States, Administration of Barak Obama 2009. Book 1. June 6th Remarks on the 65th Anniversary of D-Day in Normandy, France, p. 795. Federal Register Division, National Archives and Records Service, General Services Administration, 2009 United States Government Printing Office, Washington DC.

Orwell, G. (1946). In Front of Your Nose. In *Tribune*.

Pence, G.E. (1983). Can Compassion Be Taught? *Journal of Medical Ethics* 9(4): 189.

Petrocchi, N., Ottaviani, C. and Couyoumdjian, A. (2017). Compassion at the Mirror: Exposure to a Mirror Increases the Efficacy of a Self-compassion Manipulation in Enhancing Soothing Positive Affect and Heart Rate Variability. *The Journal of Positive Psychology*, 12(6): 525–536.

Philpot, R., Liebst, L.S., Levine, M., Bernasco, W. and Lindegaard, M.R. (2020). Would I Be Helped? Cross-national CCTV Footage Shows that Intervention Is the Norm in Public Conflicts. *American Psychologist*, 75(1): 66–75.

Post, S.G. (2011). Compassionate Care Enhancement: Benefits and Outcomes. *International Journal of Person Centered Medicine, 1*(4): 808–813.

Pronin, E., Lin, D.Y. and Ross, L. (2002). The Bias Blind Spot: Perceptions of Bias in Self Versus Others. *Personality and Social Psychology Bulletin, 28*(3): 369–381.

PwC 2021 https://www.strategyand.pwc.com/uk/en/insights/esg.html

Raes, F., Pommier, E., Neff, K. D. and Van Gucht, D. (2011). Construction and Factorial Validation of a Short Form of the Self-Compassion Scale. *Clinical Psychology & Psychotherapy, 18*, 250–255.

Ricard, M. (2013). *Altruism: The Power of Compassion to Change Yourself and the World*. London: Atlantic Books.

Richards, J. (1980). *Consul of God: The Life and Times of Gregory the Great*. Abingdon: Routledge.

Ridley, M. (2000). *Genome*. London: Fourth Estate.

Riggio, R. E. (2020). How Empathic Are You, Really? Test Which Type of Empathy You Possess. https://www.psychologytoday.com/gb/blog/cutting-edge-leadership/202010/how-empathic-are-you-really

Rippon, G. (2019). *The Gendered Brain: The New Neuroscience that Shatters the Myth of the Female Brain*. London: Bodley Head.

Rockliff, H., Gilbert, P., McEwan, K., Lightman, S. and Glover, D. (2008). A Pilot Exploration of Heart Rate Variability and Salivary Cortisol Responses to Compassion-focused Imagery. *Clinical Neuropsychiatry, 5*, 3: 132–139.

Rodell, J., Breitsohl, H., Schröder, M. and Keating, D. (2016). Employee Volunteering: A Review and Framework for Future Research. *Journal of Management, 42*(1).

Rogers, C.R. (1961). *On Becoming a Person: A Therapist's View of Psychotherapy*. London: Constable.

Rogers, C.R. (1980). *A Way of Being*. New York: Houghton Mifflin Company.

Rotter, J.B. (1954). *Social Learning and Clinical Psychology*. Prentice Hall, Inc.

Rowland, L.A. and Curry, O.S. (2019). A Range of Kindness Activities Boost Happiness. *The Journal of Social Psychology, 159*: 340–343.

Rozin, P. and Royzman, E.B. (2001). Negativity Bias, Negativity Dominance, and Contagion. *Personality and Social Psychology Review, 5*(4): 296–320

Ryan, R.M. and Deci, E.L. (2000). Self-Determination Theory and the Facilitation of Intrinsic Motivation, Social Development, and Well-Being. *American Psychologist, 55*(1): 68–78.

Rynes, S.L., Bartunek, J.M., Dutton, J.E. and Margolis, J.D. (2012). Care and Compassion Through an Organizational Lens: Opening Up New Possibilities. *Academy of Management Review, 37*(4): 503–523.

Sala, F. (2003). Executive Blind Spots: Discrepancies Between Self- and Other-Ratings. *Consulting Psychology Journal: Practice and Research 55*(4): 222–229.

Samaie, G.H. and Farahani, H.A. (2011). Self-Compassion as a Moderator of the Relationship Between Rumination, Self-reflection and Stress. *Procedia – Social and Behavioral Sciences, 30*, 978–982.

Santos, H.C., Varnum, M.E.W. and Grossman, I. (2017). Global Increases in Individualism. *Psychological Science, 28*(9), 1228–1239.

Schantz, M.L. (2007). Compassion: A Concept Analysis. *Nursing Forum, 42*(2): 48–55.

Schein, E.H. (2013). *Humble Enquiry: The Gentle Art of Asking Instead of Telling*. San Francisco: Berrett-Koehler Publishers, Inc.

Schopenhauer, A. (1839/1995). *On The Basis of Morality*. Cambridge: Hackett Publishing Company.

Senge, P.M., Kleiner, A., Roberts, C., Ross, R.B. and Smith, B.J. (1995). *The Fifth Discipline Fieldbook: Strategies and Tools for Building a Learning Organization*. London: Nicholas Brealey.

Seppala, E., Rossomando, T. and Doty, J.R. (2013) Social Connection and Compassion: Important Predictors of Health and Well-being. *Social Research: An International Quarterly, 80*(2): 411–430.

Shapira, L.B. and Mongrain, M. (2010). The Benefits of Self-compassion and Optimism Exercises for Individuals Vulnerable to Depression. *The Journal of Positive Psychology, 5*(5): 377–389.

Silani, G., Lamm, C., Ruff, C.C. and Singer, T. (2013). Right Supramarginal Gyrus Is Crucial to Overcome Emotional Egocentricity Bias in Social Judgments. *Journal of Neuroscience, 33*(39): 15466–15476.

Simpson, A. and Farr-Wharton, B. (2017). The NEAR Organisational Compassion Scale: Validity, Reliability and Correlations. Available at: http://hdl.handle.net/10453/125452

Sinclair, S., Norris, J.M., McConnell, S.J., Chochinov, H.M., Hack, T.F., Hagen, N.A, et al. (2016). Compassion: a scoping review of the healthcare literature. *BMC Palliative Care*, 15(6).

Singer, T. and Klimecki, O.M. (2014). Empathy and Compassion. *Current Biology*, 24(18): 875–878.

Smeets, E., Neff, K., Alberts, H. and Peters, M. (2014). Meeting Suffering with Kindness: Effects of a Brief Self-Compassion Intervention for Female College Students. *Journal of Clinical Psychology*, 70(9): 794–807.

Smith, A. (1759/2009). *The Theory of Moral Sentiments*. London: Penguin.

Smith, R.A. (2022). Why Is Your Boss Asking About your Feelings? Inside the Empathy Management Trend. 10 May 2022. https://www.wsj.com/articles/why-is-your-boss-asking-about-your-feelings-inside-the-empathy-management-leadership-trend–11652132040

Solomon, R.C. (1998). The Moral Psychology of Business: Care and Compassion in the Corporation. *Business Ethics Quarterly*, 8(3): 515–533.

Sprecher, S. and Fehr, B. (2005). Compassionate Love for Close Others and Humanity. *Journal of Social and Personal Relationships*, 22, 629–651.

Stewart, A.J. and Plotkin, J.B. (2012). From Extortion to Generosity, Evolution in the Iterated Prisoner's Dilemma. *PNAS*, 110(38): 15348–15353.

Strauss, C., Taylor, B.L., Gu, J., Kuyken, W., Baer, R., Jones, F. and Cavanagh, K. (2016). What Is Compassion and How Can We Measure It? A Review of Definitions and Measures. *Clinical Psychology Review*, 47, 15–27.

Sy, T., Côté, S. and Saavedra, R. (2005). The Contagious Leader: Impact of the Leader's Mood on the Mood of Group Members, Group Affective Tone, and Group Processes. *Journal of Applied Psychology*, 90(2): 295–305.

Thayler, R.H. and Sunstein, C. (2008). *Nudge*. London: Penguin.

Thirioux, B., Mercier, M.R., Blanke, O. and Berthoz, A. (2014). The Cognitive and Neural Time Course of Empathy and Sympathy: An Electrical Neuroimaging Study on Self–other Interaction. *Neuroscience*, 267, 286–306.

Tomaka, J. and Blascovich, J. (1994). Effects of Justice Beliefs on Cognitive Appraisal of and Subjective Physiological, and Behavioral Responses to Potential Stress. *Journal of Personality and Social Psychology*, 67(4): 732–740.

Tonelli, M.E. and Wachholtz, A.B. (2014). Meditation-based Treatment Yielding Immediate Relief for Meditation-Naïve Migraineurs. *Pain Management Nursing*, 15(1): 36–40.

Van den Berg, Y.H.M. and Cillessen, A.H.N. (2015). Peer Status and Classroom Seating Arrangements: A Social Relations Analysis. *Journal of Experimental Child Psychology*, 130, 19–34.

Västfjäll D., Slovic, P., Mayorga, M. and Peters, E. (2014). Compassion Fade: Affect and Charity Are Greatest for a Single Child in Need. *PLoS ONE* 9(6): e100115.

Vermeire, E., Hearnshaw, H, Van Royen, P. and Denekens, J. (2001). Patient Adherence to Treatment: Three Decades of Research. A Comprehensive Review. *Journal of Clinical Pharmacy and Therapeutics*, 26, 331–342.

Vianello, M., Galliani, E.M. and Haidt, J. (2010). Elevation at Work: The Effects of Leaders' Moral Excellence. *The Journal of Positive Psychology*, 5(5): 390–411.

Walsh, J.P. (1999). Business Must Talk About Its Social Role. In Dickson, T. (ed.). *Mastering Strategy*. London: *Financial Times*/Prentice Hall.

Warren, R., Smeets, E. and Neff, K. (2016). Self-criticism and Self-compassion: Risk and Resilience. Being Compassionate to Oneself is Associated with Emotional Resilience and Psychological Wellbeing. *Current Psychiatry*, 15(12), 18–33.

Watts, A. (no date). The Road to Hell Is Paved with Good Intentions. Available at: https://www.youtube.com/watch?v=cegl1BZ-0tI

Weinstein, N. and Ryan, R. M. (2010). When Helping Helps: Autonomous Motivation for Prosocial Behavior and its Influence on Well-being for the Helper and Recipient. *Journal of Personality and Social Psychology, 98*(2): 222–244.

Weng, H.Y., Fox, A.S., Shackman, A.J., Stodola, D.E., Caldwell, J.Z.K., Olson, M.C., Rogers, G.M. and Davidson, R.J. (2013). Compassion Training Alters Altruism and Neural Responses to Suffering. *Psychological Science, 24*(7), 1171–1180.

Wharton. (2018). LinkedIn's Jeff Weiner: How Compassion Builds Better Companies. https://knowledge. wharton.upenn.edu/article/linkedin-ceo-how-compassion-can-build-a-better-company/

White, S. S. and Locke, E. A. (2000). Problems with the Pygmalion Effect and Some Proposed Solutions. *The Leadership Quarterly, 11*(3): 389–415.

Whitehead, B. R. and Bergeman, C. S. (2012). Coping with Daily Stress: Differential Role of Spiritual Experience on Daily Positive and Negative Affect. *The Journal of Gerontology: Series B, 67*(4): 456–459.

WHO. (2001). World Health Report: Mental Disorders Affect One in Four People. Available at: http://www. who.int/whr/2001/media_centre/press_release/en/

WHO. (2022). COVID-19 Pandemic Triggers 25% Increase in Prevalence of Anxiety and Depression Worldwide. Available at: https://www.who.int/news/item/02-03-2022-covid-19-pandemic-triggers-25-increase-in-prevalence-of-anxiety-and-depression-worldwide

Wood, A.M., Froh, J.J. and Geraghty, A.W. (2010). Gratitude and Well-being: A Review and Theoretical Integration. *Clinical Psychology Review, 30*(7): 890–905.

Worline, M.C. and Dutton, J.E. (2017). *Awakening Compassion at Work: The Quiet Power that Elevates People and Organizations*. Oakland: Berrett-Koehler.

Yamaguchi, A., Kim, M-S. and Akutsu, S. (2014). The Effects of Self-construals, Self-criticism, and Self-compassion on Depressive Symptoms. *Personality and Individual Differences, 68*: 65–70.

Zinn, H. (2007). *A Power Governments Cannot Supress*. San Francisco: City Lights.

Ziv, T., Whiteman, J.D. and Sommerville, J.A. (2021). Toddlers' Interventions Toward Fair and Unfair Individuals. *Cognition, 214*, 104781.

List of figures

Figure 1.1 Common tripartite conceptualisation of compassion —— **4**
Figure 1.2 Four-part conceptualisation of compassion —— **4**
Figure 1.3 Conscious competence learning model —— **6**
Figure 2.1 New compassion construct —— **9**
Figure 2.2 Transactional Analysis: Parent – Adult – Child —— **17**
Figure 2.3 Karpman's Drama Triangle —— **19**
Figure 2.4 Compassion maths —— **28**
Figure 3.1 Empathy —— **34**
Figure 3.2 Differential neural networks for empathy and compassion (reproduced with permission from Singer and Klimecki 2014) —— **37**
Figure 3.3 Sympathy —— **39**
Figure 3.4 Pity —— **39**
Figure 3.5 Altruism —— **43**
Figure 3.6 Kindness —— **47**
Figure 3.7 Compassion —— **48**
Figure 3.8 Compassion's Mistaken Identities Summary —— **49**
Figure 5.1 New Compassion Construct and Conflict Resolution —— **77**
Figure 6.1 Cognitive Biases and the New Compassion Construct —— **88**
Figure 6.2 Theory of Mind development steps —— **95**
Figure 6.3 All the Same Underneath —— **98**
Figure 6.4 Prompts to Offset Bias and the New Compassion Construct —— **104**
Figure 7.1 Self-compassion (adapted from Neff 2003) —— **108**
Figure 7.2 Self-compassion with example statements (adapted from Neff 2003) —— **120**
Figure 7.3 Self-compassion and the New Compassion Construct —— **127**
Figure 8.1 Light and Dark Triads —— **130**
Figure 8.2 Newspaper Headlines —— **132**
Figure 8.3 Developing Compassionate Leadership with the New Compassion Construct —— **133**
Figure 8.4 Theory of Adult Development (adapted from Kegan 1983) —— **136**
Figure 8.5 Two coins —— **150**
Figure 9.1 Areas for Consideration in Designing a Compassionate Organisation —— **153**
Figure 9.2 Employee Lifecycle —— **156**
Figure 9.3 Public Compassion Commitment —— **161**
Figure 9.4 Self-Determination Theory, adapted from Ryan and Deci, 2000 —— **167**

https://doi.org/10.1515/9783110763126-013

List of tables

Table 2.1 Resourcing Ourselves —— **22**
Table 4.1 Comparison between Compassion and Empathic Distress Fatigue
(adapted from Singer and Klimecki 2014: 875) —— **63**
Table 5.1 Meyer and Allen Commitment Types —— **71**
Table 5.2 Organisational Compassion Factors (adapted from Dutton et al. 2014) —— **73**
Table 5.3 Beneficiaries of Compassion in Healthcare (adapted from Post 2011) —— **79**
Table 5.4 Post's Healthcare Approach and the New Compassion Construct —— **81**
Table 7.1 OC – AC Research Conditions —— **117**
Table 9.1 Compassionate Organisation Blueprints (adapted from Worline and Dutton 2017) —— **159**

https://doi.org/10.1515/9783110763126-014

About the author

Kirstie Drummond Papworth is a Psychologist, Behavioural Change Executive Coach and compassion researcher. She holds an MSc in Psychology (with a specialisation in business) and another in Behavioural Change. Her organisational and leadership background includes commercial roles in a FTSE50 organisation, Commercial Director for an independent wine importer and running her own successful behavioural change consultancy, Tangerine Thistle.

Kirstie has delivered leadership development interventions across many sectors including higher education, retail, software, engineering, healthcare and the armed forces. She also delivers regular webinars and workshops for the British Psychological Society and National Health Service. Kirstie is currently Executive Director of Experiential Learning at London Business School.

Kirstie has delivered keynote speaker events on compassionate leadership for professional development groups, including LeanIn, numerous NHS Trusts, Suicide Prevention conferences and BBC Radio. She is a TeDx speaker on her specialist subject of compassion, a Samaritans listening volunteer and Chair of Trustees for the Dalai Lama Centre for Compassion, Oxford. This is her first book.

https://doi.org/10.1515/9783110763126-015

About the series editor

Bernd Vogel is a Professor in Leadership and Founding Director of the Henley Centre for Leadership at Henley Business School, UK.

Bernd has more than 20 years of global experience in research, educating, speaking, and consulting with outstanding companies, business schools and universities. He supports organisations and people in life-long learning journeys that transform lives, organisations, and society. He bridges academia with practice and is an executive coach.

His expertise is in leadership and leadership development; future of work and leadership; strategic leadership to mobilise and sustain healthy energy and performance; developing leadership and followership capability; healthy and performing senior management teams; change, transformation and culture; leadership development architectures.

Bernd features regularly in media. He publishes in top-tier global academic journals and has written and edited several books, case studies and industry reports.

Throughout his career Bernd has had academic roles at the Leibniz University Hannover, Germany, and University of St. Gallen, Switzerland. He has held global visiting positions at Claremont Graduate University, USA; IESE Business School, Spain; and Marshall School of Business, USC, USA.

https://doi.org/10.1515/9783110763126-016

Index

9/11 75, 170

accountability 54, 75, 78–79, 83, 130
Adult Development, Theory of 136, 151
Affective Commitment 70–71, 82–83, 117, 131–132,
    154–155, 157, 165, 169, 171
– and Organisational Compassion 74–75, 83
– definition 71
Allen, Natalie 71–72
altruism 3, 6, 8, 21, 28–29, 33, 42–46, 49–50, 54,
    56, 62, 81, 102, 130, 133, 143, 145, 174
– at work: case study 44
– definition 42
– organisational and economic 43
appraisal 7, 9, 14, 28–29, 31, 33, 43–44, 81, 104,
    106, 121, 127, 133, 143, 158, 164, 173
– appraisal and judgement 14–15, 144–145
– definition 14
– patterns of behaviour 9, 16–21, 27
– resources 9, 21–24, 27, 49, 116
– role 9, 24–27, 116, 143–144
– safety and intention 9, 15–16, 27
Ardern, Jacinda 58, 130, 144
Aristotle 14–15, 31
awareness 4, 9, 10–11, 15, 18, 28, 35, 44, 46, 57, 59,
    68, 77, 81, 85, 88, 90, 92–95, 97, 99, 102,
    104–106, 108, 113, 121–123, 133, 139–142, 145,
    150–151
– absence of awareness 12
– awareness of others 11
– building awareness 135–138
– building self-awareness 135–136
– definition 10
– difference of perspectives 40
– language of awareness 11
– self-awareness 11, 34, 135–137, 144

behaviour 11, 13, 24–26, 38, 43, 50, 52, 60–61, 63,
    69–74, 77–79, 82, 84–85, 88–90, 92, 95–96,
    98, 102, 105, 109, 111–113, 117–119, 129–133,
    135–136, 140, 143, 145, 147–149, 151–152, 154,
    158, 165–166, 168–172, 176
– behavioural nudges 160–163, 172
– patterns of behaviour 7, 9, 15–21, 27, 29, 31–32,
    107, 149, 175
Berne, Eric 16, 18

Bodanis, David 62
Brown, Brené 31–32
burnout 36, 44, 46, 63, 78, 80, 115
– in altruism/compassion fatigue/resourcing 21

career sabotage 51, 57, 59–62, 66
Charter for Compassion 53
checking in and out 140
choice 17–18, 20–27, 31–32, 50, 59, 82, 85, 88,
    105–106, 125, 129, 136, 142, 151, 160, 175–176
– leadership choice 65, 129–133
cognitive biases 5, 8, 84–86, 88, 103, 105
– and judgement 160–161
– Authority Bias 86
– Availability Bias 34, 93–94, 99, 104
– Blind Spot Bias 84, 103, 136
– Bystander Effect 100–104
– Confirmation Bias 34, 41, 89–92, 104
– Fundamental Attribution Error 92–93, 104
– Inattentional Blindness 94–95, 104
– In-group Favouritism 6, 53, 95–97, 104
– Just World Hypothesis 5, 15, 31, 98–99, 104
– Naïve Cynicism 99, 104
– Naïve Realism 84, 99
– Negativity Bias 100, 104
– prompts to offset biases 104
– Self-Serving Bias 91–92, 104
– Superiority Illusion 84–85, 136
collaboration 113, 162
collectivist
– trends 41
– vs individualistic 41–42
commitment 31, 58, 60, 71, 154–155, 161
– Affective Commitment 70–71, 74–75, 82–83, 117,
    131–132, 154–155, 157, 165, 169, 171
  – benefits of AC 71
– Continuance 71
– Normative 71
compassion 1, 3–8, 33–34, 36–38, 43–46, 48–50,
    84–88, 106–151, 173–177
– and sense-making 4–6, 8, 14–15
– as a commercial approach 62, 80, 157, 176
– benefits of compassion (leadership) 67, 83
  – cellular inflammation 68
  – chemical balance and rewiring 69
  – reduced stress, anxiety and depression 68

https://doi.org/10.1515/9783110763126-017

- social connectedness 70
- benefits of compassion (organisational) 70, 75, 83
  - accountability and psychological safety 78–79
  - Affective Commitment 71, 74–75
  - enhanced organisational wellbeing 75–76
  - improved conflict resolution 76–78
- compassion avoidance 65–66
- compassion fade 64. *See also* psychic numbing
- compassion fatigue 51, 57, 63–64, 66, 80
- compassion maths 28, 133
- dark side of compassion 67, 81–83
- leadership and organisational outcomes 131–132
- measurement 73, 79, 146–147, 152, 169–171
- nature of compassion 7, 30, 32, 50
  - social process 32, 50, 72–73
  - verb 31–32
  - vice 30–33
  - virtue 31–32, 52–53, 131
- new construct 6–32, 35, 43–44, 59, 76–77, 80–81,
      83, 88–104, 106, 116, 121, 127, 130, 133,
      135–136, 141, 143, 145, 157–158, 160, 163, 173
- organisational 8, 26, 50, 57–58, 70, 72–75, 81–83,
      117, 119, 127, 131–133, 146, 154, 150–172
- previous definitions 9
- reputation 3, 8, 30–31, 35, 48, 50–67, 70, 77–80,
      82, 86, 109–112
competence 6, 58, 131, 158–159, 167
- unconscious/conscious 6–7, 46
Comte, Auguste 42–43, 45
conflict 2, 15–16, 82, 84–85, 96–97, 101, 130, 140,
      147, 150, 173
- and compassion 32, 77–78
- resolution 76–78, 83, 85
Coombes, Joshua 87
cooperation 61–62, 114, 132
cortisol 69, 80, 87, 112, 126
COVID-19 pandemic 2, 42, 56, 78
- and compassion avoidance 65
- impact on mental health 2, 65
culture 31, 41, 44, 62, 71, 76, 78, 95, 101, 112, 130,
      133, 139, 152, 159, 166–169, 172–173

Dalai Lama XIV, His Holiness 46, 52, 58, 173
difference 3, 5–6, 10, 14, 26, 28, 36, 38, 40, 46, 48,
      50–51, 53, 58, 63, 75–76, 86, 90, 96–97, 107,
      109, 129–130, 136, 140, 147, 150–151, 154, 157,
      164, 168, 175, 177
- vs similarity 33

Donne, John 45
dopamine 16, 20, 55, 69, 87
Drama Triangle 18–21, 24, 29, 44, 106, 110, 144, 158
Dutton, Jane 4, 14, 73, 158

economics 2, 8, 43, 51, 54–56, 61, 66–67, 75, 85,
      153
ego states 17–18, 78
Einstein, Albert 24, 45, 81, 148, 174
emotion 1, 3–5, 9, 12–13, 16–17, 22–23, 27–29, 31–32,
      34–36, 38–41, 52–53, 56–57, 63, 69, 71–73,
      75–77, 79, 81, 85, 87, 92–93, 95, 97, 99, 103, 106,
      108, 111–116, 119–120, 126–127, 130, 132, 137,
      140, 145, 149, 151, 153, 162, 164–165, 168, 175
- and contagion 141–142, 151
- emotional intelligence 142
empathic distress fatigue 55, 63
empathy 3, 6, 8, 11–13, 25, 27–29, 32–34, 40–41,
      46, 48, 50, 56, 62–63, 81, 86–87, 102, 112, 130,
      133, 143, 148–149, 165, 168, 174
- definition 34
- importance of 33
- limits of 36–38
- types of empathy 34–36
  - affective empathy 35
  - cognitive empathy 35–36, 149
  - empathic concern 35–36
employee assistance programmes 75–76, 155
employee engagement 67, 78, 131, 171
employee lifecycle 97, 146, 156–158, 172
ESG 43–44, 153–154
ethics 53, 82, 96–97, 101, 132–133, 152–154, 166,
      172–174
- of compassion 82

feeling 1, 4, 8–9, 11–14, 17, 19, 23–24, 28, 30–31,
      33–35, 38–39, 41, 46–47, 56, 59, 63, 70, 72–73,
      76–80, 87, 92, 97, 99, 104, 106, 108–109, 111,
      113–114, 117, 119, 124–126, 130, 132, 140–142,
      147–148, 160–162
- definition 12
Financial Times 35–36, 56, 58

Games People Play, The 18, 24
Game Theory 61
- evolving, dynamic populations 62
- Prisoner's Dilemma 62
- successful approaches 62

Gilbert, Paul 4, 32, 82, 107–108, 112, 141, 147
Goleman, Daniel 34–35, 142
Golem Effect 89–90
Good Samaritan, The 16, 31, 52, 101
gratitude 24, 69, 109, 132, 158

habits 85, 111, 113, 151
– compassionate habits 145–146
– Tiny Habits 145
Halo Effect 97
happiness 9, 27, 47, 54, 68–70, 111, 132, 144, 155,
    164, 169, 171
– eudaimonic 68, 165–166
– hedonic 68
Harvard Implicit Association Tests 165
healer 81
– and wounded 102, 107
– healyitis 144–145
healthcare 76
– benefits of compassion 79–80
– lessons on compassion 79–81, 83
heuristics. *See* cognitive biases
HR 157
– policies 156–158
humanising the workplace 2–3, 174–175
humble 35, 59, 109, 136, 148, 176
– humble enquiry 139–140, 151
– moderation 62
Hume, David 39

immune system 114
– and compassion 103, 115–116
– and happiness 68
Inclusion and Diversity 14, 24, 76, 85, 94, 100,
    155, 162
individual 1–2, 7–8, 10–11, 21–22, 25, 31, 33, 35,
    40–41, 43–48, 50–51, 55, 60–61, 64–66, 68,
    70–76, 78–79, 81–82, 84, 86–87, 89–91, 93,
    95–96, 98–103, 106, 109, 113–114, 116–117,
    129–132, 135–137, 142, 147–148, 150–155,
    157–159, 162–167, 169–171, 173–175
– actions and difference 5, 8, 79, 150, 157, 162,
    168, 171
individualistic 41
– trends 41
– vs collective 41–42
in-groups 6, 53, 70, 82, 90, 95–97, 104, 150–151, 174

intention 3, 9, 16, 20, 27–29, 43, 55, 61, 69, 76,
    81–82, 86–88, 99, 104, 106, 131, 142, 150–151,
    171, 175–176
– and judgement 144–145
– dangers of intention 28, 126, 144, 148
interconnectedness 41, 45–46, 50, 52, 139–140,
    150, 162
introspection 11, 138, 155

Johnson, Kevin 25
Jonson, Ben 30
judgements 4, 14–15, 85, 90, 95, 99, 104–106, 130,
    135, 138, 144, 149, 155, 160–161, 163, 175
– and intention 14–15, 144–145
– deservedness/relevance/ability to make a
    difference 5–6, 15
Jung, C.G. 81
Just World Hypothesis 5, 15, 31, 98–99, 104

Kahneman, Daniel 84–85, 88, 100
Kant, Immanuel 30–31, 54–55
Karpman, Stephen 19, 21, 24, 106, 110, 144, 158
kindness 3–4, 8, 33, 45–48, 50–52, 56, 67, 97,
    107–108, 110–111, 114, 116–117, 119, 126, 128,
    137, 144, 146, 148, 165
– benefits 47–48
– definition 46–48
– vs compassion 48
Klimecki, Olga 36–38, 46, 63
Kundera, Milan 56

leadership 1–9, 11–12, 14–16, 18, 22, 24, 27, 29,
    31–33, 35, 38, 42–46, 50–52, 54, 57–60, 62,
    65–70, 73, 76–79, 81–86, 88, 90, 93–95, 97,
    99–107, 113, 118–119, 127, 154–155, 158–160,
    168–177
– and commitment 161
– and compassionate choice 65, 129–133
– and culture 166–168
– and emotion 27, 38, 57, 69, 95, 116, 141–142,
    151, 168
– and intention 3, 16, 43, 69, 76, 86–88, 106, 131,
    142, 144–145, 150–151, 171, 175
– and meditation 46, 69
– and resourcing 21–24, 26–27, 44, 103, 106,
    115–116, 119, 158–159
– and self-compassion 116–117, 121–122

– and stress, anxiety, depression 24, 69, 91, 106, 112, 116–118, 121, 128, 144, 164, 166
– compassion, and organisational outcomes 131–132
– developing compassionate leadership 129–151
– disproportionate impact 25–26, 29, 86, 151, 158, 176
– in the firing line 148–151
– legacy 150–151
– opportunities for all 163–166
– role modelling 25, 65, 73, 106, 148, 158–159, 166
– weak 51, 54, 57–58, 61, 66, 77, 79, 130
listening 24–27, 38, 62, 87, 89, 106, 139–141, 176
– conflict 77
– Kline, Nancy 139
– Nouwen, Henri 176

measurement 27, 32, 36, 65, 80, 108, 110, 117, 142, 154
– bottom line measurement 170–171
– direct and indirect measurement 171
– of compassion 73, 79, 146–147, 152, 169–171
– of self-compassion 119, 147
– what gets measured 146, 169–170
meditation 23–24, 52, 69, 81, 86, 109, 115, 122, 142, 164
– leadership benefits 46, 69
– loving kindness 36, 45–46, 137
– self-compassion 24, 114, 121–122, 144
– to build awareness 137
mental health 2–3, 8, 23, 65, 69–70, 75, 107, 110, 116, 176
– cost to organisations 2
– trends 2
Meyer, John 71–72
Microsoft 62, 168
mistaken identities 8, 30–33, 49–50, 109–112
– altruism 3, 6, 8, 21, 28–29, 33, 42–46, 49–50, 54, 56, 62, 81, 102, 130, 133, 143, 145, 174
– empathy 3, 6, 8, 11–13, 25, 27–29, 32–38, 40–41, 46, 48, 50, 56, 62–63, 81, 86–87, 102, 112, 130, 133, 143, 148–149, 165, 168, 174
– kindness 3–4, 8, 33, 45–48, 50–52, 56, 67, 97, 107–108, 110–111, 114, 116–117, 119, 126, 128, 137, 144, 146, 148, 165

– pity 8, 33, 38–40, 46, 48, 50, 55, 86, 91, 107, 109–110, 113, 119, 128
– sympathy 3, 8, 30, 33, 38–40, 46, 48, 50, 86
monitored generosity 62

Nadella, Satya 62, 168
Neff, Kristin 107, 111, 115, 120–121, 146, 163
neural networks 13
– and In-Group Favouritism 96
– between empathy and compassion 36–37, 63
neuroscience 13, 33, 49, 107
– differences between compassion and empathy 36
– differences between empathy and sympathy 40
Nhat Hanh, Thich 31, 139
Nietzsche, Friedrich 54–55
nudges 118, 171, 175
– behavioural nudges 160–163, 172

Odebrecht 59–60
organisational compassion 8, 26, 50, 57–58, 70, 72–75, 81–82, 117, 119, 127, 131, 146, 154, 158, 163, 167, 169, 172
– and Affective Commitment 74–75, 83
– and organisational elevation 132–133
– benefits 72, 74–75
– definition 72
– designing a compassionate organisation 152–153
  – behavioural 160–166
  – cultural 166–169
  – strategic 153–155
  – structural 156–159
– measurement 169–171
– organisational character 72–73
– organisational systems 50, 72–73, 150–152, 160, 171
– six factors of organisational compassion 73
out-groups 24, 44, 90–91, 95–97, 99, 103–104, 136, 150, 155, 162, 165
oxytocin 16, 47, 69, 87

performance 8, 11, 32, 58, 62, 65, 67, 71, 74–75, 78–79, 82, 84, 89–90, 100, 103, 114, 116, 118–119, 127, 131, 136, 142, 151, 160, 163, 165, 167–168, 171
personality 9, 16, 60–61, 110, 115, 117, 125, 129, 142
– and success 91

philosophy 35, 47, 51, 168
- and compassion 54–56, 66
physiology 3, 113, 116, 128, 130, 148, 152, 165, 173
pity 8, 33, 38–40, 46, 48, 50, 55, 86, 91, 107,
    109–110, 113, 119, 128
power 3, 8, 11, 16, 27, 45, 47, 52, 59–62, 66, 73, 82,
    102, 110, 112, 118–119, 138, 142, 144, 151,
    173–176
- and corruption 60
- and personality 60–61
- perils of power 59, 62
practice 5–7, 15, 21, 28, 31–32, 35, 41, 43–44, 46,
    57, 60, 62, 69, 72–73, 81, 85–86, 91–92,
    103–104, 108–109, 114–116, 119, 123, 127,
    129–130, 133–134, 137–139, 142, 144–146, 148,
    151–152, 155–156, 159, 163–166, 168, 175–176
prompts and practices 10, 14, 16, 21–22, 25–26, 42,
    44, 46, 53, 57, 59–60, 64, 77–78, 82, 86, 90, 97,
    103, 109, 116–119, 131, 165
psychic numbing 51, 57, 64–65, 162. *See also*
    compassion fade
psychoanalysis 16, 149
psychobiology 13, 91, 101–102
psychological safety 75, 82–83, 92, 94, 99, 104, 106,
    130, 140, 143, 154, 160, 166–167, 171–174
- definition 78, 166
- how to improve 78–79
psychology 4, 6, 8, 18, 20, 24, 28–29, 33, 36, 38,
    49–51, 61, 63, 65, 69, 84, 92, 101, 106–107, 113,
    115–116, 118–119, 128, 130, 134, 144, 151–154,
    157, 165, 169, 173
psychopathy 13–14, 19, 60, 129
purpose 3, 21, 23, 60, 68, 74, 80–81, 92, 96–97,
    138–140, 151, 169–170
Pygmalion Effect 89–90

reflection and reflexive practice 137–138, 175
religion 23, 95, 135
- and compassion 3, 51–54, 56, 66
- Buddhism 45, 47, 107, 148
- Christianity 52
- Hinduism 53
- Islam 52
- Judaism 52
- Pope Gregory I 53–54, 56
- Sikhism 53
reputation (of compassion) 3, 8, 30–31, 35, 48,
    50–67, 70, 77–80, 82, 86, 109–112
- career sabotage 57, 59

- weak leadership 51, 57–58
rescuer in Drama Triangle 19–21, 106, 144, 158
resilience 70, 132
- and compassion 38, 57, 75, 82, 107, 173
- and self-compassion 10, 106, 109, 111, 118–119,
    127–128, 166
resourcing 5, 7, 9, 20–24, 26–29, 43–44, 49, 77,
    80–81, 96, 103–104, 106–107, 115–116, 119, 127,
    130, 135, 143, 158–159, 164, 174
- definition 22
- physical/social/emotional/mental/spiritual 22–23
responding 1, 4, 13, 15, 26–28, 32–33, 36, 42, 58,
    74, 92, 104, 107, 113, 127, 129, 132, 142,
    145–148, 159, 162, 166, 168, 170, 176
- definition 27
- vs reacting 27, 81, 145
- ways to respond 1, 27, 139
reward 25, 38, 59, 87–88, 98, 124, 129, 147, 152,
    158–160, 163, 165–166, 173, 175–176
Ricard, Matthieu 43, 45, 52
Robber's Cave Experiments 96
Rogers, Carl R. 15, 144, 151
role 3, 7, 9, 11, 18, 32, 33, 39, 42, 44, 46, 51–53, 60,
    63, 66, 68–69, 71–72, 74, 77, 81, 87, 89, 101,
    103, 107, 118, 124, 132, 138, 156, 158–159, 163,
    167, 173
- and resourcing 23–24
- definition 24
- Drama Triangle 19–21, 106, 110, 144
- leadership role 25–26, 134
- responses and themes 143–144
- role appraisal 24–29, 104, 116, 143–144
- role modelling 25, 65, 73, 79, 106, 144, 148,
    158–160, 166, 175
Rumi 32, 109–110

Schein, Edgar 35, 139–140
Schopenhauer, Arthur 9, 54–55
Schultz, Howard 25, 143–144
self-compassion 8, 10, 21, 23–24, 44, 69, 91,
    106–107, 134, 142, 144, 146–147, 163–164, 166,
    168, 174
- and leadership 116–117, 121–122
- and self as an instrument 106, 175
- and stress, anxiety, depression in leaders 24, 69,
    91, 106, 112, 116–118, 121
- benchmarking ad measurement 119–120
- benefits 112–113
  - growth mindset 113–114

– moderating stress, anxiety, depression 116–117
– mood regulation 115–116
– performance 118
– resilience 118–119
– social connectedness 114–115
– definitions 107–108
– developing self-compassion 119–126
– reputation and mistaken identities 109–112
– self-compassion scale 120, 146, 128, 144, 164, 166
self-criticism 108–109, 111–114, 118–120, 124, 128, 141
Self Determination Theory 167
self-esteem 10, 90–92, 107, 109–111, 113–114, 116, 119, 124, 128, 164
self-pity 91, 107, 109–110, 113, 119, 128
serotonin 16, 47, 69, 87
Sherif, Muzafer 96
Singer, Tania 36, 38, 46, 63
Smith, Adam 54–55, 67, 153, 173
social 2, 22, 25, 29, 33–34, 38, 41, 43, 47, 61, 63, 65, 79, 87, 90, 95, 97–98, 102, 107, 109, 111, 132, 142, 154, 159, 162
– dance 32, 107
– process 32, 50, 72–73
– pro-social behaviours 52, 71–72, 74, 162
social connectedness 22, 46–47, 63, 67, 83, 87, 173
– and self-compassion 114–115, 127
– benefits 70, 127
– definition 70
– risks associated with lack of 114
Social Dominance Orientation 74
Social Identity Theory 53, 90, 95
Starbucks 25, 29, 143
stress 2, 23–24, 63, 65, 67–70, 74, 82, 87, 91, 98, 106, 108, 112, 115–118, 120–121, 127–128, 131, 134, 141, 144, 164, 166, 173, 176
suffering 1–6, 8, 11–15, 21, 25–28, 30, 34–35, 38, 40–44, 48–50, 52–58, 64, 69–70, 73, 75–77, 81, 86, 91, 93–95, 97–100, 104, 106–111, 120, 123, 125–127, 129, 131, 135, 139–141, 143–146, 149–152, 155–159, 162–164, 166–167, 170, 172–173, 175–177
– alleviation 9, 15–16, 20–21, 27, 31, 34, 44, 48, 53, 55, 68, 81, 158–159
– deservedness 5, 14, 99
sympathy 3, 8, 30, 33, 38–40, 46, 48, 50, 86

Tajfel, Henri 90, 95
Theory of Mind 35, 95
training 38, 46, 52, 154, 160, 164
– compassion training 36–38, 63, 157, 163–164
– empathy training 37–38
– formalised training 165
– training for all 163
Transactional Analysis 16–18, 29, 78, 123
trust 69, 76, 86–87, 90, 102, 114, 146, 162, 166–167, 172–173
Tversky, Amos 85, 88

Unconditional Positive Regard 15, 20, 144, 166
United States of America 75, 90, 169–170
– President 64–65
– rankings 42

victim 23, 25, 28, 64, 93, 100–102, 138, 158
– and Just World Hypothesis 99
– in Drama Triangle 19–21
– locus of control 110

Wall Street Journal 56
wellbeing 2, 8, 11, 23–24, 44, 56, 66–67, 69–70, 79–80, 86–87, 106–107, 110–112, 117–118, 120, 142, 156, 163, 165, 167, 169, 171, 173
– individual 142, 166
– organisational 75–76, 83
women 58, 155
World Giving Index 41–42
World Health Organisation 2

www.ingramcontent.com/pod-product-compliance
Lightning Source LLC
Chambersburg PA
CBHW061812210326
41599CB00034B/6970